Walter Benjamin

Titles in the series Critical Lives present the work of leading cultural figures of the modern period. Each book explores the life of the artist, writer, philosopher or architect in question and relates it to their major works.

In the same series

Jean Genet
Stephen Barber

Michel Foucault
David Macey

Pablo Picasso
Mary Ann Caws

Franz Kafka
Sander L. Gilman

Guy Debord
Andy Merrifield

Marcel Duchamp
Caroline Cros

James Joyce
Andrew Gibson

Frank Lloyd Wright
Robert McCarter

Jean-Paul Sartre
Andrew Leak

Noam Chomsky
Wolfgang B. Sperlich

Jorge Luis Borges
Jason Wilson

Erik Satie
Mary E. Davis

Georges Bataille
Stuart Kendall

Jean Cocteau
James S. Williams

Walter Benjamin

Esther Leslie

REAKTION BOOKS

For Iris Rosemarine Simcha Tiley Watson,
in anticipation of her own opinions et pensées

and big up to Michael Tencer for gruntwork

Published by Reaktion Books Ltd
33 Great Sutton Street
London EC1V ODX, UK

www.reaktionbooks.co.uk

First published 2007

Printed and bound in Great Britain by
Cromwell Press, Trowbridge, Wiltshire

British Library Cataloguing in Publication Data
Leslie, Esther, 1964–
    Walter Benjamin. – (Critical lives)
    1. Benjamin, Walter, 1892–1940 2. Philosophers – Germany – Biography
    I. Title
    193

    ISBN–13: 978 1 86189 343 7
    ISBN–10: 1 86189 343 3

Contents

Abbreviations

AP   Walter Benjamin, *The Arcades Project* (Cambridge, MA, 1999–2003)

GB   I–VI: Walter Benjamin, *Gesammelte Briefe*, vols I–VI (Frankfurt, 1996)

GS   I–VII: Walter Benjamin, *Gesammelte Schriften*, vols I–VII (Frankfurt, 1992)

SW   I–IV: Walter Benjamin, *Selected Writings*, vols I–IV (Cambridge, MA, 1996–2003)

Walter Benjamin in his late thirties.

1

Benjamin's Remnants

Walter Benjamin left many remnants. There are the books published in his lifetime: four monographs, one edited collection of letters and his translations of Proust, Balzac and Baudelaire. There are the many essays and reviews written for various newspapers, magazines and journals from 1910 until 1940. Benjamin broadcast almost 90 radio shows – of which no recordings have yet been found (his voice is lost to us) – but transcripts remain. In addition to this public output, there is a mass of more intimate materials. Benjamin was a prolific letter-writer, cramming his pages with details of his life, his circumstances and his thoughts, if only because, in the many years of exile and dislocation, day-to-day exchange of information with acquaintances was impossible. His many correspondents faithfully held on to these documents of developing ideas and material circumstance. Benjamin wrote consciously for the future, constructing from early on archives of his writings, in published, manuscript, draft and photocopied form. Benjamin organized his own archive of materials meticulously. Files, folders, envelopes, boxes and cases harboured correspondence, manuscripts by acquaintances, private and business affairs, memoirs, diaries, photographs, postcards, drawings and notes, index cards, inventories, a list of books read since his school days and a list of his publications, as well as copies of his writings, in various drafts and replete with further amendments or curious markings to indicate associations and cross-references. He archived scraps of paper, sketches of essays jotted on the back of library book return reminders, diagrams in the form of compass roses and co-ordinate planes that plotted ideas in relation to each other. Even the most ephemeral objects found a place in his archive, evoking an idea from one of the poets who most fascinated him, Charles Baudelaire, who observed the twinning in modernity of the fugitive and eternal, the transitory and the immutable.

One of Benjamin's most cherished formats was the notebook. When he was without a notebook his thoughts were 'homeless'.[1] Seven of his notebooks and three notepads still remain. These are crammed with drafts of articles and letters, ideas, diagrams, quotations to be used as epigraphs, bibliographies and diary entries, and often every single centimetre of their pages is covered with tiny handwriting.[2] These books were portable. With them he could indulge his inclination to write on the move, in cafés across Europe. He fostered a cult around his notebooks, relishing in particular those with thin and translucent leaves and supple vellum covers. They survive for, once complete, they were placed with friends, with the request 'please store the manuscript carefully',[3] and the proviso that they could be recalled at any time by the author. As he wrote to his friend Alfred Cohn on 18 June 1928,

> I will continue to ensure the completion of your collection of little grasses and stems from my field. This way at least there is the benefit, more for me than you, of there being another complete herbarium somewhere apart from my own.[4]

There were many part-archives. Benjamin deposited materials with friends and institutions. In Frankfurt, Jerusalem, New York, Los Angeles, Barcelona and elsewhere, parts of the Benjamin project were strewn. The uses of the duplicate and dispersed archives was made clear on 31 May 1933, when he wrote to Gershom Scholem with the request that he arrange the replacement of some damaged papers in Benjamin's archive:

> But now that moment has arrived when you must allow me to shake a few meager fruits from the tree of conscientiousness, whose roots are to be found in my heart and whose leaves are in your archive.[5]

Some of this mass of material was lost in the exile years, along with most of his cherished book collection. But much was preserved, even by those who would destroy Benjamin. The Gestapo seized the papers and effects that Benjamin had managed to keep with him until his flight from Paris in June 1940. Bundled together with other booty, by 1945 they found their way to Moscow. Included amongst letters, contracts, photographs, radio scripts and some writings on Baudelaire was something as slight as an address book from the years of exile, with its details of friends and acquaintances offering an insight into the circles of communication in those years, its deletions a testimony to the frequent displacements of refugees. This batch of papers continued on a journey back to Berlin in 1957, when it was handed to the GDR's Ministry of the Interior, who passed it on to the German central archive in Potsdam, from where it moved in 1972 to the archive of the Academy of Arts in East Berlin. It was inaccessible for study until 1983, when it was made available to citizens of 'socialist' countries, and in 1986 it was opened for all.

This fragment of the archive was brought together with two other parts: a Frankfurt archive of the materials that Benjamin had with him on his flight from Paris which found their way to Adorno to join the manuscripts, letters and documents held by the Institute for Social Research, and a Paris archive that contained the papers deposited by Benjamin with Georges Bataille at the Bibliothèque nationale de France for safekeeping before his departure. The archive

Walter Benjamin's passport photograph, undated.

of traces continues to grow, as documents turn up from private collections or from the dissolved Special Archive in Moscow. Since April 2004 12,000 pages have resided in the archive of the Academy of Arts in unified Berlin. Even ephemera entered posterity, against all odds. Walter Benjamin's remnants in reproduced form are likewise not hard to come by. The many editions of his writings, and the commentaries on them, abound with photographs and documents. An effect as slight as his address book from 1933–40 is available for purchase now, as perfect facsimile.[6]

This book has benefited from the extraordinary efforts that German archivists have made to not only collate and reproduce as much material as exists, but also to furnish it with finely detailed commentary, elucidation and cross-references. A life, shortened but intensely lived, is reconstructable from these myriad materials:

from the *Gesammelte Schriften*, issued from 1972 to 1999, with its expansive scholarly apparatus, to the volume that appeared in 2006 under the title *Walter Benjamins Archive*, with its commented reproductions of the most curious survivals – postcards, doodles and jokes, photographs of Russian toys, drafts of ideas in minuscule writing scratched on hotel paper or a café receipt advertising S. Pellegrino water, the back of a medical prescription and a cinema ticket. In 1992 Ingrid Scheurmann, investigating the circumstances of Benjamin's death, tracked down and reproduced every document that could be found pertaining to his final days in Port Bou: the hotel bill, the doctor's bill, the cemetery and coffin bill, a letter from Max Horkheimer evidencing Benjamin's connection to the Institute for Social Research.[7] But even she could not find the one item that was rumoured to be with him at the end: a manuscript more important than his life – of what, no one knows. In a different spirit, eschewing speculation and drawing on these many available traces, this book holds rigorously to the facts of a life much fictionalized.

2

Youth Culture, 1892–1916

Walter Benjamin was born at 4 Magdeburger Platz in Berlin's
Tiergarten on 15 July 1892. His assimilated Jewish parents, Emil
and Pauline, soon moved to nearby Kurfürstenstrasse in the heart
of the old West End. Walter Benjamin was the first of three
children. His brother Georg was born in 1895 and his sister Dora
in 1901. As the children arrived and the wealth grew, the family
moved west to ever-grander homes with staff – Nettelbeckstrasse,
Carmerstrasse, finally settling in 1912 in the 'new West' at 23
Delbrückstrasse, a villa on the edge of the royal hunting grounds,
a wealthy 'ghetto'[1] far from the hectic city centre, and even further
from the poverty of Berlin's East End. Benjamin grew up with a
nanny and a French governess. On official documents, his father
gave his occupation as 'Kaufmann', dealer. He had made his
considerable fortune trading antiques and art, and by the time
Benjamin was a young boy his father was rich enough to be a
speculator, investing in firms such as a medical supplier, a wine
merchant and a skating rink. That Benjamin's upbringing was
comfortable in material terms is apparent from his own writings,
the memories of a Berlin childhood that Benjamin wrote and
rewrote, turned into verse, worked on and worked over for many
years in adulthood.

When he was forty, only finally dislodged from dependence on the
family home in Delbrückstrasse some three years earlier, he scuttled
back into his childhood. This was not as an act of self-indulgence,

Walter Benjamin at Heringsdorf, 1896.

but rather as part of his effort to understand how the impulses of the nineteenth century came to form the environments and the inhabitants of the present. Benjamin dredged up an enchanted world where the shock of sensual experiences impacts indelibly on mind and memory. He recorded the accoutrements of life in Berlin in 1900: the patterns on family dinnerware, the organic forms of garden chairs on the balconies, the intricacies of Aunt Lehmann's miniaturized quarry model. He remembered cushions, upholstery, chocolate, silk sachets scented with lavender, the smell of an apple placed in the bedroom stove by the maid on a winter morning, the clatter of shutters, the scratching of branches, the sensation of spinning on a carousel as his mother turns into a blur. The world out there, in the city, was glimpsed by a child hungry for experience and diverted into books in the quest for adventure. One vignette from his Berlin childhood, 'Boys' Books', detailed swirls of falling snowflakes tracked through the window of a warm parlour by a bookish bourgeois boy who was prone to illness and sometimes trapped in the home. The snow flurries compared, for Benjamin, to the play of words on a book's page. Books were gangways to new geographies and possible futures. These adventures under snowy conditions were inside the self, imagined, like the stuff of books. Benjamin once imagined in a dream the best books ever, with stormy things inside of them and a changing and cryptic text in effervescent and transient colours.[2]

From his own remembered childhood Benjamin extrapolated that a child's senses are receptive, as a child's world is new. The child receives the world so fully that the world forms the child. The world imprints itself, just as bodies do on the chemistry of photographs. The child is embedded in the materiality of its world. In 'Hiding Places', Benjamin wrote of being woven into curtains and banished into the hefty door. Sound – newly recordable in Benjamin's lifetime – also played a role in configuring experience. In 'The Mummerehlen', Benjamin described how clutching the nineteenth century to his ear like a shell summoned up the formative sounds of his childhood: the rustle of coal falling from scuttle

Kaiser Wilhelm II parading with troops on Unter den Linden, on a Berlin postcard of around 1900: 'To horse then, comrades, to horse and away/And into the field where freedom awaits us./In the field of battle, man still has his worth,/ And the heart is still weighed in the balance' (from *Wallenstein*, cited by Benjamin in *Berlin Childhood around 1900*).

Walter Benjamin as a soldier, 1897.

to stove, the pop of the flame igniting in the gas mantle, the clacking of the lamp globe on its brass ring as a vehicle passes, the jingling of a key basket, the bells at the front and back staircases. In 'Loggias', he revealed how the throb of passing trams and the thud of carpet beating rocked him to sleep. For his first ten years Benjamin was formed in and by the rush of an imperial city, a mollusc constrained and protected by the city as it rapidly flung its energies into modernizing, with the introduction of new technologies of transportation and labour, leisure and war.

The child has an affinity for the world of objects, an openness to sensation, an ability to invent and transform, to play with waste scraps and turn them into treasures. Benjamin identified the 'compulsion' to adopt similarities to the world of objects as a primitive impulse, reaffirmed by childish mimesis and unacknowledged in the adult world. In a vignette titled 'The Telephone', Benjamin observed that the telephone and he came into the world together, and so were twins. After early years of humiliation, when the telephone was banished to the corridor, it entered the brightly lit rooms of a younger generation who were its siblings and could accept it, becoming that generation's 'consolation for their loneliness', the ring that they longed to hear.[3] As a child, Benjamin would push his head between the heavy dumbbell-like earphones to listen to the noises that seemed as much a truth of the world outside as the noises that are trapped inside the shell. It took time for Benjamin to realise that we are also listening to the surge of our blood, to our own selves.

Benjamin as child – at least as that child portrayed in the memory of a forty-year-old man who had long lived in precarious circumstances, without ongoing employment – inhabited a world rich in sensuous experience. He was drawn as much to the luxurious objects of the bourgeois home as to its unwanted clutter. He recalled being exposed to the torrential floods of rain on a completely deserted stretch of road, as well as sitting ensconced in a well-heated room, rifling through his collection of picture postcards depicting the wooded slopes of Tabarz, the yellow and white quays at Brindisi and the bluish cupolas of Madonna di Campiglio. These were images sent by his maternal grandmother, and they kindled in Benjamin a powerful desire to travel, igniting fantasies of traversing the world's oceans, with the 'bows of the "Westerland" slicing high through the waves'.[4]

His experience of the cusp of two centuries – at least as depicted in retrospect – revealed how, for a curious child, the city and its interiors provided rich pickings for fantasy. Benjamin was exposed to the stimulations of the city, indeed the city itself as stimulant. He reported later that the first stirrings of his sexual urge occurred there on a Jewish New Year's Day, in a rare moment of his mother's adherence to religious tradition. Having lost his way to the synagogue, he enjoyed his blasphemous indifference toward the service while also exalting the street on which he stood, a setting in which his awakened drive would later enjoy

Walter, Georg and Dora Benjamin, undated.

the 'services of procurement'.[5] In this city his father's money cut paths through shops, and his childish curiosity drew him on occasion to its little-visited corners. But, this same city that could invite a person to cross thresholds, to tangle themselves himself in the ribbons of the streets, was also a city of barriers, exclusions and calamities in waiting. This was a city of 'inhuman' military brass bands,[6] of beggars and poorly paid workers,[7] of locked cabinets[8] and family secrets.[9]

An out-of-placeness, which pursued Benjamin his whole life, began early. Displaced from private tuition at home when he was nine, he attended the Kaiser-Friedrich-Gymnasium in Berlin's Savignyplatz in 1901, close to the municipal railway yard. He hated the school, whose very name evoked the imperial system and whose red-brick gave a 'narrow-chested, high-shouldered impression', exuding a 'sad spinsterish primness', such that Benjamin retained not one single cheerful memory of it.[10] Stalled outside the wrought-iron door, as the teachers passed through at will, and forced to raise his cap in a faux-intimate mode of greeting, Benjamin seethed with hatred and humiliation. The school's balustrades and mouldings, frosted windows and carved battlements, its unspeakable grey-green ornaments adorning the wall of the auditorium: all this was perceived by Benjamin as the twiddles decorating an interior of terror and nightmares. Each scroll or notching was a cipher-language reinforcing the school's own moulding of its pupils as imperial citizens. Benjamin found in his memory of school

> rigidly fixed words, expressions, verses that, like a malleable mass that has cooled and hardened, preserve in me the imprint of the collision between a larger collective and myself. Just as, when you awake, a certain kind of significant dream survives in the form of words though all the rest of the dream-content has vanished, here isolated words have remained in place as marks of catastrophic encounters.[11]

The volcanic lava of language stiffens inside the self, indicating how socialized our existences and even – or especially – dreams are. School's drills damaged him and others, just as it would later entice them into the damaging scenarios of war.

In 1905, after a period of illness when he received no tuition for several months, Benjamin was sent away to a progressive co-educational boarding school in Haubinda, Thuringia for almost two years. While there, he was taught by the educational reformer Gustav Wyneken, who promoted a doctrine of Youth Culture. Youth Culture held that the young were morally superior to the old. They were more spiritual or intellectual,[12] and so thus required

Unser Schwimmteich

A postcard of nude swimming at the Thuringian progressive school that Walter
Benjamin attended in 1905–6.

exposure to the full panorama of artistic and scientific culture.
Intellect was the aspect around which the school revolved, quite
unlike the experience at the Kaiser-Friedrich school, which left
its residue in unpleasantly recalled images of selfish and smelly
bourgeois boys thrusting themselves up and down stairwells, their
sporty and energetic bodies clumping into a massed and violent
form from which Benjamin was excluded. The boys and girls under
Wyneken's influence were encouraged in their idealism. Granted
autonomy, the young would find their way to spiritual teachers;
the teachers, in turn, relinquished power in a system of 'student
self-administration', and regarded their pupils as spiritual equals
whom they aided in a quest for knowledge and absolute values.
In this setting, Benjamin learnt that youth, the coming humanity,
could be educated as 'knights' protecting *Geist*, for whom the pro-
foundest and most important experience is that of art. Benjamin's
core philosophy developed at the school. In a letter written in
March 1915, Benjamin acknowledged that Wyneken was the first

to lead him into the life of the intellect, and he maintained contact with his mentor for a decade.[13]

In 1907 Benjamin returned to the Kaiser-Friedrich-Gymnasium for two years. During that time he made efforts to raise the level of cultural discussion, founding a literary circle to discuss the works of Shakespeare, Hebbel and Ibsen. Berlin continued to be the scene of his budding erotic fantasy, as he later recalled in *Berlin Chronicle*. One evening he was taken to the Ice Palace by his father, who held a large financial stake in the construction. It may have even been the opening event in 1908.[14] Benjamin remembered not so much the skating arena as 'a prostitute in a very tight-fitting white sailor suit' at the bar, whom he spied from afar and who determined his 'erotic fantasies for years to come'.[15]

The prospect of military service beckoned, and in 1909 he took an examination to reduce a two-year period of military service by a

The Berlin Ice Palace, in which Benjamin's father held a financial stake: 'So it happened that my attention was held far less by the convolutions in the arena than by the apparitions at the bar, which I was able to survey at my ease from a box in the circle.'

year. 1910 saw his first published writings. A follower of Wyneken had founded a magazine in 1908 called *Der Anfang* (*The Beginning*), with the subtitle 'a magazine of future art and literature'. Its initial run comprised only 150 copies and it was reproduced by hectograph. Later it reached 1000 subscribers. Benjamin published poems and prose, reflections on the possibility of a new religiosity and the questions of youth. His pseudonym was Ardor. In March 1911, with the magazine now subtitled 'Unified Magazines of the Youth', Benjamin published 'Sleeping Beauty'.[16] The essay acknowledged the age as one of Socialism, Women's Liberation, Communication and Individualism. It asked, might not the age of youth be on the horizon? Youth is the Sleeping Beauty who is unaware of the approaching Prince who comes to wake her. Youth possesses a Hamlet-like consciousness of the negativity of the world. Goethe's Faust stood as a representative of youth's ambitions and wishes. Carl Spittler's epic poems 'Prometheus and Epimetheus' and 'Olympian Spring' and his book *Imago*, 'the most beautiful book for a young person', portrayed the 'dullness and cowardice of the average person' and, in his 'universal ideal of humanity', he presented a model for youth beyond pessimism. Benjamin's essay picked out the possibilities of youth's magnificence as depicted in the 'greatest works of literature'. He and his comrades were to inject those ideal forms with living blood and energy.

In 1911 Benjamin wrote two travel diaries. He had written one before: in 1906 he wrote of a Whitsuntide journey while at Haubinda, where he noted that he was a bad pedestrian.[17] In April 1911 he wrote a daily diary of events on a short Whitsun trip, where he clambered up hills in Thuringia. He included his own poetic effort:

Out of glowing clouds arises anew
A young world;
Misty mountains ringed in purple,
Ache to bear gigantic bodies[18]

A postcard of Wengen in Switzerland, location of a Benjamin family holiday in 1911.

The second diary that year broached the question of memory, breaking with the day-to-day format. It was his first experiment in diary writing as a literary form. The 'Diary from Wengen' began with a statement on the synthesizing power of retrospection, before embarking on reflections about a family trip to Switzerland.[19] In 1912 Benjamin began to travel in earnest. A trip to Italy at Whitsun, with two friends, was a 'Bildungsreise', the 'sentimental' journey undertaken by a good bourgeois son at the beginning of his studies.[20] The friends travelled to Lucerne, St Gotthard, Milan, Verona, Vicenza and Venice. Benjamin wrote to his friend Herbert Blumenthal that the holiday proper would take place only once back in Freiburg, once it was written up.[21] The resulting journal was written in June or July 1912. The journey was in the retrospection, the writing up of experience.

On his return in the summer of 1912 he began his studies at the Albert-Ludwigs-Universität in Freiburg im Breisgau, matriculating in the faculty of Philology, but he attended lectures in General History offered by Friedrich Meinecke, and he studied Philosophy with Heinrich Rickert. It was a disappointing experience. He voiced his frustrations about university to Blumenthal, mocking scholarship as a mooing cow to which students were compelled to listen in lecture theatres.[22] In August, he took a trip to Stolpmünde on the Baltic coast, to regain his 'G.N.I.', his 'general normal intellectuality', though 'snakes of stupidity' still plagued his hair, while a 'diffident smile of maturing experience' curled on his lips.[23]

In the same letter, Benjamin wrote to Blumenthal about an awakening commitment to Zionism and Zionist activity, which appeared to him for the first time as a possibility or even perhaps a duty. He did not, however, intend to abandon his political efforts at school reform.[24] The new obligation to consider the significance of Jewishness emerged from a personal encounter – on holiday in Holzmünde he spent many hours with Kurt Tuchler, founder of the first Zionist youth movement, Blau-Weiss, which, in similar fashion to the other youth groupings, undertook hikes and outings through the German countryside. Tuchler spoke of Zionism, while Benjamin tried to persuade him of the correctness of his Free School doctrine. There were at the time intense debates about Germanness and Jewishness in the intellectual press. In March 1912 Moritz Goldstein published an essay in the journal *Der Kunstwart und Kulturwart*. It was titled 'German Jewish Parnassus', and it exhorted Jews to become conscious of their own traditions, to retreat from German culture, where they were unwanted, despite their domination of it. German culture owed so much of its existence to the Jews, and yet their love for Germany remained unrequited. Jews should respond, Goldstein urged, by developing their own cultural and intellectual life. Ninety positive and negative reactions to the polemic were also recorded in *Der Kunstwart*, a journal whose circulation at that time was over 20,000. Was Goldstein's assertion of a Jewish 'character' to be embraced? Was assimilation unachievable? The article irreconcilably divided Zionists and anti-Zionists amongst German Jewry.

Benjamin wrote about the debates in a series of letters to Ludwig Strauss, who supported – and wanted to institute – Goldstein's plan for a German language magazine for Jewish culture. He requested Benjamin's help. Benjamin approved of a journal documenting Jewish spiritual life and dealing with such themes as Jews and luxury, Jews and the love of Germany, and Jews and friendship. He noted in his letter of 11 September 1912 that he and others do indeed possess a 'two-sidedness', the Jewish and the German side, and how, up till then, they have oriented to the German side: 'the Jewish side was perhaps often something foreign, a Southern (worse yet, sentimental) aroma, in our production and our life'.[25] He agreed that Jewish forces in Germany would be lost by assimilation, though he noted that the entry of Russian Jews would postpone that. But he drew back from embracing a Zionism that involved the formation of Jewish enclaves or indeed the establishment of a Jewish state. Against a nationalist and political Zionism he advocated a cultural Zionism, a cultural Jewish state and not a territorial state. Such a Jewish state might provide a solution for Eastern Jews who were fleeing persecution, he conceded, but for Western Jews there was another solution. German Jews might reach the necessary 'Selbstbewusstsein', 'self-consciousness', a salvation of Jewish characteristics in the face of assimilation, through the organization of Jewish intellectual life in Germany.

In October he returned to the theme of modern Western European Jews in a letter to Strauss, which meant he reflected on his own situation. Zionism was one way forward, but he had already been led far along another path, represented by his liberal upbringing, which meant that his 'decisive intellectual experience' – with Wyneken – occurred before Judaism struck him in any sense as important or problematic.[26] Benjamin described himself as a 'strict and fanatical pupil of G. Wyneken', and he told Strauss of his plans to continue promoting Wyneken's ideas of Pedagogical Eros and Youth Culture by issuing a brochure of essays criticizing contemporary schooling, addressing topics such as teaching and assessment and relationships between teachers and pupils, schools and idealism.[27] It would include letters from pupils, in order to document lives that had previously only been fictionalized in novels and stories. Wyneken's educational precepts drew on Kant, Hegel, Goethe and Nietzsche. This political doctrine squeezed out any other.

Benjamin could not countenance the argument for a Jewish state, as he and his assimilated progressive Jewish peers were tied to Europe and the non-Jewish European cultural heritage. That was their duty, and it was one that they were born to bear. Jews were an elite because Jewry was the 'most noble bearer and representative of the *Geistigen*', the intellectual spirit.[28] The cultural energy of Jews was needed in Europe.[29] 'Cultural Zionism' should work for Jewish values wherever Jews are, and Jews are international. But, he argued, the quality of these values was uncertain. Benjamin expressed dismay at the intellectual capacities of most Zionists, who 'propagandize Palestine and booze in German', these 'half-humans' who have never considered the important questions, 'schooling, literature, the life of the mind, the state', from a Jewish perspective. He revealed to Strauss that it was with Wyneken that that he found his Jewishness, 'not on the basis of speculation or mere emotion, but from outer and inner experience. I have discovered that that which is most important for me in terms of ideas and individuals is Jewish'. Wyneken left Hermann Lietz's school to found his own Free School Community Wickersdorf:

In Wickersdorf I see something that has affected me and other Jews internally. Two conclusions exist: either this idea is in essence Jewish (even though a German had conceived it ten times over!) or I and the other Jews are no longer true Jews because we have been possessed in our most personal core by something not Jewish.[30]

In January 1913 a letter from Benjamin to Strauss articulated his dilemma: was his political home with Left Liberalism or Social Democracy? In either case, while Jewishness played a role in the 'whole complex' of his 'convictions', he restated that his Jewishness was not that of the National Jewishness of Zionist propaganda but rather that of the contemporary intellectual literary Jew that such Zionism fights. Ultimately, he acknowledged, his political energies lay with the Left, and the key political fight for him at that point was attaining a Left majority, so that across Germany the Wyneken model of education could be adopted. Zionism and the intellectual Jew might play a role in this task, but for Benjamin it was the organization of the Left parties that was of crucial importance.[31]

If debates with friends in letters and elsewhere were stimulating, university was far less so. Benjamin signed into the university in Berlin for the winter semester of 1912/13, but returned to Freiburg to study philosophy from April to July 1913. He read Kant and Kierkegaard. In June 1913 Benjamin described Jonas Cohn's seminar on the aesthetics of Kant and Schiller as 'chemically thought-free', and Heinrich Rickert's seminar on Bergson as unsatisfactory.[32] In addition, he was isolated. He had one dependable friend, the poet Christoph Friedrich Heinle, whose motto was 'booze, guzzle and make poems', but university provided no real peer group; in contrast to Berlin, the Free Student Association, a student organization quite different in temper to the aristocratic and upper-middle class fraternities, was inactive.[33] He wrote to his friend Carla Seligson about his study of philosophy and attendance at a reading circle of specialist philosophers. He told her that he felt odd in their company at this 'grotesque pageant' because his philosophy stemmed from and constantly returned to his first teacher Wyneken.[34] He fought hard to convince the 'Student Pedagogic group' to accept some ideas derived from Wyneken on Youth Culture. Over the next few months these ideas did indeed spread across a number of university pedagogic groups.

Respite came in travel. In 1913 Benjamin took trips to the Black Forest, the Tirol, Breslau and Weimar and, at Whitsun, visited Paris for the first time. He reported on his experiences in a letter to Carla Seligson in June. The two weeks were lived intensely, 'such as only a child lives'. He was out and about all day, almost never reaching bed before 2 am. Mornings were spent at the Louvre, Versailles, Fontainebleau and the Bois de Boulogne. In the afternoons, the streets, churches and cafés beckoned. Evenings were spent with friends, at the theatre and on the boulevard. Paris presented itself on his first visit as it would for the rest of Benjamin's life: 'In the Louvre and on the Grand Boulevard I am almost more at home than in the Kaiser-Friedrich Museum or in Berlin's streets.'[35]

Paris renewed Benjamin's sense of life's exciting possibilities. In June he wrote an essay entitled 'Experience' for *Der Anfang*. 'Experience' launched an attack on adults, the philistines who snort at spirit, ideals and compassion. He argued that adults wore a mask called 'experience'. This mask is 'expressionless, impenetrable and ever the same'. Adults claimed to have experienced everything already – youth, ideals, hopes, woman – only to find it was all illusion, and they despised youth because it reminded them of the dreams they once shared and in which they lost faith. Such adults find no meaning in the world, no 'inner relationship to anything other than the common and the already-out-of-date'. They were without *Geist*. But Benjamin and his ilk knew 'a different experience', 'the most beautiful, most untouchable, most immediate, because it can never be without spirit while we remain young'.[36]

That same year saw more essays on school reform. 'Romanticism' appeared in *Der Anfang*, followed shortly after by a second part that responded to criticisms made in the same pages.[37] Once again Benjamin admonished the youth for sleeping, for not mobilizing their potential. School damaged any innate idealism, presenting Romantic ideals as the unattainable qualities of extraordinary and long past fictional heroes. Art was 'an opium' inhibiting the suffering will. Youth succumbed to tawdry films and cabarets, designed to arouse the exhausted sexual feelings of fifty-year-olds, because there was no other realm in which the specific eroticism of the young might be explored. Benjamin's Romanticism, rooted in present life and effective human activity, reformulated the 'narcotic imperative' of 'wine, woman, song' so that wine signalled 'abstinence', woman a 'new eroticism' and song not a drinking ditty but a new school hymn.

In July 1913 Benjamin walked in the Swiss Jura, reading philosophy, literature by Heinrich Mann, Hermann Hesse and Guy de Maupassant, and examining Dürer prints in Basel. A short holiday in Italy ended his Southern sojourn and he, along with Heinle, returned to Berlin for the winter semester of 1913/14. He remained there, resident in the family home, for two years, though the educational merits of the university were lacking and Benjamin found it difficult to endure the 'attacks of the lectures'.[38] Study in Berlin brought Benjamin closer once more to the students around Wyneken and *Der Anfang*, including Grete Radt, a Youth Movement activist who became his girlfriend.

On 19 February 1914, seeking a platform for greater dissemination of the Wyneken doctrine, Benjamin put himself forward for the presidency of the Free Students' Association. He won and took up the post in May 1914. His acceptance speech, part of which was included in the essay 'The Life of Students', provoked controversy. He launched an attack on those students who saw their academic study only as a vocational training. But, Benjamin noted, 'scholarship, far from leading inexorably to a profession, may in fact preclude it'.[39] Genuine study would not lead students to embrace the partial lives represented by the official professions of doctor, lawyer or university professor. That seats of learning took up these vocational objectives showed how much the modern disciplines were forced to 'abandon their original unity in the idea of knowledge, a unity which in their eyes has now become a mystery, if not a fiction'. The universities adapted themselves to bourgeois conditions and the students did not resist. Students gestured at criticizing social conditions, but this was just a spare-time activity. Students failed in Benjamin's eyes because they were not representatives of the Tolstoyan spirit of total commitment. Students, irrespective of specialism, should confront the 'great metaphysical questions of Plato and Spinoza, the Romantics and Nietzsche', to deepen the concept of life and prevent the 'degeneration of study into the heaping up of information'.[40]

'The Life of Students' appeared late in 1915. By then Benjamin was no longer president of the Free Students, and the situation had changed dramatically, for the First World War had begun. In protest, nineteen-year-old Heinle committed suicide by gassing in the kitchen of the Berlin youth movement's meeting house, together with his girlfriend Rika Seligson. These two deaths reinforced for Benjamin the hostility of the city to the ideals of the young, and the limits that the modern city and its social systems set on social and political intercourse, policing its spaces, inhibiting any room for manoeuvre. The vain attempt to find a joint burial ground for two dead young lovers reinforced Benjamin's awareness of the many uncrossable moral, political and social limits, as he later recalled in *Berlin Chronicle*:

And when finally, after August 8, 1914, the days came when those among us who were closest to the dead couple did not want to part from one another until they were buried, we felt the limits in the shame of being able to find refuge only in a seedy railway hotel on Stuttgart Square. Even the graveyard demonstrated the boundaries set by the city to all that filled our hearts: it was impossible to procure for the pair who had died together graves in one and the same cemetery. But these were days that ripened a realization that was to come later, and that planted in me the conviction that the city of Berlin would also not be spared the scars of the struggle for a better order.[41]

The struggle at that time was not just between warring national enemies. Benjamin felt compelled to break his links with Wyneken in March 1915. Wyneken had delivered a public lecture entitled 'War and Youth' in Munich on 25 November 1914, and it was published a few months later. Wyneken assumed that Germany would win the war and that, through this victory, the various factions of the nation – excepting the proletarian parties – would be united. The coming peace would allow orientation to 'the idea, to that which absolutely must be'.[42] After reading Wyneken's discourse on the 'ethical' experience afforded to youth by war, Benjamin wrote a letter detailing his disagreements and his severance of all connection 'without reservation'. Benjamin accused Wyneken of sacrificing youth to the state, and this a state that had taken everything from Wyneken, when it had denied him the directorship of Wickersdorf because he had taught religion in a Hegelian manner. Benjamin reminded him that he had taught that boys and girls were 'comrades' in the 'holiest work of humanity'. In supporting the sending of German youth to war, Wyneken betrayed the women who loved his pupils, as well as the men torn from those women and from humanity.[43] Wyneken had betrayed his own ideals. For his own part, Benjamin feigned palsy at the call-up of his age group, and was allowed a year's reprieve.

Little was written in the second half of 1914. War jolted Benjamin, soured his experience and silenced him for a while. As 1914 turned into 1915 he completed a study of two poems by Hölderlin, demonstrating an interest in poetry's inner form, the dense weave of words known in German as 'das Gedichtete', 'the versified' but also 'the sealed' or 'the consolidated'. Poetry was a working-out of material and form, life and art, task and solution, each element fluidly transforming into the other. To interpret poetry meant to indicate truth.

The essay was not published, but it was distributed amongst a small circle of friends, the bright minds who constituted Benjamin's peers in the youth movement.

In July 1915 Benjamin met Gerhard Scholem. The two young men attended a lecture by the socialist Kurt Hiller and, upon bumping into each other a few days later in the catalogue room of the university library, they agreed to meet to further discuss Hiller's vehement denunciation of history. On a visit to Benjamin's home, where Benjamin's room appeared as a 'philosopher's den' full of books,[44] Scholem gave Benjamin a copy of the first issue of Rosa Luxemburg and Franz Mehring's journal *Die Internationale: Zeitschrift für Theorie und Praxis des Marxismus*, from April 1915, which Benjamin thought 'excellent'.[45] Scholem had been attending clandestine anti-war meetings staged by those sympathetic to a faction within the German Social Democratic Party, organised around Luxemburg and Karl Liebknecht – the International Group, nucleus of the future Communist Party of Germany. Benjamin was keen to be involved, and reading the journal was a first step.[46] There was, however, no subsequent association, just as there was no second issue of the journal, for it was suppressed by the government.

War once again impressed itself on Benjamin. Scholem aided him in his efforts to evade war when he was summoned a second time. The two stayed up until 6 am drinking black coffee on 20/21 October. There was much to discuss: philosophy, Judaism, Kabbalah, politics – and the next day Benjamin presented himself as an undesirable soldier to the authorities and was deferred for another year.[47]

In the winter semester of 1915/16 Benjamin transferred his studies to Munich. He reported his disappointment with the art historian Heinrich Wölfflin in letters to his friend Fritz Radt in November and December 1915.[48] The literary historians and critics were also unsatisfactory. The only good lecture series was on the history of the old-church penance, attended by Benjamin and three or four monks. He was also impressed by a lecture series on ancient Mexican culture and language, which took place in an elegant private apartment where participants sat on pretty white and black silken chairs around a large table with a Persian cloth. Codices were passed around to the handful of people attending, amongst whom was the poet Rainer Maria Rilke.[49] Benjamin's then-fiancée Grete Radt was enrolled at the university in Munich, where she was a youth movement activist, and that was reason enough to be there, though Benjamin's affections were transferring to the older Dora Kellner (who was married at the time to Max Pollak). By the summer of 1916 Benjamin and Kellner were a couple, and she began her divorce proceedings. In any case, Munich provided Benjamin with the peace he needed to carry out his work, by which he meant his writing.

In 1916 the pace of writing picked up again. The shock of war had jolted Benjamin into a new set of concerns, and he did not resume the political and ethical ruminations on youth that had so dominated his life since his attendance at Haubinda in 1905–6. Instead there were some reflections on antiquity, happiness and Socrates, but the main pull on his attention was literary form and language. Benjamin drew together impulses from German Romanticism, which had long fascinated him, and mysticism, stimulated by exchanges with Gerhard Scholem. Three essays emerged in 1916: '*Trauerspiel* and Tragedy', 'The Role of Language in *Trauerspiel* and Tragedy' and 'On Language as Such and the Language of Man'. This last essay, a disquisition on experience, translation and language in its broadest sense (including the language of nature, things and the divine), endeavoured to find the essence of language. It asked what language communicated. Was there an original sin in language? Could spiritual being in the world be expressed in language? Words that had been so instrumentally abused in war propaganda were reconceived by Benjamin as non-instrumental, divine vessels of something other than mere communication. As he wrote in a letter to Martin Buber in July

1916, Benjamin sought in language a 'sphere of wordlessness', wishing to awaken interest in what was denied to the word.[50]

The same letter declined Buber's invitation to write for *Der Jude*, for the journal carried articles that enthused about the experience of war, and Benjamin did not agree with Buber's stance towards Zionism. Writing, Benjamin insisted, was not to be mobilized for political ends, for the genuine relationship between word and effective action was attainable only in the expression of the ineffable. Language's interest lay not in the communication of content, but rather in the disclosure of magical effects, in its mystery. Benjamin's mystically inflected linguistics developed as a very different type – Ferdinand de Saussure's *Cours de Linguistique générale* – was doing the rounds in Europe. Benjamin's thought was filtered through the work of 'counter-Enlightenment' linguist J. G. Hamann, who proposed the idea that language was a broken remnant of a divine primordial articulation of unique and non-arbitrary proper names.

In light of his new linguistic concepts, Benjamin pondered the role of writing and critique. He informed Blumenthal at the end of 1916 that true criticism was like a chemical element that affected something only in the sense that it revealed, through disassembling, its inner nature. It did not destroy or go against its object. The suprachemical element that affects *intellectual* things in such a way is light. In the midst of war, Benjamin and friends were stranded deep in the darkest of nights. Once he had tried to fight the night using words. He realized that to vanquish night it was necessary to let light flood in. But light did not appear in language. Language could not illuminate. Criticism illuminated. Benjamin defined criticism as the differentiation of the genuine from the non-genuine, and again this was not the commission of language, except perhaps in humour. In humour a critical magic brought its object in contact with light and so it decomposed: 'For those who radiate excessively, the rays will undertake that heavenly exposure that we call criticism.'[51]

Criticism was the decomposition of language, not the positive assertion of its efficaciousness.

At the close of the year Benjamin was called up for military review again and was classed as fit for light field duties. Using hypnosis, Dora induced a sciatica attack and he avoided service a third time. The two began preparations for their marriage, which took place on 16 April 1917.

3

Making a Mark, 1917–24

In 1917 Benjamin's future was unplanned. He thought he might
continue studying in the hope of an academic career, but the
discipline was unclear. With his new wife he moved to a clinic in
Dachau to recover from sciatica. They visited friends in Zurich
and took a holiday in St Moritz. For his own amusement, Benjamin
wrote essays over the summer. One considered Dostoevsky's
Idiot, another assessed Balzac. In August 1917 a one-page article,
'Painting and the Graphic Arts', pondered the spatial alignment
of different types of imagery.[1] These thoughts were the result of
Benjamin's intention 'to follow the difference between painting
and graphics to its very root'.[2] A picture stood vertical before the
observer. A mosaic lay horizontal at the viewer's feet. Benjamin
argued that drawings were too often viewed as paintings, that is
to say, in the upright plane. This might be possible in the case of
a Rembrandt study, but it violated the plane of children's drawing,
whose inner meaning relied on its horizontality. These planes
revealed something about the world. It had a substance and could
be cut two ways. Painting presented a longitudinal image of the
world, representational and containing the world's objects.
Drawing showed the world's cross-section, a flat plane, and so was
symbolic – it was comprised of signs, like writing. But would writing
rather stand? he asked. Is the original place of writing upright,
the position adopted by engraving on a headstone? This short
piece proposed themes that would stay with Benjamin: historical

shifts in the role of signs and imagery, as they bed down or rise up, a changing relationship between humans and cultural artefacts, the mythic roots of art, sensitivity to the experiential and the context of cultural reception.

He followed this with the longer 'On Painting or Sign and Mark'.[3] Its title exploited the ambiguity of signs, for *zeichen*, the word for sign, is the root of the word for drawing (*Zeichnung*), and *mal*, mark, is the root of the word for painting (*Malerei*). For Benjamin, the sign, always an imprinting, was characterized by the role that the line plays in it. Benjamin distinguished the line of geometry, the line of the letter, and two other more interesting lines. The graphic line was defined by its contrast with both the 'background' and the paper's plane, from which it separated itself in order to exist. The magic line was the line of the 'absolute sign', the mysterious signal operative in the world of myth. His examples included Cain's sign, the sign on the Israelites' doors in the tenth plague of Egypt and the chalksigns on the door in Ali Baba and the forty thieves. All these contrasted with the absolute mark, which emerged onto a surface. This mark, often related to guilt or innocence, appeared on the animate – Christ's wounds, blushes, birthmarks, leprosy. What held for the mark, *Mal*, also held for the medium of painting, *Malerei*. Painting eschewed background and graphic lines. It did not conceive the picture plane in layers. Paint fused rather than was layered. But, in being titled, the painting points outside itself. As composition it points to something transcendent, a 'higher power in the medium of the mark': It points to the word.

The transfer between image and word provided Benjamin with a paradigm of contemporary art. For Benjamin, Paul Klee was one of the few worthwhile modern artists, and his art was positioned somewhere between painting and drawing, an art in which the 'linear structure' dominates the image.[4] Klee's scratches were hieroglyphs ready for decipherment, writing and image at once. Sometimes this passage between media was obviously achieved,

as in *Einst dem Grau der Nacht enttaucht . . .* [1918], in which each
letter of the poem occupies a coloured square of the divided grid,
divided through the middle by a strip of silver paper. The image
is the letters, the letters are the words and the whole is a picture.
Klee's line – as word and as image simultaneously – was dynamic.
It signalled its self-transformative power by moving freely between
word and image, between painting and drawing, colour and line.
Such transfer between layers, articulations, lines and signs, was a
utopian aspiration: the world can be made whole again; names and
things, words and their representations, can be brought back into
unity once more. And perhaps through this, Benjamin's developing
longing for an Adamic language of things and the judging language
of humans' can be approached. Objects name themselves. Nature
is no longer mute. Language is a vessel of communication for all of
God's creation.

These thoughts emerged from Benjamin's continuing specula-
tions on language, but his fascination with images made him wonder
if he might become an art critic. For the moment, though, the urgent
question was where to study for his doctorate. He was anxious about
returning to Germany as military service posed a continuing threat.
Neutral Switzerland offered a refuge and a place to study, in Berne.
The couple moved there in October 1917. 'Colourless' but pleasant
Richard Herbertz accepted Benjamin as his doctoral student in philosophy, but exerted no influence over his pupil's thinking. In the
first semester Benjamin wrote papers on Bergson and on Hegel's
phenomenology, but this was simply preparation for his own work.
He told Scholem that he hoped to investigate fields closer to him
that those he was forced to 'hack through' at the university.[5]

The initial doctoral plan was a consideration of Kant and the
philosophy of history, but Benjamin took no pleasure in materials
he had to read.[6] Indeed, he sketched a 'Program of the Coming
Philosophy', which interrogated Kant's pale, categorical and 'lifeless'
definition of experience. With its roots in Newton's mechanistic

and mathematical enlightenment physics, Kantian experience was 'reduced to a nadir'.[7] Its restricted co-ordinates of space and time imposed the finite on the infinite. Benjamin's counter-delineation of an experience and his 'new concept of knowledge' were sensitive to manifestations of the 'absolute' in space and time, undreamt by (neo)Kantianism's conformal strictures and unrestricted to the spatio-temporality of the individual subject. Language, not 'formula or numbers', would play an important role, for language is where philosophy has 'its unique expression'. Kant remained, however, a starting point for a philosophizing beyond philosophy, expanded to fit the warping and distortions of absolute experience.

In March 1918 Benjamin registered a new dissertation topic – on the Concept of Art Criticism in German Romanticism. The dissertation emerged from his studies, which he described as an 'interest in the philosophical content of poetic writing and art forms'.[8] He was drawn to the Romantics' notion of critique as something productive and creative. At his leisure he read in a quite different tradition: Baudelaire's *Artificial Paradise* and his *Paris Spleen*. He reported to his friend Ernst Schoen that Baudelaire's writing on drugs was an effort to see what the psychological phenomena of hashish and opium teach us philosophically. But its beauty and value lay in the childlikeness and purity of the author.[9] An interest in children's expression and experience was burgeoning, perhaps impelled by the arrival of Benjamin's son, Stefan Rafael, on 11 April 1918.

In May 1918 Scholem moved to Berne, having completed his military service. The Benjamins moved to the village of Muri in the summer, and Scholem followed them. The two friends invented a playful University of Muri, which, with its ludicrous and parodic courses and faculty, remained a running joke between them for some years. Scholem's family connections were useful to the biblio-phile Benjamin. Through Scholem's printer father, Benjamin ordered countless books at discount rate, and he pressed ahead

Muri bei Bern

Muri in Switzerland, where Benjamin and Scholem lived for while and established their playful university.

with his studies. His letters to friends discussed his reading and the progress of his studies. One, to Schoen, on 31 July 1918, uncharitably assessed Luise Zurlinden's *Platonic Thought in German Romanticism*, testifying to the 'indescribable' horror that overcame him when women hoped 'to participate in conclusive discussions of these things. It is sheer baseness.'[10] This despite the progressive Wyneken co-education.

His letters reflected little on the turbulent events in Europe. One rare reference to war noted his brother's wounding in 1918. The turbulent politics of Russia and Germany found little resonance. There was some mention of the proclamation of the Bavarian Soviet Republic of November 1918, and the resultant 24-hour general strike in Switzerland as protest against military call-up to defend the state against revolutionary actions. But Benjamin's concern was with its impact on a book auction in which he was bidding for some Grimm fairytales, some Schlegel and some Shakespeare.[11] He feared that the ending of war would lead to interruptions in the regular payments he received from his parents in Germany, used to pay the rent. The ending of war did not, indeed, see an alleviation of the Benjamins' financial hardship. On 29 January 1919 Benjamin told Schoen that he and Dora were disadvantaged by the 'change in German circumstances'.[12]

On 27 June 1919 he passed his doctorate brilliantly, with the award summa cum laude. But Benjamin was not at one with the university. He proclaimed that he had had to conform to academic demands unwillingly. A letter to Schoen noted that the dissertation was about the 'true nature of Romanticism' – unknown to the existing literature – but only in a mediated way, because he was unable to address things that he wanted to without undertaking the 'complicated and conventional scientific attitude', an attitude that Benjamin distinguished 'from the genuine one'.[13] He inserted an esoteric afterword on Goethe, the real matter.[14]

Despite academic accomplishment, there was bad fortune in 1919. Still reliant on his parents – and when they failed, Dora's – for money, he withheld news of his successful qualification from them, so that he might extend the period of their financial support. This entailed subterfuge in the form of secret holidays, and a degree of tension. The baby, who never cried or screamed without a good reason, fell seriously ill in May for three months, infected by streptococcus – Mahler's cause of death, Benjamin grimly noted.[15] Two operations left a scar on the child's face.

New friends offered some diversions. Benjamin met the Dadaist Hugo Ball and his wife, Expressionist poet Emmy Hennings. In July he told Schoen that he had bought some pictures by Annemarie Hennings, Emmy's daughter, who had first exhibited in the Galerie Dada in 1917. She was thirteen and had been making pictures of her dreams and of ghosts. These reminded Benjamin of what he considered the only art of interest, the Expressionism of Chagall, Klee and Kandinsky. Hennings had a 'new and justified technique' for painting ghosts, but Benjamin feared it might not last through puberty.

Keen to promote children's art, he pressed for Schoen to persuade the gallerist Friedrich Möller to arrange an exhibition in Berlin, and he suggested the title 'Expressionist Children's Pictures'.[16]

In July 1919, with Dora musing on the composition or translation of a detective novel and Benjamin translating Baudelaire, they left for the peaceful setting of Iseltwald, a retreat from the noise at home that so disrupted Benjamin's work. Baby Stefan went into hospital. In peace, Benjamin wrote reviews of André Gide's *Strait Is the Gate* and *Lesabéndio* by a utopian writer newly introduced to him by Scholem, Paul Scheerbart.

While on holiday in Lugano, he wrote a short study, 'Fate and Character', which mused on the reading of the future and character from signs such as the alignment of planets, fortune telling cards, facial traits and lines on the palm. This dense reflection revolved the themes of mantic symbols and physiognomics in relation to character in its ethical context and fate in its divine context. Benjamin sought a notion of character severed from fate and its implied questions of guilt and morality. He approved of the stance of 'the ancient and medieval physiognomists', who recognized 'that character can be grasped only through a small number of morally indifferent basic concepts'.[17] Exemplary was the comic hero: his actions derived not tragically from his moral failings but simply from his character and, as such, he presented the possibility of free action against the determinism of fate and its guilt complex. Benjamin's treatise approvingly cited Hermann Cohen, whose thought fused Neo-Kantianism and Judaism and formed a reference point for Benjamin in those years.

Another stimulus was Ernst Bloch. Hugo Ball introduced Benjamin to Bloch, who was living nearby in Interlaken. Bloch later recalled Benjamin's 'secluded life', spent 'up to his ears in books'.[18] One of those books was Bloch's *Geist der Utopie*. On 19 September 1919 Benjamin informed Schoen that he had been thinking about politics in relation to Bloch, the only person of any significance that he had met in Switzerland. Bloch challenged Benjamin's rejection of all contemporary political tendencies.[19]

In November the Benjamins transferred to a sanatorium in Breitenstein, Austria, owned by Dora's aunt. It was warm, with good food, but the electric lights switched off at half past nine each night. Herbertz invited Benjamin back to Berne for his second doctorate, the 'Habilitation', a necessary qualification for anyone pursuing an academic career – and he dangled the possibility of a teaching post. Benjamin required financial backing from his parents, but the rocketing inflation in Germany resulted in his father refusing to fund further study for the foreseeable future. In December he wrote to Scholem from Vienna complaining about the lack of coal and the lack of a room of his own at the home of his parents-in-law.[20] Under such difficult circumstances, he thought concretely about leaving for Palestine. As he mentioned to his friend Hüne Caro, who was about to depart, 'all the decent – unearning – Jews talk of nothing else'.[21] His options otherwise appeared miserable: earn a bitter bread in Switzerland, or look for crumbs on the street in Germany.

But they remained in Austria, shuttling between the convalescence home and Dora's parents in Vienna, while Benjamin worked on a review of Bloch's *Geist der Utopie*. In January 1920 he told Scholem that in the course of preparing his review, he realised that its context was Expressionism, and so he read Kandinsky's 'wonderful' theory of painting, 'Concerning the Spiritual in Art' (1912).[22] In March the family returned to Berlin to live with Benjamin's parents at Delbrückstrasse. The first weeks were dreadful as Benjamin had to endure financial negotiations with his parents, which brought him little joy. Benjamin refused to make their house his permanent home and they responded by withdrawing his monthly allowance, offering him instead an advance on his inheritance, but set at such a level that the couple needed employment to supplement it.[23] In addition, it pained Benjamin that he did not have his library there in Berlin to show off to people, for it was all packed up in crates and stored in three places.[24]

On 26 May he told Scholem that he was enduring one of the most miserable times of his life. His father was depressed, because of financial losses suffered and the fear of more to come. His mother was jealous of Dora, on behalf of the other Dora, Benjamin's sister.[25] His parents' poor treatment of his wife and their refusal to strike an adequate financial deal culminated in a rift. Benjamin received a prepayment from his inheritance of 30,000 marks, plus another 10,000 marks and not a single piece of furniture from the house. It was, he concluded, the decay of all the maxims of bourgeois civility. Leaving Stefan at Delbrückstrasse, they moved into the home of friends Erich and Lucie Gutkind in Grünau-Falkenberg. Dora took on translation work, while Erich gave Benjamin his first lessons in Hebrew. Their main material backing came from Dora's parents, who, despite the sacrifices made on behalf of the younger couple, had little to offer. They insisted that Benjamin become a bookseller or a publisher, but for that Benjamin needed his own father to provide capital, and this was an impossibility. Miserably, Benjamin revealed that he would have to do his studies secretly and at night, alongside some sort of 'bourgeois activity' of yet undetermined type. However, he did earn 110 marks that month with three analyses of people's handwriting.[26] And one bright moment was Dora's birthday present to him, a small original by Klee, his favourite of all the Klees he had seen, titled *Introducing the Miracle* from 1916, in tempera, pen and ink on canvas, first owned by the Expressionist Herwarth Walden. He needed his own walls – four rooms was the wish – to hang it on. But in September they were compelled to return to his parents' house once again. He had completed little that summer. In the autumn he attended classes at the University in Berlin – Hebrew Grammar for beginners – and, in order to gain access to the library, he signed up for Troeltsch's seminar on Simmel's philosophy of history.[27]

By December a long depression was lifting, and an industrious period began.[28] The review of Bloch's book was complete. Bloch recalled visiting Benjamin, who was 'living unhappily and unsuitably in the family villa'. Indicating how Benjamin might lose his cares in thinking, Bloch continued: 'Our meetings were therefore all the more lively and frequent.'[29] A letter from Benjamin to Scholem mentioned plans for a book on 'true politics'. It was to include a philosophical critique of *Technik* in Scheerbart's *Lesabéndio*, an essay on 'The Dismantling of Violence' and another essay titled 'Teleology Without a Final Goal'.[30] The essay on violence became 'Critique of Violence', completed in January 1921, a response to Georges Sorel's reflections on violence. There Benjamin considered the proletarian general strike an act of 'revolutionary violence' or a 'divine violence of pure means', as a means to destroy the endless and fateful cycle of state-backed 'mythical' violence, inaugurating 'a wholly transformed work, no longer enforced by the state, an upheaval that this kind of strike not so much causes as consummates'.[31]

Benjamin's concern with linguistics and language persisted. He reflected on the process of translation, beginning work on a preface to a collection of his renditions of Baudelaire poems. This became 'The Task of the Translator', completed the following year.[32] It explained what a translation communicated: not the imparting of information, but something that developed from the original – as an echo – emerging in its 'afterlife', its renewal through its existence in another language, another epoch. The essay demanded that everything that persists through time be accorded a life, and that all life be understood not as a natural process but an historical one. Benjamin had updated – or 'actualized' – Stefan George's language in his renditions of Baudelaire's *Tableaux Parisiens*, for 'just as the tenor and the significance of the great works of literature undergo a complete transformation over the centuries, the mother tongue of the translator is transformed as well'. Translation was not a striving for literalism, but rather the communication of the pure linguistic essence or signification of a poem in present-day language.

Benjamin's own plans to learn a new language for a possible migration to Palestine were shelved. He gave up Hebrew to concentrate on his Habilitation, hopeful still for an academic career. He was perhaps negatively spurred by his reading of Heidegger's own student effort, expressing astonishment, in a letter to Scholem, that what was essentially a 'translation' of Duns Scotus could pass. Furthermore, that the author engaged in a 'miserable grovelling to Rickert and Husserl' did not 'make reading it any pleasanter'.[33]

Dora had plans for the future too – she was hoping to develop a career as an actress.[34] By the spring of 1921 what had been at times a turbulent marriage was now in crisis, and something of its dissolution could be discerned in the essay on Goethe's *Elective Affinities* that Benjamin commenced in the summer. The exercise was to focus on a single work, in what Benjamin regarded as an exemplary piece of criticism, and to illumine it immanently, rather than reading it through a life or a context. Benjamin described the essay as 'an execution of Friedrich Gundolf',[35] a prominent Jewish-German literary critic from the Stefan George circle, who counted as one of his admiring students in 1921 the young Joseph Goebbels. Gundolf banished Goethe to the retrogressive sphere of myth, with an interpretation that was no different from 'fortune-cookie mysticism', were it not for the 'bloodthirsty mysticism of its wording'.[36] For Benjamin, the novel displayed how myth worked negatively to spoil any aspirations of the characters to self-determination and free action. Benjamin excavated from the novel of 1809 its modernity.[37]

But the essay was also a study of the collapse of two relationships and their recombination in a new constellation. In the spring of 1921 Dora fell in love with Ernst Schoen and Benjamin transferred his affections to Schoen's girlfriend, Jula Cohn, a friend's sister whom he had known since 1912. It was to her that Benjamin dedicated the essay on *Elective Affinities*. Dora's view as expressed to Scholem was that Jula was too naïve to know what love is.[38] While Dora suffered from a severe pulmonary disorder, Benjamin spent the summer in Heidelberg with Jula Cohn.

In late summer 1921 a surprising and welcome offer to conceive and edit a magazine arrived from the publisher Richard Weissbach, who was set to publish Benjamin's Baudelaire translations. Benjamin selected the name of another favourite Klee water-colour, purchased that April from the Hans Goltz Gallery in Munich for 1000 marks: *Angelus Novus*. Klee remained, with Macke and possibly Kandinsky, the only reliable contemporary artist. Even when their work was weak, Benjamin could see its weakness and so could orient his aesthetic sense by it.[39] Benjamin planned the journal's contents for the next year and a half. Negotiations with Weissbach were complex. Benjamin wanted the journal to reach significant numbers, and secured plans for a number of 'proof copies' to donate to those who would not buy it but who, Benjamin thought, had to read it. Wealthier readers would subsidize the journal through a highly-priced subscription.[40] Benjamin was to receive 2000 marks a year as editor of the 120-page journal, which was to appear every three months. He designed a cover: italic bold Antiqua capitals in deep blue, with the press's name in black and printed smaller than the title.[41] A letter to the author Fritz von Herzmanovsky-Orlando revealed what sort of literary work Benjamin wished to present in its pages. He denounced the epigonic and classicist attitude in favour of radical and eccentric prose pieces.[42] He rejected 'vulgar literary Expressionism', instead intending to showcase completely unknown authors of his acquaintance, namely C. F. Heinle and his brother Wolf. Benjamin was faithful to his friend, even unto death.

Friendship was crucial for Benjamin, as attested in his many letters rich with gossip and intellectual matters to small circles of selected correspondents in different periods of his life. He could not endure maintaining contact with those who offended him or who behaved improperly in some way. His boyhood friend Blumenthal was shunned at one point. Another, Werner Kraft, was cut off at the beginning of 1921. A letter announcing the close of the friendship stated: 'For me intercourse and conversation with my friends belong to that which is most serious and most to be protected.'[43] In April he and Scholem began to address each other in the informal manner, using the word 'Du' for 'you'.[44]

Benjamin returned to a still poorly Dora in Berlin at the end of the summer. They attempted to live again as man and wife, and as parents. Benjamin enjoyed the company of Stefan. He recorded the affectionate early names that they had devised for Stefan.

> Stefanze Stefanserich Houselion (when he was laying on his
>   stomach after bathing in Berne) Mr Silly Mr Treasure (after
>   a wooden doll that I had named in the same way)

> Wauzi wauzi
> Schnauzi schnauzi

> One foot is called Felefoot (Philip Foot), the other is Franz Foot.
> When he was brought in the room in swaddling clothes he was
>   called Babysausage
> Snüll, Snüllen, Zeppel [?], Soul, Gob, Sweetielamb. In very early
>   days, in Switzerland also: Buschi, Buschonnili[45]

Benjamin also jotted down a page of mangled words that Stefan had uttered from birth until 27 November 1921. These included such formulations as 'Bildschwein' – image pig – for Wildschein – wild pig – for he had seen it in a picture; 'kiss' for anything damp that touched his face; or 'letter' for any piece of paper; 'oulish' for ugly or evil, derived from ghoulish, but co-determined by owl; and 'bagschool for satchel'.[46] He continued this with another page of coinages after December 1921. These included 'Rice eagle' for

Dora and Stefan
Benjamin.

Reich's eagle, and 'Gratophoph' for photograph.[47] He noted scenes
from Stefan's acquisition of language – how, for example, the first
word he spoke meaningfully was a version of the word 'quiet',
spoken with a finger raised in the air, just as Dora did when she
requested he be still. The recordings of his son's first sentences
indicate both the tenderness of the father and the fascination of
this scholar of childish thought processes and subjectivity: 'After
Stefan had been undressed he was left alone in the room and he
cried. When Dora came in to see him after a little while he said:
Wipe nose and dry tears all by self.'[48]

On another occasion Dora showed him a page in Friedrich Justin Bertuch's twelve-volume *Picture-book for Children*. Berries were depicted on it. Stefan asked, as he always did: 'May I eat that, yes?' Dora replied: 'Yes'. To which Stefan responded: 'Little Steffe should eat that.'

Dora: But you are little Steffe.
Stefan: No, little Steffe in the book (points to an empty space on the page) should come and eat it.[49]

The regime of the house in 1921 is indicated in one vignette. There had been several days of enforced quiet in the house so that Benjamin might work. When Benjamin was away, though, Stefan went to the kitchen and told his nursemaid Grete to be very quiet, for 'he must do his work now'. Then he climbed the stairs and opened two doors to enter his own room. He stood there immobile in the dark for some time, and when Grete arrived he pleaded, having internalized the presence of his absent father, 'Grete do not disturb him. He really has to work.'[50]

For several days in November 1921 Stefan mimicked lifeless objects such as a pear rolling on the ground or a clock striking.[51] Benjamin also noticed telepathic abilities when Stefan was in a half-sleep.[52] These observations of words, sentences and behaviours, recorded intermittently until March 1932, found their way into Benjamin's 'Doctrine of the Similar' and his theories of the 'mimetic capability' of 1933.[53] Words, he found, are slippery. They accrue extra significance through childish reasoning and agglomeration. 'Potatoes' [*Kartoffel*], for example, Stefan called his own little bones [*Knöchel*]. April 1922 brought the following entry from Benjamin:

Miss Burchard says: The hare tried as hard as he was able, to which he responded with lots of laughter and repeated again and again: 'hard as he was able – hard as he was able. That is not able, that is vegetable'.[54]

Another entry described how Benjamin's friend, Florens Christian Rang, gave Stefan an image on which there was a saint. Stefan called this figure the ship's kobold.[55] Rang, a curious acquaintance made through Ernst Gutkind in 1920, was a much older man who had studied protestant theology and planned to become a minister of the church, but became instead a conservative-nationalist. Benjamin wished to publish him in *Angelus Novus*. But in October 1922 he informed him that the journal was unlikely to appear, as the publisher was in financial difficulty. He also told Rang that his father-in-law had arrived to mediate with his parents, for his father was about to disinherit him if he did not take up a position in a bank. Benjamin still hankered after an academic career – and so still needed the Habilitation. He claimed to be happy to earn his keep as long as it did not prevent him from pursuing this goal.[56]

To ease the immediate financial crisis, Benjamin deployed his extensive knowledge of old books and their markets, buying books in markets and antiquarian bookshops in the north of the city and selling them for a profit in the west.[57] Benjamin hoped for some capital from his relations in order to open his own antiquarian bookshop, but it was not forthcoming, though his in-laws agreed to help as much as they could. Indeed, the appearance of his father-in-law set his father even more intransigently against him. Benjamin was compelled to break off relations, rejecting an 8000 mark monthly 'charity handout', for it could not be received without 'unbearable pestering and surveillance'.[58]

There was more bad fortune. Benjamin hoped to return to Heidelberg to take up a Habilitation place, but instead the lucky recipient was Karl Mannheim.[59] Benjamin wished to present a purely philosophical project somewhere, but he suspected it might be easier to find a sponsor if he were to write on post-mediaeval

German literature. In December Benjamin considered a Habilitation in aesthetics with Hans Cornelius, in Frankfurt, and he visited the city, meeting there with the theological philosopher Franz Rosenzweig. Frankfurt was also the hometown of an acquaintance, the literary editor of the *Frankfurter Zeitung*, Siegfried Kracauer, through whom in the summer of 1923 he met a young doctoral student, Theodor Wiesengrund Adorno.

The outside world and the 'grim situation in Germany' pressed ever more on Benjamin.[60] In letters in January 1923 he referred to the French and Belgian occupation of the Ruhr and the 'terrible mental infection' that accompanied it.[61] In these months there was much talk of illness in the family, and amongst acquaintances, such as Wolf Heinle, who was dying. Retreating from the chaos, the Benjamins went back to the sanatorium at Breitenstein, so that all three might convalesce. Benjamin was happy to be out of Germany but he felt alone, as he told Rang on 27 January, in a letter encouraging Rang to donate money to the Heinle family, as he himself had done.

> And so it seems as if there is well nigh no good news at all to be expected from whatever corner of Germany. Most of my correspondents have left me completely in the lurch. In a certain respect we are quite glad of our isolation here, however not untroubled, as we have been greatly disturbed in the last few days by Stefan's minor but unfamiliar and painful ailments. Since this morning things seem to be somewhat better. Dora has put on a lot of weight, but there still needs to be much more improvement in her bodily state, as well as that of her nerves.[62]

Germany was a place without hope. The dream of *Angelus Novus* was over. Again he raised the prospect of learning Hebrew as a prelude to emigration.[63] A trip through Germany in February, on his return yet again to his parents' home, took him to the edge of hopelessness and provided a good view of the abyss.[64] Habilitation in Frankfurt offered a possible escape route from the parents' home, if not from Germany. A new interest – in *Trauerspiel*, Baroque mourning plays – was taking shape. Benjamin visited the fearfully 'expensive town' once more, staying with a great uncle for some weeks.[65] On 12 March 1923 he travelled to nearby Giessen for the first meeting of the Frankfurter Kreis, a grouping around Rang and Buber, with some Quakers and a Catholic striving for political and social change out of religious conviction. 'An unsuspected side of Germany appeared to me', Benjamin wrote afterwards to Rang.[66]

Back in Berlin in the autumn, conditions worsened. There was hunger in the city and the tram network was collapsing. Dora took work as a personal secretary to Karl von Wiegand, German correspondent for Hearst newspapers.[67] There was hopeful news from Frankfurt. Cornelius rejected Benjamin's proposal to write his Habilitation in aesthetics, but Franz Schultz, a literary historian, took him on; still, Benjamin's hope simply to submit the essay on Goethe's *Elective Affinities* was dashed.[68] The thoughts on Baroque mourning plays needed to be developed into something worthy of submission to a university. However, in September Benjamin described working on 'refractory material', characterizing his thought process as 'subtle' and, as such, liable to go awry.[69] Still he was determined to complete a manuscript, noting he would 'rather be chased away with shame and dishonour than withdraw'.[70] If he failed, he planned to go abroad, perhaps following Scholem, who had left for Palestine.

In September Benjamin depicted the parameters of existence in inflationary Germany. The tract included a protest against money:

All close personal relationships are hit by an almost superhuman, piercing clarity in which they are scarcely able to survive. For on the one hand, money stands ruinously at the centre of every vital interest, but on the other, this is the very barrier before which almost all relationships malfunction; so, more and more, in the natural as in the moral sphere, unreflected trust, calm, and health are disappearing.[71]

His bitter assessment of current conditions, 'Descriptive Analysis of the German Decline', was a parting gift for Scholem, written on a scroll. Little worthwhile remained in Germany, and what did – his energy and some valuables – was depleting rapidly.[72] Dora, who earned the household's money, was ill again, her work proving too exhausting. Benjamin was concerned by newspaper reports of anti-Semitic unrest in the centre of Berlin.[73] On 6 November 1923 the *Frankfurter Zeitung* reported on how the hike in bread prices had been used as a pretext to whip up crowds, loot shops and beat up Jews. Few Gentiles had resisted these attacks, observed the newspaper.[74] While embittered and helpless Berliners scrabbled for bread, Benjamin fed his intellect by exchanging books to acquire new books by Stendhal and Balzac and the first German translation of Dante.[75] The study of the Baroque brought bibliographical oddities daily. Through his burrowing into the obscure collections of the Berlin state library, he salvaged some several hundred extracts from little-considered mourning plays, theological tracts and philosophical reflections. Germany in decline clashed with the other Germany that Rang had unlocked. Benjamin told the Gentile Rang that he represented 'true Germanness', and that he himself was bound to his own Germanness, ' for nothing leads deeper and binds more dearly' than the 'rescue' of old literature.[76]

But, in explaining why he could not sign Rang's treatise about reparation payments, *German Shelters*, on behalf of 'We Germans', he revealed that Jewishness compromised his position. The Jew could not speak for the German people at a time of crisis, for he did not belong in the same way. The issue of Jewishness and Germanness had returned forcefully, after the assassinations of the anarchist Gustav Landauer and the foreign minister Walther Rathenau by Rightists. Both were Jews. Rathenau had brokered reparation agreements for the German nation, and Benjamin discerned a certain 'necessity' in his murder. Landauer, initiator of the Munich Soviet Republic in 1919, had 'screamed' against the newly constituted nation rather than spoken in its name, and he had been killed in prison, after the bloody suppression of the republic by the army and the Freikorps. The visibility of these Jews, Benjamin contended, had damaged the relationship of Jews and Germans under current conditions. For the time being, only secret personal relations were possible: 'today, the noble natures of both peoples are obligated to silence regarding their association'. There was, still, a quiet task to undertake: the updating of Germany's cultural inheritance and its past. Germany was allowing its intellectual treasures to rust, for Germany was languishing in isolation, and so its culture could only wither if it remained unnourished by the present.[77]

Benjamin was reaching the limit of what he could endure. The hyperinflation was dizzying: on 1 May 1923 $1 cost 31,700 marks. On 1 July it cost 160,400 marks, and on 1 August 1,103,000 marks. From then on, prices doubled every few hours. Workers rushed to spend all their money before it bought only half as much again. Million-mark notes were used as wallpaper. A single German mark in 1913 was the equivalent of 1,261,000,000,000 in December 1923. Benjamin was compelled to calculate where he could live longest on the smallest amount. He hoped for a price collapse. Dora lost her post, but, mercifully, was offered it again, which was good fortune as its hard currency wage was the only one that really bought anything.

The book of translations of poems by Baudelaire, *Tableaux parisiens*, appeared in October 1923, published in a small print run of 500 copies. To his immense frustration, Benjamin received no honorarium and no copies.[78] There were delays in sending the books out for review and, once they were sent, there were only two reviews. These, one by author Stefan Zweig, were negative.

Benjamin's modern and urbanist renditions were criticised as 'metrically naïve' and too literal.[79] This blow to his reputation unleashed a childish streak of rudeness in Benjamin, who privately blamed 'big-nosed' Siegfried Kracauer, the literary editor of the *Frankfurter Zeitung*, for picking the wrong reviewer.[80] Another writer was prepared to deem Benjamin a genius though. At the end of 1923 Hugo von Hofmannsthal picked up on the *Elective Affinities* essay and published it in his journal, *Neue deutsche Beiträge*, in two parts over the next two years.

In 1924 the influx of dollars stabilized the mark. Benjamin left in the spring for Capri, where he could afford to live for several months. While there, he translated Balzac's supernatural novella *Ursule Mirouët*. He hoped to complete his Habilitation, but difficulties arose. Noise pursued him, and it was too hot for him to work during the day.[81] He continued to be unimpressed by academia. Reporting on an international congress of philosophy, occasioned by the 700th anniversary of the University of Naples, he sneered: 'Philosophers are the worst paid lackeys of the international bourgeoisie, because they are the most irrelevant.' Benjamin was shocked at their eagerness in flaunting their subaltern status.[82]

Benjamin used the language of the Left – and on Capri he read the most important book for his generation of disaffected Communist-leaning intellectuals, Georg Lukács' *History and Class Consciousness*. Contrarily, though, he took out a subscription to a Royalist journal of the Right, *Action Française*, claiming that it relayed details of German political developments despite its brittle stance.[83] But his immediate intellectual milieu was quite different. He was developing connections to the post-Dada avant-garde, proponents of a 'new configuration' in art and architecture, collectivist, industrialized, constructivist and destructive (of tradition). In June his translation of 'La Photographie à l'Envers' ('Photography Inside-out'), Tristan Tzara's introduction to Man Ray's *Les Champs délicieux*, appeared in Hans Richter's magazine *G. Zeitschrift für elementare Gestaltung* ('G. Journal for

Elementary Form'), alongside contributions by Mies van der Rohe, Ludwig Hilberseimer, Raoul Hausmann, George Grosz, Hans Arp, Kurt Schwitters and Ernst Schoen.

In June too he met Asja Lacis. A letter to Scholem mentioning this 'most remarkable acquaintance', whom he met in the renowned Café Hiddigeigei, described her as a Bolshevik Latvian, a Christian, who acted and directed, and with whom he chatted long into the night.[84] His next letter to Scholem repeated the news – he told of meeting a Russian revolutionary from Riga, 'one of the most outstanding women' he had ever met.[85] He also noted that through her he had gained an 'intensive insight into the actuality of a radical communism', a 'vital liberation', even though it disturbed his work and his 'bourgeois rhythm of life'. Lacis was in Italy with her daughter, Daga, and her lover, the German playwright and theatre critic Bernhard Reich. A doctor had recommended the trip to Capri to improve Daga's poor state of health.

A less significant meeting was with the leader of Italian Futurism, Marinetti, who was in Capri visiting Franz Werfel. Marinetti was a 'character', and he performed a 'noise poem' with horse whinnying, cannon thunder, rattling carriages and machine gun fire.[86] In July Benjamin found himself stranded on the island. Madame Curie had explained Capri's curious attraction by its increased radioactivity, but Benjamin's immediate reason for staying was blood poisoning, having been bitten by an insect. He needed money urgently, and hoped that Weissbach could provide cash drawn from sales of the Baudelaire book or an advance.[87] Weissbach sent no money, and in October Benjamin was pressing him once more.[88]

Mussolini visited the island in September. There was surprise that the leader had visited South Italy, where, Benjamin noted, he was unpopular and the coldness of the population had to be masked by plentiful bunting and decoration. It was rumoured that six thousand secret agents had shielded him in Naples. Benjamin observed a discrepancy between Mussolini in the flesh and the heartbreaker of the postcards. In reality he was inert and haughty. Benjamin relished describing the fascist. Mussolini seemed liberally smeared in rancid oil. His body was plump and unarticulated, like a fat grocer's fist.[89] If Naples repelled Mussolini, it opened itself up fully to Benjamin and to his paramour Lacis. The two visited the city, and wrote a city sketch that was published in the *Frankfurter Zeitung* the following year. 'Naples' ruminated on spatial and temporal porosity, whereby public and private zones of experience were intermingled, as exemplified in the Neapolitan arcade – an architectural form that would soon gain in importance for Benjamin – and in the bustle of the streets that so contrasted with deserted Berlin. Naples is a city crosscut by routes and intersections where things and places – a staircase jutting from a building, for example – appear and disappear unpredictably. Through old paths new streets were hacked, attempting to inject revised modes of living and order into historical accretion.

Scholem reacted with alarm to Benjamin's growing interest in communist politics – both Scholem and Benjamin had activist Bolshevik brothers, which provided a measure of the meaning of engagement. Benjamin felt compelled to defend his stance in a letter. His relationship to communism had developed through his reading of Lukács. He was impressed by Lukács' philosophically adroit combination of theory and practice, and he was drawn to the 'political praxis of communism' as a 'binding position', though he knew that there must come tensions between Lukács' Hegelian dialectics and what he conceived as his own nihilism. In practical terms, Lacis provided a context for his developing thought. Through her, prospects opened of publication in Moscow and a dialogue with the Soviet intelligentsia.[90]

After a journey through Rome and Florence, Benjamin returned to Berlin in December, where everyone agreed there had been a change in him, following the 'communist signals' from Capri. These, he admitted to Scholem, 'awoke in me the will not to mask the actual and political moments in my thought as till now in the Old Franconian fashion, but to develop them, as an experiment, in an extreme way'.[91] This meant the retreat of literary exegesis, with its attempts to conserve the best and restore what is genuine in the German tradition. But until he was able to find texts of quite different significance and totality, he was forced to 'spin "politics" out of' himself. He also admitted how surprised he was at his 'proximity to various aspects of an extreme Bolshevik theory'.[92]

Such new concerns did not preclude consideration of literary marginalia, such as Karl Hobrecker's *Old Forgotten Children's Books*. It was a book that Benjamin should have written, given his extensive collection of children's literature. It prompted two reviews, for a bibliographical circular and a Leipzig-based illustrated newspaper. Such small-scale reflections on minor publications could still provide opportunities to develop significant stances. Some books, he decreed, were an invitation to the world of language – not through words as such, but through images, or rather through line images, the forceful edges of woodcuts, for example. Through these, children are led out of themselves (out of the dreamy self-sunken worlds evoked by coloured illustrations) into the world, inducted into language by the 'compelling invitation to describe' the strong outlines. In any case, aesthetics find a new footing – away from illusionist mimeticism. The world is apprehended not as a passive contemplative display, but rather as a thing recreated in the imaginative activity of children – in what Benjamin termed the 'poetry of their own' – and re-enacted in a child's inhabitation of the images' surface, which was 'readily filled out'.[93] Imagination plumbed depths beyond those of the flat page. It joined dots and scattered them, spinning curlicues between strewn fragments.

Childish imagination worked, Benjamin decreed, on the lowliest objects. Children, he claimed, loved to haunt any site where things were being visibly worked on, irresistibly drawn by the detritus generated by building, gardening, housework, tailoring or carpentry: 'In waste products they recognize the face that the world of things turns directly and solely to them.' By playing with the broken-down and the unwanted, children combine 'materials of widely differing kinds in a new, intuitive relationship', and so 'produce their own small world of things within the greater one'. The fairy tale itself is a waste product, emerging from the growth and decay of the saga:

> Children are able to manipulate fairy tales with the same ease and lack of inhibition that they display in playing with pieces of cloth and building blocks. They build their world out of motifs from the fairy tale, combining its various elements.[94]

Armadillos in F. J. Bertuch's *Bilderbuch für Kinder*, a favourite book in the Benjamin household.

Just as children were attracted to scraps, they assailed the books they read, turning them into waste matter, using them up. Books were marked by the patina of grubby children's hands, which made them of no interest to book collector snobs.[95] Some books allowed themselves to be further destroyed. Monochrome woodcuts – simple, plain illustrations – introduced children to the waking world of script. The images drew children out, making them complete the image, for instance by scribbling on it. In addition, Benjamin spoke with wonder of Bertuch's *Picture-book for Children*, published in Weimar between 1792 and 1830, with its one thousand coloured and high-quality copperplate illustrations and countless other images, from the eruption of Vesuvius to the patent of an English washing machine, all mobilized in the service of 'spreading out the knowledge of the epoch before the child'. It was a book that Benjamin and Dora often showed to Stefan. Incredibly, Bertuch invited children to snip out pictures from the volumes. To appropriate knowledge meant grasping it actively, with the hand that scribbled, and with the scissors that tracked the outlines and clipped out the figures.

The fairytale world, as much as the abandoned wood shavings on a shed floor, allowed the child to imaginatively construct the world anew. Shavings and fairytales presented themselves as scrap, as waste, ripe for reappropriation. The emergent core of Benjamin's own practice was thus discernible. From this point on, fundamental to Benjamin's thought was the idea of montage, of juxtaposition, of sticking this motif next to that. Montaging, for Benjamin, cannot be disassociated from the act of rescuing, the efforts to recycle rubbish, detritus, scraps that appear to have no value. He deployed for the purposes of critical enlightenment what he called 'rags and refuse', a procedure later described in his *Arcades Project*.[96] He planned a series of illustrated publications written by himself and others, such as Bloch, investigating degraded forms of material. His notebook from the period includes a list of topics, such as studies of the aesthetics of postcards, waxwork cabinets, kitsch, cabaret and advertising.[97] Benjamin's procedure involved less a rescue of tradition than the rescue of experiences unacknowledged, experiences under threat, rejectamenta, materials on the point of disappearance.

4

Books after Books, 1925–9

In 1925 Benjamin's Habilitation was still to be completed. The conclusion and much of the most intricate material, notably the first third, were unwritten, and there remained plenty of fiddly bibliographical work. Benjamin searched for a typist, someone who could cope with the 'indescribably delicate' work, a 'highly educated lady' to whom one could dictate for a week.[1] His object of study was the ghoulish mourning play, which exhibited a predilection for ruination and intrigue, used language fatally as a curse or command, and imbued melancholic drama with a 'world-sadness' and boredom in a timeless time. He also investigated emblem books, those fragmentary and riddle-like hieroglyphic combinations of word and image set together for purposes of moral instruction. Through these he pondered the hierarchies of aesthetic form, specifically allegory and symbolism. He examined how classical tragedy emerged from myth, while these mourning plays drew their energies from history itself. Their specific historical period was one of gloom and wreckage and endless war, which expressed itself in doomy timelessness, but also proposed – contra the fatality of myth – that historical agency does exist, even if the protagonists were unable to realise this fully and their *Real*-politicking collapsed back into myth and paralysis. The heroism and transcendence of the classical world was denied to these political worldlings.

Benjamin told Scholem of his plans for the introduction, a prolegomenon to epistemological theory, which he described as 'unmitigated chutzpah'.[2] It was esoteric and self-reflexive. It digressed. It used quotations as detonators of ideas that blasted against the analytic context to produce a montage as fragmentary and aphoristic as the body of material under study. It fractured texts into many meanings and none, refusing to pin things down, and determining that very inconclusiveness to be of prime significance. It confounded reading, drawing to its aid simultaneously Kabbalist language theory and Platonic idealism, Croce's 'universal singularity' and Leibnizian Monadism. It set the interpreter's moment in relation to the moment of the text.

Benjamin had grounds to imagine that his Habilitation might pass – his supervisor was dean of the faculty. But equally he feared success because that meant remaining in Frankfurt, dealing with students and writing lectures: aspects of an academic career that 'murderously attack time', the time needed to fulfil a long-cherished plan to write on Goethe's 'New Melusine' and to compose his collected essays on politics. It would also eat into the time that he needed to devote himself earnestly to the study of Hebrew, he told Scholem.[3]

In Frankfurt a new medium for his thoughts opened up, as he was casting around for opportunities in the uncertain knowledge of his Habilitation's fate. He noted that Ernst Schoen had become a programme assistant at the Frankfurt radio station, and would very likely offer him the chance to participate in programmes, for 'all the university lecturers are blabbing on the radio here'.[4] Frankfurt radio was especially interesting during the Weimar era. It was populated by innovators such as Hans Flesch, brother-in-law of composer Paul Hindemith, who in his first broadcasts in 1924 carried out live sound experiments to make the audience aware of the mediation of the material. Flesch also transmitted courtroom trials, commissioned radio plays by Brecht and Weill, used mobile studios and, in 1931, set up the first German studio for electronic radio work. Schoen encouraged Benjamin to work for a magazine that accompanied the radio listings, as a move into the ambit of radio might offer promising new types of employment.

Journalism beckoned Benjamin, and he pressed for publishing opportunities in the *Frankfurter Zeitung* and in literary journals. He told Scholem that he was reading the latest French literature – the Surrealists and Valéry – in order to familiarize himself with the techniques of criticism.[5] He was invited to contribute regularly on French art theory for the German cultural journal *Die literarische Welt*. A plan was hatching to co-translate with Franz Hessel a volume of Proust's *In Search of Lost Time* – *In the Shadow of Young Girls in Flower*. His work on Baroque tragedy had a promise of publication – until the publishing house collapsed in April.[6] He was also pursuing the publication of a collection of writings that he had collated since the beginning of 1923, *One-way Street*. Written originally as a very personal testament that used friends' names as section headings, the book was a 'manuscript of aphorisms',[7] a cryptic guide to the Berlin of Benjamin's adult years that recorded the city of modernity as a place of street signs, asphalt roads, underground works, construction sites and petrol stations.

In late May 1925 Benjamin wrote to Scholem about his miserable financial circumstances and the 'deeply deplorable collision of literary and economic plans'. He noted that if his journalistic efforts turned sour he would 'probably accelerate' his 'involvement in Marxist politics and – with the view in the foreseeable future of going to Moscow at least temporarily – join the party'.[8] Benjamin was seeking other routes, for the prospects of a successful Habilitation were diminishing. The work on Baroque mourning plays accorded well enough with academic form: it was rich with footnotes; it had tracked down many obscure and overlooked primary sources; it drew on the work of some emergent theoreticians, notably Lukács' *Soul and Form* and Panovsky and Saxl on Dürer's *Melencolia*. But it was idiosyncratic. The study of cultural form in the sixteenth and seventeenth centuries had unearthed arcane material that exerted a 'vertiginous attraction' on Benjamin.[9] Such a force could hardly be accommodated within the usual academic format and according to the usual academic methodologies. Benjamin revealed that the thesis was intended to bring down the stiff walls of separation between disciplines. He showed it to Schultz, only to find the professor unprepared to accept it as a submission in literary history. Benjamin was told to submit it to Cornelius as a work on aesthetics.

In May he handed it in with heavy heart, and told Scholem that there were a thousand reasons why it seemed ever more distant that he might take up a university career. Cornelius found the work incomprehensible and passed it on to two colleagues. One was Max Horkheimer, who deemed it impenetrable. Benjamin was advised to withdraw his application, in order to be spared official rejection. The work had already received plaudits elsewhere, from the writer Hofmannsthal and a Professor of German Literature in Vienna. But university accreditation appeared hopeless. Benjamin felt betrayed by Schultz, but he mused that all in all he was glad. The long trek through provincial universities was not for him, and Frankfurt appeared as the 'most bitter desert' since the death of his friend Rang in October 1924.[10]

Benjamin's thoughts turned away from old German literature to French modernism – the Surrealists, the Proust translation and a translation of 'Anabasis', a long poem by Saint-John Perse written in China. He pursued the controversy unleashed by Lukács' *History and Class Consciousness* with hostile contributions by Communist Party men, Laszlo Rudas and Abram Moiseyevich Deborin.[11] His brother gave him the first German collation of Lenin's writings, and Benjamin waited impatiently for the next, philosophical, volume.[12] And he planned his autumn holidays.

On 19 August 1925, the day that the *Frankfurter Zeitung* printed the city sketch of Naples co-written with Lacis, Benjamin boarded a ship in Hamburg. Passing through Barcelona, Seville, Genoa, Pisa,

Lucca and Livorno, he alighted finally in Naples in late September. On board the ship he made friends with the captain, a man who longed for learning. Benjamin promised to send him his translation of Balzac.[13] Sailing past Genoa, he glimpsed Africa and decided to visit there soon, obtaining a visa for Libya. But he did not reach Africa. In Naples and Capri he wrote a 'barbaric polemic' against Fritz von Unruh's 'pacifist' travelogue, *Wings of Nike*, devouring the author's 'skin and bones'.[14] The attack had to be 'formidable', he told Scholem, for it was to mark out his place in *The Literary World* as a political critic.[15]

> The great prose of all evangelists of peace spoke of war. To stress one's own love of peace is always the close concern of those who have brought about war. But he who wants peace should speak of war. He should speak of the past one (is he not called Fritz von Unruh,[16] the one thing about which he would remain silent), and, above all, he should speak of the coming one. He should speak of its threatening plotters, its powerful causes, its terrifying means. And yet might this be perhaps the only discourse against which the salons, which allowed Mr von Unruh entry, remain completely hermetically sealed? The much pleaded peace, which is already there, proves, when seen by daylight, to be the one – and the only 'eternal', known to us – which those enjoy who have commanded in war and who wish to be setting the tone at the peace party. Mr von Unruh has become one of these.[17]

In November he headed north to Riga to meet Lacis, who was devising political theatre at a club for Leftist trade unions.

One section in *One-way Street*, titled 'Stereoscope', presents a description of everyday life in Riga. This description was one heavily coloured by Benjamin's fascinations – commerce, public activity, a childlike plenitude of experience that might be glimpsed in the modern urban realm. Benjamin described the market, the stalls and traders, housewives and shoppers, the small steamers on the river Dvina, docked in the 'blackish dwarftown'.[18] Benjamin was drawn to the little shops of the town, selling undergarments and hats, leather goods, coal, sugar, boat tackle and ironware. The city laid itself out as visual intrigue. Benjamin observed how, on signboards and walls, each shop depicted its wares, but these depictions were oversized:

> One shop in the town has cases and belts larger than life on its bare brick walls. A low corner-house with a shop for corsets and millinery is decorated with ladies' faces complete with finery, and severe bodices painted on a yellow-ochre background.[19]

The giant wares existed alongside the miniaturized steamers. Much was toylike, out of perspective, too big or too small. Commodities became playthings or swelled to the proportions of fairytales and myth. The town recalled one of the children's picture books that Benjamin collected.

> Somewhere else shoes rain from horns of plenty. Ironmongery is painted in detail, hammers, cogs, pliers and the tiniest screws on one board that looks like a page from an outmoded child's painting-book. With such pictures the town is permeated: posed as if from chests of drawers.[20]

Colours were either flat or dramatic. Playthings could be bought from 'petty-bourgeois women', multi-coloured paper rods glowing against the grimy boards. Flashes of colour leapt out to his eye – stereoscopically – such as the red and white piles of apples, trivial goods slashing the grimy drabness of the setting. Nearby sugar sacks and mounds of coal pulsed in grey and black. Amidst all this, the seemingly eternal time and values of the deep red church rose above the ever-shifting values of commerce and the lived time of human bustle. Between the pictures, the 'memory-images' carried in Benjamin's imagination, something else loomed, not reducible to a picture as such, not portable or appropriable. Benjamin warned ominously of the 'desolate fortress-like buildings evoking all the terrors of czarism' – the tenuous present of newly independent Riga trapped in the oppressive past, whose forces might yet recur in the future.

Such a montage of city images, with its sudden flares of red colour, generated in writing an effect similar to that produced by Sasha Stone's dust jacket for *One-way Street* when it appeared in 1928: a jumble of urban signs, buildings, transportation. Modernist montaging of the city reacted to the energy of city life, including its ludicrous juxtapositions, its Surrealist connections, its seemingly arbitrary logic. The modernist montage city was a pile-up of buildings jostling in cramped urban centres and interspersed with street signage and trams and, sometimes, people. The world was made image, or image upon image, each synaptic visual connection tumbling into dreams or memory, stimulating, playful, multivalent.

Benjamin went to Riga full of hope. Another entry in *One-way Street*, titled 'Ordnance', explained how he arrived in Riga unannounced and walked the unfamiliar streets for two hours trying to find his bearings. Sparks sprayed from each cornerstone and flames darted from every gate, for from any place the beloved might have suddenly emerged. He had to catch sight of Lacis before she saw him, for 'had she touched me with the match of her eyes, I would have gone up like a powder keg'.[21] He appeared at the rehearsal rooms. Lacis was surprised to see him, but not pleasantly. She was absorbed in the theatrical production and irritated by police interference. He stayed a few weeks and worked on translating Proust. In December 1925 he returned to Berlin.

On 14 January 1926 he told Scholem about the booklet he had been compiling since Stefan's birth on the 'opinions et pensées' of his son. He admitted that his absences made it patchy, but there were several dozen strange words, coinages and vignettes that he intended to have typed up and distributed to a few chosen individuals. It was not a parodic gesture. This was evidence of the thought processes of a child, and deserved a place in Scholem's archive of Benjamin's works.[22] Entries from around that time delighted in the child's 'logic':

At the table Stefan says in every book it is always the case that the people one loves come off well. I say: 'In your books that is always the case – later on for grown-ups there are books where that is not the case [']. In response he laughs out loud and says: 'Yes, a lover is killed!' (By 'lover' he means, as it transpired, someone who is loved {by the reader} and the sentence 'a lover is killed ['] he had read to his great amusement a few days previously on the cover of 'The Profile'[.][23]

Stefan holds colourful shiny paper against the light and calls out again and again: 'German illusions'[.][24]

Mammy, the cat is laughing. It is really laughing. But I don't know why it is laughing. It is laughing even when I don't say anything funny. But perhaps cat jokes are different.[25]

He is lying in bed, pulls his pyjamas up. I ask: why? 'It is modern, you know . . . One has to see the stomach, the navel, at all times, because then one knows what holds one together. ('It is modern, you know' has been one of his turns of phrase for a while.)[26]

The Baroque book, the essay on Goethe's *Elective Affinities* and the collection of aphorisms *One-way Street* were all scheduled for Ernst Rowohlt's imprint. In the interim, Benjamin wrote short reviews and reflections to be published in the *Frankfurter Zeitung* and literary magazines. He kept himself abreast of political events in Europe, reading French newspapers and Trotsky's *Where is England Going?* He read the theorist of matriarchy Johann Jakob Bachofen and the phenomenologist Ludwig Klages. He mused on cultural developments in France, writing 'Dreamkitsch', a gloss on Surrealism and the historical nature of dreams, the medium that catches all that is cast into the past by technological change. Commonplace objects were stars of dreams once they fell into disuse. The rapid industrial changes of the second half of the nineteenth century exacerbated the process of technological remaindering. For this reason, there was much that was kitschy and sentimental in the dream world – and it was with this that the Surrealists struck up a dialogue, deciphering 'the contours of the banal as rebus'. Surrealists, he claimed, quite correctly executed not psychoanalysis of the self but of things, for the energies of extinct things bristled at our core as well. Benjamin noted that what formerly counted as art stood two metres away from the body, but through kitsch the thing-world shifted towards the person. Kitsch offered itself to the groping touch of the 'new man' – one struggling to emerge from the nineteenth century – and built its figures inside him to form a being, who could be called the *mobilierte Mensch*, the 'furnished person' or 'lodger'.[27]

In March 1926 Benjamin took off for Paris, invited there by Franz Hessel, with whom he was translating Proust. He described the first day of the trip in a letter to Jula Cohn, now wife of his friend Fritz Radt and a sculptress – she made a bust of Benjamin's head earlier that year. Writing from the Hotel du Midi, Paris on 22 March, he described how he left Hagen at 5 am by train and played poker with a Spaniard, an Egyptian and a Berliner. He arrived in Paris and went to the Café du Dôme in Montparnasse, a new bohemian quarter populated by Russians. Then there was a meal with friends and on to a 'bal musette'. Finally at 4 am he visited a nightclub. The next morning, without interruption to his routine, he woke early – for Paris was so familiar – in order to translate Proust.[28] His small Paris library was 'mainly composed of communist

Walter Benjamin. Bust by Jula Radt.

things'.[29] He continued following the Lukács controversy in *Arbeiter-Literatur* and the debates initiated by Bogdanov and Bukharin on a 'general Tectology', or the universal science of organization, which considered the commonalities in the human, biological and physical systems. Benjamin was intrigued by this 'fragmentary first attempt at a Marxist universal history'.[30] He would have to prove himself in this arena too, for he had managed to get a commission to write 300 lines on Goethe 'from the standpoint of Marxist doctrine' for the *Great Russian Encyclopaedia*.[31]

The streets of Paris continued to exert their pull and compensated for such 'dreadful' events as a Surrealist soirée that he happened to see in a small private theatre. The Hessels enjoyed the raunchy delights of night-time Paris – and Benjamin complained about the flirtatious behaviour he endured from Hessel's wife, the journalist Helen Grund.[32] He saw Bloch daily, 'or especially nightly', for half a year, which Bloch interpreted as a 'true symbiosis':

> So close, in fact, that as is usual with excessive proximity and enforced dependence upon one another in a great city (even being Paris, her intellectuals and celebrities had turned a cold shoulder to Benjamin at that time), our relationship gave rise to a sort of trench fever, or at least this had its place in our relationship. I mean: we had a bit too much of one another due to this enforced proximity.[33]

Benjamin also enjoyed walks and car trips with his friend Thankmar Freiherr von Münchhausen through the markets that dropped 'like bombs' into an area, with their tents and waffle stands, shooting ranges, butchers' stalls, antiques and picture dealers. In one he found three wonderful glass snow shakers.[34] Such were the trivial, everyday things and spaces that attracted Benjamin. In April he wrote to Kracauer about future writing plans, and mentioned some work on the history of toys and the preparation of some notes under the title 'Ships and Stalls', revealing the secret affinity between fairgrounds and harbours.[35] Another letter to Kracauer in June 1926 stated:

> If you pursue further the skewed bits of the petty bourgeois stage of dreams and desires, then I think you will come across

wonderful discoveries and perhaps we will meet each other at a point which I have been gauging with all my energy for a year without being able to hit it in the centre: the picture postcard. You may perhaps one day write that salvation of the stamp collection for which I have been waiting for so long without wanting to chance it.[36]

Benjamin was called away from Paris by his father's death on 18 July 1926. He spent a month in Berlin, then returned to Paris for three weeks, where he met the reform Rabbi and post-Zionist Judah Leon Magnes, founder and chancellor of the Hebrew University of Jerusalem, to whom he poured out his frustrations about his lack of recognition in Germany. Then he headed south with Jula Radt. Enjoyment came in the form of reading *Tristram Shandy* and walking with Kracauer in Marseilles. Kracauer's observations appeared in an essay titled 'Two Planes', his thoughts crystallized around Marseilles' bay and one of the squares that they stumbled upon.[37] The backstreets were barely legible for the walkers, the narrow alleyways convoluted and complicated by winding stairways and, from the outsider's perspective, equally opaque jumbles of Arabic signs. This was an unstable geography, where unfamiliar walkers traversed the quarter as in a dream, for illogically it seemed as if the 'improvised backdrops' were torn down and resurrected in other places. In the midst of all this, a square was found. It emerged suddenly for the walkers released from the clutches of the crinkled alleyways. Against the tangle of backstreets, this square's lines appeared drawn with a ruler. Visitors were compelled to move to the square's centre, into a position of exposure, subjected to the stares of those behind windows and walls. The square was never sought purposefully, but once found 'it expands toward the four sides of the world, overpowering the pitiful, soft, private parts of the dream'.

Benjamin was in search of peace and quiet. He moved on to Agay. There were plans to translate more of Proust's odyssey of memory with Hessel, but the process made him ill. He was spending too much time with an author whose intentions were too close to his own. He felt he was being poisoned. But his hope was that as a translator of Proust he would be accorded some status in France.[38] Back in Berlin in October he was still ailing and felt depressed about publication delays. *One-way Street* was completed in September, but Rowohlt had still not published the book on Baroque drama or the study of Goethe's *Elective Affinities*. He read René Fülöp-Miller's *The Mind and Face of Bolshevism*, which presented Bolshevism as a form of religious sectarianism. Acknowledging its inaccuracies and bias, he recommended it to Kracauer because the author had a 'nose for extreme and eccentric manifestations'.[39]

Various reviews and glosses – on Poe, travel writing, nature symbolism in Bachofen, on the writers Valéry, Hessel and J. P. Hebel, Russian soldiers' thoughts, Lenin's letters to Gorky, colour in children's books – appeared in *Die literarische Welt*, *Der Querschnitt* and the literary supplement of the *Frankfurter Zeitung*. Benjamin reviewed books, but, in addition, the book itself as form was under review. 'A Glimpse into the World of Children's Books' acknowledged the transformative impulse of children as they play to learn. The trick-books that Benjamin cherished, and which were so fragile, had shifting page-orders where hidden flaps revealed concealed figures, characters moved across the scenery and ribbons or tabs were tugged to trigger or resolve episodes. These demonstrated how much seeing and knowing were tied to touch. Indeed the best books reinforced the sense in which knowledge of the world was practical, interventionist. Such imaginative work in the renewal of matter signalled to Benjamin the child's originary impulse to revolutionary overhaul. And where colourful books drew the child into reverie, black-and-white illustrations invited them to scribble, imaginatively completing the illustrations. Rebus books introduced children to writing, but through hieroglyphics.[40] These books reinvented the book for those who were not yet readers.

At the other end of the spectrum too – within advanced poetic practice – writing became image. Stéphane Mallarmé predicted the future, as he was one of the first to recognise the graphic nature of script, incorporating in his 1897 poem 'Un coup de dés' all of 'the graphic tensions of the advertisement'. In a review published in *Die literarische Welt* in August 1926, and adapted in 'Arrested Auditor of Books', an entry for *One-way Street*, Benjamin noted of Mallarmé:

> One day he invited Valéry to be the first to see the manuscript of 'Coup de dés'. 'Take a look at it and tell me whether I have gone mad!' (This book is known from the posthumous edition of 1914. A quarto volume of a few pages. Words are distributed across the pages in changing typefaces, separated by quite considerable distances and irregularly.) Mallarmé – whose rigorous immersion in the crystalline construction of a quite traditional writing saw the true image of the future – has here processed the graphic tension of the advertisement, for the first time (as a pure poet), in the actual image that the writing forms.[41]

Apollinaire took this further in his *Calligrammes* in the second decade of the twentieth century with his ideographic logic of spatial rather than narrative disposition. And the Futurists participated too, with Marinetti insisting on typographical revolutions to express the disruption of syntax, metre and punctuation in pursuit of instantaneous telegraphic 'lyrical intoxication' in his efforts at abrupt communications. After these poetic reinventions of the word and the line, picture writing more fully invaded urban space. Newly expelled from the bed-like sheets of a book, 'a refuge in which script could lead an autonomous existence',[42] words flickered across the night skyline, glimmering their neon messages above shops, or they stood upright on posters, newspapers and cinema screens. Such visual stimulations deterred contemporary people from entering the world of the book: their eyes were exposed to such a 'blizzard of changing, colourful, conflicting letters' that the chances of 'penetrating the archaic stillness of the book are slight'.[43] 'Locust swarms of print' densified each year. The urban dweller required cityscape literacy.

The intellectual's work was not unchanged in this new world of 'international moving script'.[44] The card index became the new version of scriptural multi-dimensionality and mobility. It too revealed the redundancy of the book, for all that mattered in the book was to be found 'in the card box of the researcher who wrote it' and the card box of the scholar who studied it. Commercial and bureaucratic methods exerted their pressures on writing, but Benjamin hoped poets would take writing's development 'ever more deeply into graphic regions of its new eccentric figurativeness'.[45] The spread of the typewriter also altered things. However, the mechanical transposition of the typewriter or other future machines would be chosen over handwriting for composition only once flexibility in typeface choice was available. The pliancy of the hand in writing allowed the recording of meaning in the form of a trace, which possessed a shape, a size, an amount of pen pressure. The standard characters of the typewriter barely imitated this. Benjamin imagined a future machine, suggested by the present one, but far exceeding its capacities. Only with that would typed writing be adequate for purposes of expression. With his fantastic machine, the energetic dance of the innervated 'commanding' fingers, jabbing away at a keyboard of variable typefaces sensitive to hues, tones and shades of meaning, would type at high speed but relinquish none of the extra-linguistic subtlety intimate to handwritten characters. These extra-linguistic aspects amounted to a type of scriptural unconscious, and they were what made graphology possible. Were the writer to compose directly on the variable machine, 'the precision of typographic forms' could directly enter the conception of his books. Books would be composed according to the capabilities of the machine, much as photographs eventually found their own aesthetic rather than imitating the aesthetic of painting.[46]

The book was condemned to reinvention as writing liberated itself from old forms. The author would be compelled to engage with a machine aesthetic. Such processes of de- and re-composition were revolutionary in nature, and to be pursued fully perhaps required quite different social conditions, a place where experiment was the order of the day. Benjamin hoped to pursue a radicalism in thought, production and being in a place where changes occurred in accelerated form, where 'each thought, each day, each life' lay 'as on a laboratory table'.[47] Benjamin headed hurriedly to Moscow in December 1926, his trip financed by a journal co-edited by Martin Buber titled *Die Kreatur*, which was to publish an account of his experiences in the post-revolutionary capital. He went there to be with Lacis, who was then at a sanatorium in the capital, suffering with neural illness. In the event, Benjamin spent as much time with Lacis as with the person who had informed him of Lacis' serious illness, Bernhard Reich.

The visit was a test of the Party and an experiment in life under the Party's control at a significant time. The end of the 1920s saw ferocious struggles over official economic, social, political and cultural positions. The opposition was experiencing its final but vigorous gasps, and it was clear to Benjamin that 'the restoration' had begun and 'militant communism' was being suspended.[48] 'Everything is being built or rebuilt and almost every moment poses critical questions', he wrote.[49] Benjamin struggled to learn a new language, but more than that, it seemed that he had to review and relearn things and thoughts that had become habitual. For the first time in many years he wrote a diary. Away from the asphalt of Berlin streets, which seemed to him like a 'freshly swept, empty racecourse on which a field of six-day cyclists hastens comfortlessly on', the bustling streets of Moscow in the winter, under slippery ice, forced him to learn to walk again.[50]

In Moscow the eye was infinitely busier than the ear. The colours did their utmost against the white:[51]

> in the evening they switch on brighter lights than are permitted in any other great city. And the cones of light they project are so dazzling that anyone caught in them stands helplessly rooted to the spot. In the blinding light before the Kremlin gates the guards stand in their brazen ochre furs. Above them shines the red signal that regulates the traffic passing through the gate. All the colours of Moscow converge prismatically here, at the centre of Russian power.[52]

Experience is coloured – in Moscow maybe most of all, for life, hustling bustling life took place against the white of snow, in the blinding light of power that invaded all spaces and tolerated no private life. The red light that regulated traffic was the light of the East, communism. It picked up the colour of glowing coloured rags, Chinese paper fans, paper kites, glazed paper birds and solid coloured wooden toys, the stuff for sale on the boulevards.

Experience was augmented, and what counted as experience was expanded too. As the avant-garde redeployed found materials of daily life in order to make material experience significant – rejecting the blandishments of the sublime – so too Benjamin demanded an openness to contingency, searching for meaning rumpled in the constellations of experience. In Moscow the Kantian fundamental of time was remoulded, for its unit of measurement was *seichas*, 'at once', heard a hundred times a day, until the promise was eventually carried out.[53] Each hour was 'superabundant, each day exhausting, each life a moment'. If time was shattered by too much fullness, too much activity, then space too was disrupted – Benjamin wondered at the icy North, palms, marble staircases and southern seas appearing on screens at a photographer's stand on the boulevard beneath bare trees.[54] This was one sign of how the new Soviet existence evoked improbably its geographical counterpart, life in the South, under a less favourable sky, but just as porously public.

The love affair with Lacis did not proceed easily: her feelings towards Benjamin altered constantly. Lacis was ill. And, at times, she displayed 'hostile elements', a 'hardness' and 'lovelessness', which scared him. In December, he declared that he wished to have a child by her. He did not note her response to this – though, some days earlier, she had blamed him for the fact that they were not currently living on a desert island with two children. He had not 'run off' with her in Capri. He had not joined her on trips to Latvia or Assisi. He had not stayed in Berlin in the winter of 1925, awaiting her arrival. Still, he observed that her spontaneous gestures showed she was at least 'fond' of him. Her kisses and gazes were the longest he had ever experienced. She 'often' said his name and, on occasion, ran her fingers through his hair.[55] But Reich was always there, and one day, Benjamin feared, they would live together again.

Various cultural opportunities opened up for Benjamin in Moscow. He held meetings with officials and cultural figures and met Trotsky's sister, Olga Kameneva, who had worked with the theatre director Meyerhold. He was interviewed on art and culture for a Moscow newspaper. In his diary Benjamin recorded encounters with intellectuals and his fears for the future of the revolutionary society. He told Jula Radt, in one of a number of very intimate letters, that what Russia would become was unclear: perhaps a genuine socialist society, perhaps something quite different. 'The struggle which will determine this is in process without interruption.'[56] He hoped that he could write for Russian magazines in the future, but suffered a blow when informed that his Goethe article was 'too radical'.[57] Karl Radek, his German-speaking editor on the *Great Soviet Encyclopaedia*, was unimpressed by all the talk of class struggle. Soviet cultural politics was purging what might be thought of as the expected lines of Marxist inquiry. And the only thing of significance in the theatre was Meyerhold, declared Benjamin.[58] Before leaving, on 1 February 1927, he gathered material for a number of journalistic pieces on Russian film art, the political groups amongst Russian authors, new poetry in Russia and Meyerhold. His impressions in the diary were worked up into a lengthy essay for *Die Kreatur*. His representation of Moscow was devoid of theory, deductive abstraction and prognostics.[59] It presented vignettes of daily life as picture puzzles to be deciphered by the reader.

Benjamin returned to the living space provided at his parents' villa for himself, Dora and Stefan. The translation of Proust's *In the Shadow of Young Girls in Flower* appeared under the Berlin imprint 'Die Schmiede' [*The Smithy*], and was favourably received. Benjamin wrote reviews and pushed Kracauer for commissions for newspaper articles. He was curious about the possibilities of political analysis in the journalistic arena, and wrote to Kracauer expressing amazement that he could accomplish such political film criticism in bourgeois newspapers – Benjamin was responding to Kracauer's 'The Little Shopgirls go to the Movies', a 'political exposure' as well as 'sociological detection'.[60] For his part, he engaged in polemic with author Oscar A. H. Schmitz on the merits of Eisenstein's *Battleship Potemkin* and the possibilities of film, a 'dramatic' fracture in artistic formations. He proposed that film opened up a 'new realm of consciousness' through which people come to grips with the ugly, incomprehensible and hopelessly sad world, comprehensively, meaningfully and passionately. The object of the best films – those of the Soviet Union and American slapstick comedy – were superior because they dealt with modern technologies, the former exposing its lethal power, the latter provoking laughter that 'hovers over an abyss of horror'.[61]

On 23 March Benjamin debuted on Südwestdeutscher Rundfunk, the radio station in Frankfurt, speaking on new Russian literature. On 1 April he left Berlin for Paris, ready to immerse himself in French cultural developments. In June he told Hofmannsthal that he felt isolated from his generation in Germany and closer to the Surrealists in France.[62] He dared to chance the 'salvation' of the stamp collection in 'Stamp Shop', which appeared in the *Frankfurter Zeitung* on 9 August 1927.

> Stamps bristle with tiny numbers, minute letters, diminutive leaves and eyes. They are graphic cellular tissue. All this swarms about and, like lower animals, lives on even when mutilated. This is why such powerful pictures can be made of pieces of stamps stuck together. But in them, life always bears a hint of corruption to signify that it is composed of dead matter. Their portraits and obscene groups are littered with bones and riddled with worms.[63]

Summer came and with it Dora and Stefan and travel in the South of France. He won enough money in the casinos in Monte Carlo to visit Corsica for a few days, and flew back from there to Antibes, excited to be using the latest mode of transportation. After a return to Paris he set off again in August for a trip along the Loire. He mused on a Parisian woman with whom he had fallen in love and who had not reciprocated. The landscape presented empty frames for a love stalled.

Autumn came and, on his return to Paris, a new realm of study beckoned. He had meant to devote his attention to contemporary French literature, but reading Flaubert's *Sentimental Education* had drawn him into Paris's past, and he spent every moment in the Bibliothèque nationale researching a newspaper article on Paris. He hoped to have all the documentation collated before he left the city. This was the beginning of the *Arcades Project*, Benjamin's card index, a never-to-be book of quotations copied from hundreds of old and mainly obscure books, peppered by paragraphs of insight and query. It would become an unwieldy pile-up of quotations and notes on streets, department stores, panoramas, world exhibitions, types of lighting, fashion, advertisements, prostitution, collectors, flâneurs, Baudelaire, gamblers and boredom. It began as some more or less polished jottings, reflecting on the Parisian mealtime and aperitif, the disappointments of Bastille Day celebrations, streets and architecture, silk, cashmere, gas and electricity, mirrors and optical gadgets. Through all this ran reflections on the history and remnants of the arcades.

Arcades were passages through blocks of buildings, lined with shops and other businesses. These montaged iron and glass constructions housed chaotic juxtapositions of shop-signs, window displays, mannequins and illuminations. The arcade was the *Ur-form*, the originary form, of modernity, for it incubated modes of behaviour – distraction, seduction by the commodity spectacle, shopping as leisure activity, self-display – that would come to figure more prominently as one century passed into the next. The Paris arcades sheltered the first modern consumerism. They were built, for the most part, in the decade and a half after 1822. A guide from 1852 described each glass-roofed and marble-lined passageway as 'a city, a world in miniature'.[64] Such description attracted Benjamin, who had long harboured a fascination for the small, the child's tiny facsimiles of things and the miniature worlds in snow shakers or on stamps. Parisian arcades were a miniature dramatization of the wider world, that is to say, of the antinomies of capitalism. These covered walkways had evolved out of the galleries of the Palais-Royal. The arcades were an international architectural form, crammed with colonial plunder and incongruous pile-ups: souvenirs, umbrellas, orthopaedic belts and bandages, collar studs, naked puppet bodies with bald heads, frog-green and coral-red combs 'as in an aquarium', trumpets like conches, ocarinas like umbrella handles and 'lying in the fixative pans from a photographer's darkroom is birdseed'. There 'the odalisque lies in wait next to the inkwell; priestesses in knitted jackets raise aloft ashtrays like vessels of holy water', 'a bookshop makes a place for manuals of lovemaking beside devotional prints in colour'.[65]

With their jumble of diverse commodities from across the Empire, the arcades turned shopping into an aesthetic event. They were perfect sites in which to loiter and to learn how to window-shop and be amazed by the absurdities of commerce, the same uncanny jumble of obsolescence that attracted the Surrealists. Benjamin uncovered decayed and forgotten things and impulses. He followed the Surrealist procedure to the letter, montaging disparate industrially produced fragments, trash and parodies of natural form. Rags and refuse were deployed – waste came into its own. One such curiosity was visible in hairdressers' windows, where 'one sees the last women with long hair; they sport richly undulating masses, petrified coiffures. How brittle appears the stonework of the walls beside them and above.'[66]

Those permanent waves, fashionable relics from a past epoch, reversed values, in that they seemed more lasting than the very fabric of the buildings that contained them. The efforts of hair technology – which made advances in the 1920s just as Benjamin wrote his Parisian studies – were directed towards the artificial generation of organic, shell-like forms. Nature was emulated by artificial means. The permanent wave was an archetype of a new modern mythology. Modern myth was designed as contradiction. The modern should be exactly unmythic, for myth is that which is ancient and unchangeable. At the core of modern mythology lay the fact that fashion was never far from death, for what always changed was always expiring too. There, ironically, the old mannequins hold onto an image of past fleeting beauty for ever.

Benjamin's project hoped to chart the arcades and the world in which they existed comprehensively, and this included the perspective of the marginalized types who inhabited them, such as prostitutes and flâneurs. One note in the early jottings compared the flâneur, eagle-eyed habitué of Parisian streets and cafés, with the hashish eater: 'In hashish intoxication, the space starts winking at us: 'What do you think may have gone on here?' And with the very same question, space accosts the flâneur.'[67]

Benjamin was also recording his own expansion of experience, as he had made his first experiment with hashish on 18 December 1927, under the medical supervision of friends Ernst Joël and Fritz Fränkel. He documented the effects, in what he called 'protocols', at 3.30 am. One note reported the following:

> One is very much struck by how long one's sentences are. This, too, connected with horizontal extension and (probably) with laughter. The arcade is also a phenomenon of long horizontal extension, perhaps combined with vistas receding into distant, fleeting, tiny perspectives. The element of the diminutive would serve to link the idea of the arcade to laughter. (Compare the *Trauerspiel* book: miniaturizing power of reflection.)[68]

The arcades, a disappearing nineteenth-century form, shed light on an obscure seventeenth-century dramatic form, when perceived through the fuzz of drugged consciousness. The rush of drugs allowed glimpses of a unity in his thinking: 'You follow the same paths of thought as before. Only they appear strewn with roses.'[69] Benjamin sought to think the entire world all at once. He recorded his dreams too, monitoring modes of perception more generally discarded in the light of day.

At the end of the year his publications were finally ready. The book on mourning plays faced backwards, a product of his abandoned attempts to gain an academic position. Even *One-way Street* was the completion of past work, the closure of a 'production cycle'.[70] Reviews of *One-way Street* were mixed. The *Magdeburgische Zeitung* criticized the 'indecisiveness of a work, whose subtle observations settled high above rather than in between the chairs of Paris and Moscow'. But communist Willi Munzenberg recommended the book to 'proletarian circles', perceiving it as a 'headlamp which douses the world of pre-revolutionary thought' with the blinding light of revolutionary insight in respect of state, education, love, writing, poetry and politics.[71] Bloch's reflections on the book compared it to a 'store-opening of philosophy, something wholly unprecedented, with the latest spring models of metaphysics in the window display'.[72] He passed a copy of his review to Benjamin in one of the large cafés on Berlin's Kurfürstendamm, where they met in the evenings. Recalling this meeting later, Bloch noted what the book tendered:

> A slice of the surrealism of lost glances, of the most intimate things; and just for this reason the best thing lay behind or among the others, disturbing and unhappy, inviting, challenging, enticing, avoided, sought again, the best found again in the unlikely, but also this: 'Don't forget the best' – a small, distant, hushed-up glimmer of the heavenly Jerusalem. I mention this because of Benjamin, because of the sight of his joy at that time, a tiny joy, as was proper, at such an unexpected comparison, a comparison with the 'final condition' which lay embedded everywhere, as Benjamin wrote pointedly elsewhere, because this tiny joy at such an extraordinary and lofty comparison at the same time reveals the elegance of Benjamin's understatement.[73]

Benjamin had no major commissions, beyond the odd review, and so no income. He met Adorno again in February and struck up a friendship with Adorno's companion Gretel Karplus. In April he received a renewed request to write an entry on Goethe for the *Great Soviet Encyclopaedia* under quite favourable conditions. He accepted but delayed its composition, preferring instead to spend every possible moment scouring books in the library and transcribing quotations for the *Arcades Project*, which he characterized as a 'dialectical fairy spectacle'.[74] He moved away from the family home in Grünewald for a couple of months. Lodged in a room amidst the greenery of Tiergarten, he watched provincial people rolling past in ice-grey cabs. He spent four or five hours a day thinking about old Paris in the nearby State Library, and mused that this immersion in the past had prevented him from securing a means of getting to modern Paris for the summer.[75] A small advance from Rowohlt for a projected book on Kafka and Proust was used to finance his *Arcades* studies; the outlines of the Paris study were as yet unclear, but the scope was expanding beyond the remit of an article.

In May Benjamin told Scholem that he had decided to visit Palestine in the autumn, enthused by Rabbi Magnes's offer of a teaching post at the Hebrew University. Scholem was negotiating with Magnes for a stipend for Benjamin so that he might learn the necessary Hebrew. While in Frankfurt for the funeral of an uncle, Benjamin told Buber that he needed a stipend of 300 marks a month. From Frankfurt he went on to Königstein im Taunus, where Adorno was spending the summer. After that he took off for Weimar, to investigate at close quarters some Goetheana. Back in Berlin he met Magnes to discuss finances and awaited the motivating pressure of the deadline for the Goethe article, for he found it difficult to relate 'a popular Goethe from a materialist standpoint' in so few words.[76] He preferred to read books on arcana, such as Anja and Georg Mendelssohn's *The Person in Handwriting*, on graphology. This led to bold thoughts about language in a review for *Die literarische Welt*.

For Benjamin the graphologist, the scratches in the surface of articulation, the plane of writing, could be literally probed to reveal a deeper significance. Benjamin claimed that any scrap of writing, any few handwritten words, might be what he called a free ticket to the 'great theatre of the world', for it was a microcosm of the 'entire nature and existence of mankind'.[77] Each little bit of scrawled nonsense was a gateway to an unconscious that was bigger than that of the individual. Benjamin rejected the notion that handwriting was a surface phenomenon:

We can see from the impression made in the paper during printing that there is a sculptural depth, a space behind the writing plane for the writer; on the other hand, interruptions in the flow of writing reveal the few points at which the pen is drawn back into the space in front of the writing plane, so as to describe its 'immaterial curves'. Could the cubic pictorial space of writing be a copy in microcosm of a clairvoyant space? Is this the source of the insights of telepathic graphologists like Rafael Scherman? Whatever the answer, the cubic theory of writing opens up the prospect that one day it may be possible to exploit graphology to investigate telepathic events.[78]

Handwriting presented not only a way of analysing the character of the writer, but also the possibility of accessing what was only considered or maybe not even considered. Captured in the features of the script were unconscious, unarticulated elements, things prior to language, perhaps extraneous to expression.

Benjamin's microscopic writing, with letters sometimes just a millimetre high, crammed the sheets of his *Arcades Project* with his own thoughts and the found thoughts of countless texts. Benjamin insisted that to know texts you had to write them out. The handwritten word expressed the world. Words had to pass though your mind, your body, your hand, completing a full circuit from body into language and from language back through the body again. In *One-way Street* he had indicated that only the copied text

commands the soul of him who is occupied with it, whereas the mere reader never discovers the new aspects of his inner self that are opened by the text, that road cut through the interior jungle; forever closing behind it: because the reader follows the movement of his mind in the free flight of daydreaming, whereas the copier submits it to command. The Chinese practice of copying books was thus an incomparable guarantee of literary culture, and the transcript a key to China's enigma.[79]

The plans to translate more of another's words into German stalled. The Proust translations ran into difficulties because of a change of publisher – Munich's Piper Press took over from 'Die Schmiede'. And the question of where to be raised itself again. In the autumn of 1928 he told Scholem that he planned to spend at least four months in Jerusalem, and pressed Scholem again for money from Magnes. He dreamt of travel, drawn by the idea of a lonely journey to the frozen North.[80] But instead he made it to Lugano, Genoa and Marseilles in September, and managed to finish the Goethe article. In Marseilles he experimented with hashish again, stimulated by Hermann Hesse's *Steppenwolf*. It possessed 'the power to persuade nature to repeat the great squandering of our own existence that we enjoy when we're in love'. Alienated from the strictures of his education, he 'permitted' himself to mark the 'rush switches' of a jazz band with his foot.[81]

While in Marseilles he read Johannes V. Jensen's *Exotic Novellas*, and he found the line: 'Richard was a young man, who had a sense for all that was kindred in the world'. This line resonated with Benjamin, and he applied it to the conglomerative effects of drugged experience – where correspondences and analogies emerge – as well as to mass reproduction and mass experience, where all is so thoroughly mechanized and rationalized that the particular lies only in nuance. Another line in the book stirred the impulse to write to Lacis:

> And yet there was a single moment during which they hesitated, one of those soundless pauses of fate of which one notices only subsequently that they contained the kernel of an entirely differently life course than that which is allotted to us.[82]

Money arrived from Magnes in October. The 3642 marks were intended to finance Hebrew lessons and initiate the move to Palestine for a trial year. But Benjamin took no steps towards either obligation. The following weeks, as he waited for Lacis to arrive, were spent 'wildly reviewing',[83] on topics as diverse as the Berlin Food Exhibition, a novel by Princess Bibesco, philosophical tendencies in France and Karl Blossfeldt's photographs of plants. In addition he wrote thirteen theses on 'the path to success': 'in the grammar of success, chance plays the same role that irregular verbs do in ordinary grammar. It is the surviving trace of primeval energy.'[84]

Concurrent with his production of *feuilletons*, he lost himself further in the arcades. Benjamin had finally to broach divergences from Surrealism, whose influence could be 'fatal'.[85] This required a broadening of his themes, making the project's 'tiny frames as universal' as possible, so that it became 'with all the authority of a philosophical Fortinbras the heir of Surrealism'.[86] In other words, the project's deadline was not in the foreseeable future.

He wrote an assessment of the Surrealists, which appeared in *Die literarische Welt* in February 1929. He observed that Surrealism's intoxicated, ecstatic and occultist perspective stressed the mysterious. For example, much of the third issue of *La Révolution Surréaliste*, largely edited by Antonin Artaud in the spring of 1925, presented 'a hosannah in honour of the East and its values'. Artaud, Robert Desnos and others promulgated a 'new kind of mysticism', and 'believed they had found the mysterious East of the Buddha and the Dalai Lama'.[87] In contrast Benjamin forwarded a 'dialectical optic', equally gripped by the response to mystical phenomena such as extra-sensory perception or mind reading, but discovering them in commonplace activities. In actual fact, he decreed, there is nothing more extraordinary than the processes of thought itself, a mind-warping narcotic, or the activity of reading, 'an eminently telepathic process'. Mystery was situated in life, not the otherworldly: 'the everyday as impenetrable, the

impenetrable as everyday'.[88] The essay voiced political criticism
of the Surrealists, who promoted a radical concept of freedom as
revolt, but did not weld this to 'the constructive, dictatorial side
of revolution'.[89] And such revolutionary rigour was essential, if
Benjamin's bleak diagnosis of European developments was correct:

> Surrealism has come ever closer to the communist answer. And
> that means pessimism all along the line. Absolutely. Mistrust
> in the fate of literature, mistrust in the fate of freedom, mistrust
> in the fate of European humanity, but three times mistrust in
> all reconciliation: between classes, between nations, between
> individuals. And unlimited trust only in I. G. Farben and the
> peaceful perfection of the air force.[90]

Lacis arrived in Berlin in November and worked in the film section
of the Soviet trade representation. For two months she and Benjamin
lived together at 42 Düsseldorferstrasse, until she left and he moved
back to his parents' villa, where Dora and Stefan were living.
Benjamin wrote a great deal in this period, small skits on Chaplin,
on Marseilles, a programme for a proletarian children's theatre,
schizophrenia and poetry, Darwinism and other diverse topics.

In 'The Critic's Technique in Thirteen Theses' from 1925 he had
noted that: 'The critic is the strategist in the literary struggle.'[91]
He had forwarded the role of the critic as polemicist, as side-taker,
as partisan. In his journalistic pieces he was beginning to engage
in intellectual skirmishes. For example, 'Once Again: The Many
Soldiers' challenged another critic's feeble analysis of war in which
the discussion shifted 'from the terrain of the political to the
abysmal pit of the ethical'. Benjamin argued for the necessity of
the armed uprising against pacifist idealism.[92] In a recomposition
of affiliations, he distanced himself from Ernst Bloch, whom he
suspected of pilfering his thoughts and terminology. He joked that
he needed two police officers to prevent him from speaking any

'unpublished' words.[93] He struck up new alliances – for example, he wrote enthusiastically to Siegfried Giedion in February 1929 after the electrifying experience of reading *Building in France, Iron and Ferro-concrete*.[94] And through Lacis, in May, he inaugurated a significant friendship with Bertolt Brecht.

Much time was spent discussing art and politics at Brecht's home. In June Benjamin mentioned Brecht in a piece titled 'Lyrics for Everyday Use? But Not Like This!', which was a critique of satirist Walter Mehring's poetry. Brecht's base sexual and economic materialism took the form to a new level. In Brecht, the chanson emancipated itself from the Brettl or cabaret, making decadence historical: 'His hooligan is the hollow mould in which some day the image of the classless person is to be poured with better, fuller stuff.'[95] For Benjamin, Brecht represented a new literary type – Benjamin was most excited by his didactic 'learning plays'.[96] New associations opened up: through Brecht, Benjamin met the Marxist Karl Korsch. Nonetheless, the escape route from Europe to a post in Jerusalem still enticed Benjamin. He began to study Hebrew with Max Mayer, an Orthodox rabbi, in the summer, reporting to Magnes in June that he had a month's study behind him and that he hoped to be in Palestine in the autumn.[97] From a driving holiday in Bansin on the Baltic in June, spent with the author Wilhelm Speyer, whom he knew from the days at Wyneken's Wickersdorf Free School, Benjamin reported to Scholem that he was dissatisfied. He could not devote all the necessary time to learning Hebrew: his journalistic career was proceeding all too well (though he complained bitterly that Bloch's new books *Traces* and a collection of essays were to deliver 'a not insubstantial part of my immortal works, partially rather battered to posterity').[98] In July he took off for Italy on a car tour with Speyer, and that was the end of Benjamin's Hebrew lessons.

In San Gimignano he continued the intellectual civil war, composing an attack on a right-wing writer from the Stefan George

A view of some of the towers of San Gimignano in Tuscany; Benjamin owned a copy of this postcard. 'In the evening the women congregate at the fountain by the town gate in order to fetch water in large jugs' – only once I had found these words did the image emerge with hard dents and deep shadows out of what had been experienced all too bedazzlingly.' (*GS*, IV.1, 364–6)

school, Max Kommerell. But he also continued to reflect on the relationship between perception and writing. A travelogue called *San Gimignano*, dedicated to the memory of von Hofmannsthal, observed: 'To find words for what one has before one's eyes – how difficult that can be. But once they come they batter with tiny hammers against reality, until they have pressed a picture from it as from a copper plate.'[99] Time came to be experienced differently in the South. It was an 'exaggerated present'.[100] The very environment – arches, battlements, shadows, the flight of doves and crows – make an individual forget his or her needs. Travel put Benjamin in contact with cosmic forces, away from the rush of the city:

I have never previously seen sunrise and moonrise in my window like this. When I lie on my bed at night or in the afternoon there is only sky. Out of habit I begin to wake shortly before sunrise. Then I await the sun's ascent from behind the mountains. There is first one brief moment when it is no bigger than a stone, a tiny glowing stone on the ridge of the mountain. What Goethe said of the moon: 'Your edge gleaming as a star' – has never been thought of the sun. But it is not a star but a stone. Early man must have possessed the ability to harbour this stone as a talisman and thereby to turn the hours to good account.[101]

This postcard shows one of eight mosaics on the floor of the cathedral in Siena. She and her siblings are represented on similar postcards in Benjamin's collection. Benjamin made a short visit to Siena in July 1929, but why he collected these cards remains a mystery.

Five years of German radio listening figures; a poster reproduced in the 1929 German *Radio Handbook*.

When Benjamin returned to Germany he engaged in a conversation for publication with Ernst Schoen, now Head of Programming at Südwestdeutscher Rundfunk, about the possibilities of radio as a popular, educational and political instrument.[102] Regular radio lectures commenced, with twelve appearances in 1929 on topics including the novels of Julien Green, children's literature, J. P. Hebel and Gide. Also in a more popular vein, he wrote a little essay titled 'What Our Grandparents Racked Their Brains Over' on picture puzzles from the previous century for an illustrated magazine.

> We might yet be able to recognize that our grandparents amused
> themselves with these – but how they knew the ways to steal the
> secrets of this emaciated Corps de ballet of devices and letters
> remains obscure to us. But only for as long as we set out from
> our own perceptual world, which corresponds to the crossword
> puzzle so well, its standardized architecture, statistical schemes,
> the unambiguousness of neon advertising signs and traffic
> symbols.[103]

'What Our Grandparents Racked Their Brains Over'. In *Das illustrierte Blatt*, July 1929 (No. 28), p. 795: 'The picture puzzle is not quite as old as those obscure and lofty riddles of folklore, the best known of which is that of the Sphinx. Perhaps the awe of man before the word had to decline a little, before he dared to loosen the connection of sound and meaning – which had seemed so strong – and invited them to play with each other.

Such commissions notwithstanding, Benjamin's existence was precarious. After some strained months with Dora, he left his parents' villa in August to stay with Franz Hessel in Berlin, and he initiated divorce proceedings in order to marry Lacis. In the middle of September he informed Scholem that his visit to Palestine in November would have to be delayed. There was the chance of some unrefusable paid work with Speyer. In addition Lacis fell ill with encephalitis just before returning to Moscow after a year in Germany – it was just after a visit from Reich and Daga. Benjamin sent her to the neurologist Kurt Goldstein in Frankfurt.

Stuck in Germany, Berlin was on Benjamin's mind. In October he published a review of his flatmate's *On Foot in Berlin*, titled 'The Return of the Flâneur'.[104] Benjamin trailed the Berlin flâneur Hessel, who drifted into a past made present and transformed the town into a mnemo-technical device. He concluded that the native and the tourist experienced environments differently. The city book written by the native always had something of the memoir about it – for the writer did not spend his childhood there in vain. Where the tourist sought the superficial, exotic and picturesque, the native, travelling into the past and not just through space, found in corners and nooks the dusty and forgotten moments of childhood, encrusted in the very paving-stones like mislaid gems. Space became a doorway into time.

In November Benjamin began a series on Berlin for Berlin radio's Youth Programme, foraying into Berlin past and present, composing his own coded memoir of the city of his childhood. His first lecture was on Berlin dialect, and he began in a strikingly direct mode: 'Right, today I am going to chat with you about the big Berlin gob: this so-called big gob is the first thing that strikes anyone when they talk about Berliners.'[105]

That same month Benjamin told Scholem that the divorce had taken on 'cruel forms'. The judge was vicious, he claimed.[106] Dora fought hard to trounce Benjamin's claims of infidelity on her part

Walter Benjamin around 1929.

and was furious at his efforts to take Stefan from her. She shifted the weight of the blame towards him, revealing that he had not contributed to his son's upkeep and insisting, despite his protestations, that Lacis and Benjamin had indeed shared a room.

Benjamin felt lonely in Berlin. Hessel left to be with his wife in Paris and Benjamin had a breakdown, which meant that he was incapable of doing anything for ten days.[107] Happier times were spent in Frankfurt, where, in between visits to Lacis, he saw Adorno and Horkheimer in Königstein, and read to them drafts of material drawn from the *Arcades Project*, which led to 'unforgettable conversations' that influenced all participants hugely. In December *Die literarische Welt* financed a trip to Paris to write about some encounters with prominent literary figures. Ensconced in Paris, he abandoned plans to visit Palestine. He wrote to Scholem in French in January 1930 and told him of his new ambition – to be considered as the premier critic of German literature. And not only that: he wished to 'create criticism as a genre', and, indeed, had already contributed to this process of reinvention.[108]

5

Man of Letters, 1930–32

That aspiring 'premier critic' was busy in 1930, with reviewing and *feuilletons*. The Paris diary appeared in spring and recorded his encounters with numerous figures, including André Gide; the Surrealists Louis Aragon and Robert Desnos; the bookseller Adrienne Monnier; the symbolist poet Léon-Paul Fargue who provided anecdotes about Proust, James Joyce and M. Albert, who was Proust's guide to the homosexual world of Paris and who met Benjamin in a public bathhouse. The *Arcades Project* still drew Benjamin and his concern was to erect a 'solid scaffold' by drawing on the work of Hegel and Marx. A discussion of the theory of historical knowledge was inevitable: he imagined a sparking confrontation with Heidegger, whose approach on similar terrain was so different.[1]

But study of the Parisian arcades was interrupted for a while. Once back in Germany in February, living at Franz Hessel's, Lacis was no longer a distraction from work: she returned to the Soviet Union before the completion of the divorce proceedings and never saw Benjamin again. His attention was largely focused on remunerative radio work in Frankfurt and Berlin: 37 radio appearances in that year alone. At the beginning of January he spoke in his Berlin series on Berlin radio's Youth Programme. On 23 January he was on the radio in Frankfurt speaking on 'Paris Heads', which drew on his diarized encounters with André Gide and Emanuel Berl. The following day he considered Friedrich Sieburg's recent book on

Russian Toys. Of the straw doll in the centre Benjamin noted its recall of an ancient fetish of the harvest.

France. And February and March brought seven lectures for the Berlin Youth Programme on Berlin themes. Then there were more Frankfurt broadcasts – one on Baroque author Christian Reuter and one on E.T.A. Hoffmann. In March he informed Piper Press that he no longer wished to be involved in translating Proust beyond checking proofs.[2]

His energies were freed up for radio work: four more Berlin-based lectures for the Berlin Youth Programme in April, before another trip to Frankfurt to speak on comedy and on Siegfried Kracauer's recent study of the fantasies and anxieties of white-collar employees.[3] And so the pattern continued throughout the rest of the year. On 4 April Benjamin wrote to Schoen about his radio work and about devising his customary number of thirteen theses for an article on the politics of radio for the *Frankfurter Zeitung*.[4] The unwritten article was to address the institutional structures of radio; its failure to take poetry seriously; corruption in the mutual relationship between press and radio; the demagogic role of the press, which values stupidity; exemplary aspects of radio practice in Frankfurt, Berlin and Königsberg, and censorship, the radio station's 'surveillance council' and the sabotage of Schoen's progressive plans.

On 16 April Benjamin signed a contract for a collection of essays on Gottfried Keller, J. P. Hebel, Franz Hessel, Karl Kraus, Proust and the Surrealists. It was to be fronted by a reflective piece on 'The Task of the Critic'. Such good news was counterbalanced a few days later by the receipt of the divorce case documents. The judge decided against him, and he was forced to relinquish his inheritance and to sell his collection of children's books in order to pay back the 40,000 marks Dora had lent him from her inheritance. The loss of the books was wounding. In a review of Gabriele Eckehard's *The German Book in the Baroque Epoch*, published in *The Literary World* in June, Benjamin wrote in praise of collectors, for this breed cultivated a passionate attachment to their objects, which represented 'transformations of coincidental fate in mimetic expression'.

> It would be better to characterise the community of genuine collectors as those who believe in chance, are worshippers of chance. Not only because they each know that they owe the best of their possessions to chance, but also because they themselves hunt down the traces of chance in their riches, for they are physiognomists, who believe that nothing so illogical, wayward or unnoticed can befall things without leaving behind its trace in them. These are the traces that they pursue: the expression of past events compensates them a thousand fold for the irrationality of events.[5]

A collection brought together through chance and fate was now dispersed and with it was lost what he termed elsewhere 'a form of practical memory'[6] and a 'primal phenomenon of study'.[7]

Scholem, who was close to Dora, pressed Benjamin on other matters. Frustrated and embarrassed by Benjamin's failure to learn Hebrew and come to Palestine or to pay money back to Magnes, he demanded a statement on the 'Gordian knot' that was his relationship to Judaism. Benjamin answered that he related to Judaism only through the figure of Scholem, and that he could only 'unknot' his relationship to the Hebraic once he had unravelled the 'very tangled twine' of his existence. He left open the possibility of a trip to Palestine.[8] Turning to literary matters, he informed Scholem that he had composed some ideas on his 'interesting intercourse' with Brecht, and revealed plans, currently thwarted because of Brecht's absence, to initiate a small reading group in order 'to demolish Heidegger'.[9] Heidegger, he claimed, promoted a philosophy opposed to their praxis-oriented thought.

Domiciled in a summerhouse in the Meineckestrasse, Benjamin approached his forties 'without property or position, dwelling or resources'.[10] Summer came and the usual pull away from Berlin, as irresistible as magnetic forces, exerted itself. In *Berlin Chronicle* he noted that the desire to undertake journeys was kindled by his maternal grandmother's postcards from far-flung travels.[11] This time he fulfilled the two-year-old wish to take a lonesome journey to the frozen North. In July 1930 he boarded a boat in Hamburg and set off for several weeks on a voyage across the North Sea to the Arctic Circle and Northern Finland, returning to Germany via the Baltic Sea. A postcard sent from Trondheim to Gretel Karplus quipped that he was following in the footsteps of Schelmuffsky, the comic hero from Christian Reuter's novel of the same name, published in 1696, which he had discussed on radio the previous March.[12] In a sense the distance travelled on this journey was not just through space but through time – backwards. As a landlocked Berliner, the Northern coast had long represented for Benjamin a place without limits, and he noted in *Berlin Chronicle* that since childhood, when at the hub of the city,

the dunes of the Baltic landscape have appeared to me like a
fata morgana here on Chausseestrasse, supported only by the
yellow, sandy colors of the station building and the boundless
horizon opening in my imagination behind its walls.[13]

Heading northwards, his imagination swelled. He wrote on the
postcard: 'Once out of Berlin, the world becomes beautiful and
roomy.'[14] Space, room, was precisely what Benjamin was lacking
in July 1930, or at least what he, as a homeless man, sought. The
travel sketch 'Northern Sea', based on diary notes and published
that September in the *Frankfurter Zeitung*, opened with the thought
that time, in which lives even the person who has no home, becomes
a palace for the traveller who leaves no home behind.[15] The significance of homelessness was greater than the fact of not having a
room, akin to Lukács' observation of a modern 'transcendental
homelessness' in his *Theory of the Novel* from 1916. In a Germany in
which every day the consequences of the defeat of the 1918, 1919,
1920 and 1923 revolutions and the decrepitude of Weimar's democracy – reinvented by Brüning as 'authoritarian democracy' and
rule by emergency decree – became more conspicuous, Benjamin
felt increasingly out of place. What space to occupy? Where to
situate the self ? A journey provided respite, allowed Benjamin
to play for time.

   He described the journey in 'Northern Sea': 'a series of halls,
stretching northwards, filled with the sound of waves', and on their
walls seagulls, towns, flowers, furniture, statues and always, day
and night, light streaming through the windows.[16] This domestic
decor provided the headings for each of the sections of the travelogue, a piece of writing that exemplified his characteristic form:
the *Denkbild*, thought-image. The *Denkbild*, a word introduced into
German by Stefan George in a discussion of Mallarmé, is a concen-
trated depiction of experience, filtered through images, where the
objects' depiction was their own philosophical commentary.[17]

To write *Denkbilder* meant insisting that what appears to the trivial mind as merely subjective and arbitrary was actually a manifestation of the objective.

In diary notes for 'Northern Sea' he observed how, on this journey, events and objects evaded usual categories. He watched as a man, half-clown, half-intellectual, directed a curious busking performance, then collected money, not amongst the well-heeled tourists but from the banks of poor people who had gathered to watch. Responding to this event in the harbour at Rörvik, Benjamin wrote: 'What happened there was uncertain and overdetermined at once, like all things appear here, when the white dusk captures them.'[18] Benjamin's writing in the *Denkbilder* – description as theory – is an imprint on the whiteness of memory, here mirrored in the Northern white nights. The fight against blanking out involves holding on – with difficulty – to the specificity of experience; or to use another two of his images, like reading the signs in the sand that have been written in salt or deciphering letters in the flurries of snow.

Benjamin decoded the unapparent and the everyday. The flowerpots in houses presented a wall against the over-bright outside, and the houses themselves, at war with the unfriendly outside, had developed too many corners and stairways, all reinforcements of the barrier between inside and out. These forms developed in a place where idleness and art were never really tolerated, where people once slept in chests-of-drawers, where women crouch at the thresholds of their homes. And the seats, more enclosing, and closer to the ground than 'ours', were always pushed forwards as if the occupier had just been forced off the crest of a wave, suddenly, on to the shore that was the room's floor. Personal and objective histories were compacted in these observations. The isolating harshness and gruelling work ethic of the North, embodied in the everyday materials of life, corresponded to Benjamin's personal situation. And, while his Northern sketches were equally a challenge to Kantian space-time categories, they contrasted with his vivacious and chaotic city sketches of the South, where public and private spheres interpenetrated – in the happier days when he was in communication with others and newly in love.

One section of 'Northern Sea' was titled 'Statues'. It detailed a museum of wooden figures collected by a man who searched for them across sea and land, in the knowledge that only collected together and with him could they find peace. Not a lover of fine arts, but a traveller, he sought happiness in remoteness and made his home with figures broken by distance and voyaging, their faces weathered by salty tears, eyes straining upwards: they were ships' cutwaters. Their bodies revealed the passage of time.

In Bodø, Norway, Benjamin discerned a deadliness in the town. The fishing museum was closed. The thirteenth-century stone church was too far away. And he did not even buy the travel souvenir that he wanted like no other – a three-piece porcelain smoker's set depicting, on a background of sepia and cobalt, black palm trees in the desert.[19] The desert and fjords, far from each other, were both seen by Benjamin in his youth at the imperial panorama, a late nineteenth-century optical entertainment device with multiple viewing windows, set in a circle, that allowed an automatic, fixed-time viewing of hand-coloured postcard-size 3-D images. His autobiographical sketch of this device described how his desire hooked to images of fjords and coconut palm trees, as they rested while awaiting the bell signalling their departure.[20] These sights, of extreme Northern Europe and an undefined South, existed at the edges of his world. And so the travel souvenir he wanted more than any other did not render the place that he was, but a scene of the warm, if desolate, South – signifying not a place but desire itself, not experience, but its absence.

In 'Northern Sea' Benjamin recalled his observation of the gulls above the ship. They circled in the air, forming patterns against the sky's backdrop, which Benjamin took as signs. Suddenly two groups of gulls appeared, one in the east, one west, left, right, and so different that he wondered how both sets could still be called gulls. The birds on the left held on to some of their brightness against the background of the extinct sky, and flashed with each turn up and down, a never ceasing series of signs. But he kept slipping away to look at the other group. It did not speak to him. The puzzle to the left remained unresolved, but his fate hung on its every nod. That on the right was resolved long ago and remained only a soundless beckoning. Benjamin presented himself as the threshold across which envoys exchanged black and white in the air.[21] The memory reads as political allegory. To the left, the east, some signs of vitality and many questions, including ones that involved his future. To the right, the west, no questions but a lingering fascination, and one he followed up on board the ship as he read Ludwig Klages' *The Mind as Adversary of the Soul*, along with other 'mythologicis' by Erich Unger.

The ship docked in Sopot in the middle of August 1930 and Benjamin was grateful to be joined by Fritz and Jula Radt, because, no longer alone, what seemed like the first convalescence in years could begin.[22] He had worked too hard on the ship, writing the 'Northern Sea' cycle and translating Marcel Jouhandeau. On his return to Berlin, occupying temporary accommodation sublet from an artist called Eva Boy in the Prinzregentenstrasse, he composed a critique of Rightist myth-making, as perpetrated by the Fascist modernist Ernst Jünger. It was titled 'Theories of German Fascism'. He completed his attack on Stefan George – 'Against a Masterpiece'. He also polemicized against left-leaning liberals such as Erich Kästner and Kurt Tucholsky in the article 'Left-Wing Melancholy'. Criticism was a political task. To seriously wage the intellectual civil war against reactionary or incompetent fellow critics, it was deemed necessary to publish a journal.

Krisis und Kritik [*Crisis and Criticism*] was planned in the autumn of 1930. Rowohlt was to publish it monthly and Benjamin and Brecht were to edit it, with foreseen input from Bernard von Brentano, Herbert Ihring, Alfred Kurella, Paul Hindemith, Weill, Bloch, Korsch, Marcuse, Adorno, Kracauer and Lukács amongst others. Its character was political, 'standing on the ground of class struggle', and 'its critical activity anchored in clear consciousness of the basic critical situation of contemporary society'.[23] The journal was not conceived as an 'organ of the proletariat', but rather it would 'occupy the hitherto empty place of a organ in which the bourgeois intelligentsia renders its account of the demands and insights, which alone allow it under current conditions to produce in an interventionist manner and with consequences, as opposed to the usual arbitrary and inconsequential modes'.[24]

The many forms of crisis – social, economic, political, cultural – were ever more manifest. There was increased censorship, a loss of academic posts and a considerable advance in fascism's fortunes. On the cultural front, for example, in Thuringia in 1930, the Beer Hall Putschist and State Minister for Education and the Interior Wilhelm Frick eradicated from the Weimar Schlossmuseum works by Paul Klee, Otto Dix, Ernst Barlach, Wassily Kandinsky, Erich Heckel, Karl Schmidt-Rottluff, Lionel Feininger, Emil Nolde and Franz Marc. Benjamin witnessed the fascists first-hand. In October he attended a 'fascinating debate' at a session of the Strasser Group.[25] Gregor Strasser and his brother Otto were inside Hitler's NSDAP (National Socialist German Workers Party) but they represented a different ideological tendency that stressed anti-capitalism alongside anti-Marxism and anti-Semitism. In 1928 Georg Strasser joined Alfred Rosenberg and Heinrich Himmler in the call to establish a 'Fighting League for German Culture'. The organization, devised to attract the educated bourgeoisie to the NSDAP, fought 'bastardizing' and 'negroizing' in all areas of the arts and life, for a return of 'Germanic values'.[26]

Germany was ever more uncomfortable – and on 2 November Benjamin's mother died – but the Wilmersdorf sublet flat, where

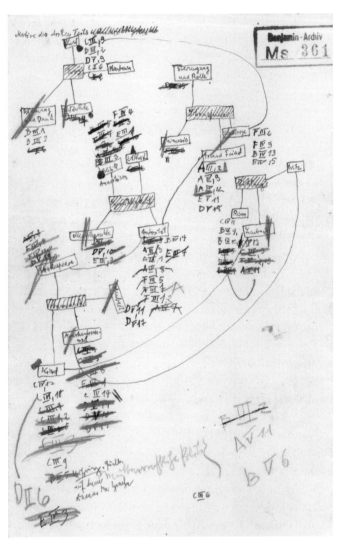

Layout sketch for the essay on *Karl Kraus* (1930). Five motifs appear to be central in this graphic rendition of the third part of his essay: 'Eros', 'Actors', 'Justice', 'Poetry' and 'Monster'. Connections are drawn between motifs and keywords, indicating something of Benjamin's working procedures.

he enjoyed the gift of a gramophone and managed to scrounge a number of records,[27] at last provided a welcome home for his 2000 books. He read Korsch on Marxism and philosophy, and he concluded his study of the Viennese satirist Karl Kraus, who mocked the degraded language of the press. Benjamin was employed as a reader for Rowohlt, and the translation of Proust's *The Guermantes Way* by Benjamin and Hessel appeared that winter. Amidst the skirmishes in the intellectual civil war – for example 'A Critique of the Publishing Industry' – he mused on arcana. 'Graphology Old and New', written for a radio magazine, bemoaned the fact that the academy had still not accepted this scientific method and had appointed to date no chairs for the interpretation of handwriting.[28] He outlined the three main schools of German graphology: Klages's Stefan George-influenced existential interpretation of handwriting as gesture, as expressive movement of character; Robert Saudek's physiological and psychophysical approach, and the Freudian approach of Pulver and Mendelssohn, which interpreted script in terms of unconscious graphic elements.

If writing had an unconscious, its matter, language, also allowed for the fathoming of extra meanings for those who were receptive. At the end of the month Benjamin's short story 'Myslovice-Braunzweig-Marseilles' appeared in the Berlin monthly *Uhu*. Relating elements from one of Benjamin's drug protocols, it was the story of a hashish-induced trance in Marseilles, and it rendered myriad transformations of spaces and self, catalysed by language's inherent paronomasia.[29]

Benjamin continued to cultivate unpredictable alliances. In December 1930 he sent a letter and a copy of the Baroque book to the authoritarian theorist Carl Schmitt, for he had used Schmitt's *Political Theology* to expound the doctrine of sovereignty in the seventeenth century. There were tensions with his old ally Brecht. Early in 1931, having seen manuscripts for the first issue of *Krisis und Kritik* by Brentano, Kurella and Plechanov, Benjamin withdrew his association. The journal, he reminded Brecht, was planned as 'an organ in which specialists from the bourgeois camp undertook to represent the crisis in science and art'. This was in order 'to demonstrate to the bourgeois intelligentsia that the methods of dialectical materialism are dictated to them because of their own requirements – requirements of intellectual production and research'.[30] What they had received, however, was not specialist commentary in relation to essential questions of the day – or if it was, as in the case of Plechanov, it was twenty-five years too late.

But the break from the journal was not with Brecht. Benjamin wished to contribute a short piece to the journal, and he urgently needed to see Brecht to discuss with him an article he was writing for the *Frankfurter Zeitung* on Brecht's *Man Is Man*.[31] This became the study 'What is Epic Theatre?', completed early in 1931 but rejected by the newspaper editor after an intervention from the newspaper's theatre critic, Bernhard Diebold. Brecht's epic theatre used an armoury of distancing techniques and appealed to the audience as critical, thinking individuals. For Benjamin, Brecht's theatre was exhilarating because it treated the stage in a technical way: 'The forms of epic theatre correspond to new technical forms, cinema as much as radio. Epic theatre corresponds to the modern level of technology.'[32] Epic theatre, film and radio enabled spectators to enter at any point – epic theatre consisted of self-contained scenes; film was likewise montaged, amenable to projection on a continuous loop, and viewers' entrance and exit did not discombobulate the pre-recorded cast; and radio was switched on or off at will. The basis in montage, the reproducible nature, the activating appeal to audiences, the simultaneous distancing and intimacy – all these were elements promised by the new media. But their possibilities were rarely explored, or worse, were ignored.

In 1931 Benjamin wrote 'Reflections on Radio', in which he theorized radio as a form of mass culture that potentially used montage and experimental techniques better than any other method to produce a genuinely modern art form. But, crucially, current radio culture failed by perpetuating 'the fundamental separation between practitioners and the public, a separation that is at odds with its technological basis'.[33] In Russia, he noted, 'they are in the process of drawing out the logical implications of the different apparatuses'. In Germany there is only the 'mindless notion of the "offering", under whose aegis the practitioner presents himself to the public'. The public was helpless, inexpert in its critical reactions, and its only active contribution to radio was an act of sabotage – switching it off. Benjamin argued that even a child knows that 'it is the spirit of radio to put as many people as possible in front of a microphone on every possible occasion'. Radio was a democratic forum in which as many voices as possible should be heard. Benjamin's judgment on contemporary radio was harsh: 'There has never been another genuine cultural institution that has failed to authenticate itself by taking advantage of its own forms or technology – using them to create in the public a new expertise.'[34]

Other forms produced their expert publics, but radio, wrote Benjamin, 'with its unrestrained development of a consumer mentality in the operagoer, the novel reader, the tourist, and other similar types', had produced 'dull, inarticulate masses'. Radio had the opportunity to create a public sonically-attuned, actively engaged in what they heard and excited by the possibilities specific to radio, rather than people who see reflected in the medium their already existing interests – novels, classical music, travel reportage. The root of the problem lay in the types of voices on radio, which, as uninvited visitors in the house, were judged immediately by listeners.

No reader has ever closed a just-opened book with the finality with which the listener switches off the radio after hearing perhaps a minute and a half of a talk. The problem is not the relentlessness of the subject matter; in many cases, this might be a reason to keep listening for a while before making up one's

mind. It is the voice, the diction, and the language – in a
word, the formal and technical side of the broadcast – that
so frequently make the most desirable programmes unbearable for the listener.[35]

For the same reason, a listener might continue to entertain – as
guest in the home – the voice reading the weather forecast, simply
because of its sonic qualities.

That same year Benjamin undertook some radio experiments
of his own, known as 'hearing models'. This was a form developed
with Ernst Schoen, whose fascination was with radio drama that
explored sociological and everyday situations. Benjamin decreed the
purpose of the hearing models to be 'didactic', in much the same
way as Brecht's 'Lehrstücke' or 'learning plays' were didactic. They
dealt with 'typical situations taken from everyday life'. The format
was prescriptive as befits a model. There were never more than four
participants, and the speaker appeared three times. First the speaker presented the topic and introduced the public to the participants
appearing in the first half of the hearing model, which was conceived as a 'counter-example', an example of how not to proceed.
The speaker returned after the first half to point out errors in procedure. The speaker then introduced a third figure who appeared in
the second half of the model, in order to demonstrate how one
might proceed correctly in the same situation. At the close the
speaker compared the false and the correct mode of proceeding and
drew out the moral.[36] Each show was followed by live discussion.

The first hearing model, written together with Wolf Zucker and
broadcast on 26 March 1931, was called 'Pay Rise?! What Are You
Thinking Of?'[37] Two scenarios were played out, involving a naïve
and an adept worker in their efforts to secure increased wages. The
moral of this model was that in order to achieve success an individual needed 'an attitude of mind', polite but not subordinate, con-
sisting in 'clarity, determination, courage', a consciousness of one's

worth and dignity. The successful worker regarded his 'struggle' as a kind of sport, a game, 'fighting in a comradely fashion with the difficulties of life', maintaining a clear head, even in defeat. For all the bad luck that life brought, noted the speaker, the person who was ultimately successful was never demoralized and always ready to fight again.

In a letter to the Swiss critic Max Rychner on 7 March 1931, Benjamin discussed his own analytical practice and how it related to that of communists and Marxists. Rychner had praised his reading of the Swiss writer Gottfried Keller, juxtaposing it with the bone-headed reading of orthodox communists who dismissed his work as bourgeois and antiquated. Benjamin was concerned, however, to emphasize to Rychner that his own position also relied on material-ist insight. He agreed that his path to a materialist conception came not from communist brochures but rather through the best bour-geois studies in literary history and criticism of the last twenty years. These were not, however, academic works. Indeed the desola-tion of what passes for academic study was attested in the fact that no academic had noticed his Baroque book. This book, he noted, was not materialist, though it was dialectical. Yet what he did not know at the time of its composition, though it became clearer soon after, was that from his 'very particular position on the philosophy of language, there exists a relay – however strained and problematic – with the viewpoint of dialectical materialism'.[38] This was because he strove to focus his thought always on those objects in which truth was most compacted, which meant 'not the "eternal ideas", not "timeless values", but there where historical study ushers in contemporary revelation'.[39] Keller was significant inasmuch as he illuminated current conditions, and was indeed not antiquated.

Once again Benjamin differentiated his thought from 'the Heidegger School', with their 'profound circumlocutions of the realm of ideas', in order to place himself closer to the 'scandalous and coarse analyses' of the Marxist Franz Mehring, who, like him, sought in literature 'the true state of our contemporary existence'. Benjamin also conceded that he had 'never been able to research and think other than in, if I might say it in this way, a theological sense – namely in accord with the Talmudic teaching of the 49 levels of meaning in every passage of the Torah'.[40] Still, the recognition of the 'hierarchies of meaning' was more present in the most clichéd communist platitudes than in the apologias of bourgeois profundity.[41]

Benjamin nevertheless continued actively pursuing an older, now depleted, bourgeois tradition of real humanism. From April 1931 to May 1932 he made available, anonymously, 27 letters in the *Frankfurter Zeitung*, written between 1767 and 1883, representing another Germany as embodied in the Romantic natural philosopher Johann Wilhelm Ritter, the experimental physicist G. C. Lichtenberg, the poet Annette von Droste-Hülshoff, the chemist Justus Liebig, the radical dramatist Georg Büchner and others.

On 17 April he found himself defending his materialist approach once more to Scholem.

> Where is my site of production? It is – and I do not cherish the slightest illusions about this – in Berlin w. ww if you wish. The highest civilization and the 'most modern' culture belong not only to my private comfort but are also, in part, precisely the means of my production. That means that it is not within my power to move my site of production to Berlin E or N.[42]

He continued that there might be moral grounds for transferring to Berlin E or N, but he would not do anything differently in another, more proletarian part of Berlin than he did in the bourgeois West of the city. Did that mean though, he asked, that Scholem should forbid him from hanging the red flag from his window on the grounds that it was nothing but a ragged scrap? Scholem accused him of composing 'counter-revolutionary'

writings from the perspective of the Communist Party, which
Benjamin conceded. But did that mean that he should 'expressly
place them in the service of the counter-revolution'?[43] Benjamin's
solution was to 'denature' his writings, 'like spirits', with the risk
that they might become unpalatable for everyone. This was the
only way, he argued, to distance himself from the bourgeoisie.
It placed him in an extreme position. He compared himself to
a traveller on a shipwreck who puts himself in yet more danger
by climbing to the top of the crumbling mast, from where he can
at least signal and have the chance of being rescued.[44]

It was summer. Benjamin took off for the South of France with
the Speyers and his cousin Egon Wissing and wife Gert. Brecht was
holidaying there with a group of friends while working on his play
The Holy Johanna of the Stockyards. An exhausted Benjamin – tired
of the struggle for money and his miserable personal life – commenced a diary, but because he thought there would be little to
write about, he decided to concentrate on the past, dredging up
memories from his state of fatigue. His dissatisfaction was spurred
by his lack of confidence in the methods whereby people of 'his
kind' chose to 'assert control over the hopeless situation of cultural
politics in Germany'. He was tormented by the unthought-through
division into factions of those close to him.[45] He was considering
suicide. This was an outcome of the 'struggles on the economic
front', but it was also conceivable because he felt he had already
'lived a life whose dearest wishes had been granted'.[46]

Later in the diary he wrote about wishes and the fact that our
dearest wishes are unknown to us, unconscious, as fairytales with
their stories of squandered wishes make clear. We recognize our
true wishes only later, once they have been granted. He wrote of his
own wishes – the first that he recognized was 'the wish for distant
and, above all, long journeys'.[47] Benjamin recognized this just in the
moment of it being granted. He recounted an episode from 1924. He
had saved enough money to spend some time abroad. He arranged

to meet some friends in Capri. With a shock he saw the headline in the evening edition of the newspaper held by the paper seller at the corner of Friedrichstrasse and Unter den Linden: 'Ban on Foreign Travel'. A decree had been issued restricting foreign travel to those who could leave a deposit around ten times the sum he had available. The decree was to become law in the next couple of days. He decided not to wait for his friends, but packed immediately and rushed to Italy. Only once at his first stop – he forgot in the retelling whether it was Capri or Naples – did he realize how badly he had packed in his panic, having snatched superfluous items, forgetting essential things. However, the true realization came some five or six weeks later when he recognized he would endure any deprivation not to have to return to Berlin, including living in a cave.[48]

The next entry in the diary turned the theme of privation into a positive, modernist gesture. He wrote up a discussion with his cousin on the aesthetics of the Bauhaus. He compared the sleek and bare rooms of Bauhaus with the cluttered bourgeois interior of the 1880s, with its antimacassars, monogrammed cushions and upholstery, traces of the owner's possession of the space. Brecht's 1926 *Reader for City-dwellers* coined the phrase 'Erase the Traces'. This was apt for the Bauhaus room, which was no more than a bare lodging that disallowed habits. Empty rooms, often adjustable at will, were dwellings of the new times.[49] Reduced versions of these had been Benjamin's habitat for some time. If the dwelling of the insecure individual was provisional, Benjamin speculated, so too might be the self. On 6 May the diary reported a discussion with his cousins about love. For he had loved three different women – presumably Dora, Jula Cohn and Asja Lacis – and each had made of him a different man.[50]

In June he spent three weeks in Le Lavandou with Brecht and friends. On 14 June 'How to Explain Great Book Successes' appeared in the literary supplement of the *Frankfurter Zeitung*. There, undeterred by Scholem's accusations of inauthentic materialism (levelled against the Kraus essay),[51] he called for a materialist-oriented criticism, more concrete, closer to reality and more political.[52] Discussions with Brecht were lively and diverse: they discussed Lenin's proposition from 1922 to form 'the international society of materialist friends of the Hegelian dialectic', as well as ideas for a detective play, the trial of Friedrich Schiller and Proust. On another occasion they mused on Trotsky, exchanging episodes from his books. Brecht, buoyed by news from Berlin about political riots, expounded his theories, which Benjamin recorded: The intelligence of capitalists grows in relation to their isolation, that of the masses in relation to their collectivism. The collective, Brecht claimed, needed to be forged: Brecht had tried to actualize this during the Munich Revolution, when he was a junior doctor in charge of a venereal diseases ward. The situation was extreme and promising now. To forge a collective, Brecht insisted, it would be necessary to kill 200,000 Berliners in order to draw 50,000 proletarians together.[53] They discussed Kafka. Benjamin was amassing notes on this figure who intrigued him especially because of his straddling of the ancient and the modern, the popular and the avant-garde.

Chaplin holds in his hands a genuine key to the interpretation of Kafka. Just as occurs in Chaplin's situations, in which in a quite unparalleled way rejected and disinherited existence, eternal human agony combines with the particular circumstances of contemporary being, the monetary system, the city, the police etc, so too in Kafka every event is Janus-faced, completely immemorial, without history and yet, at the same time, possessing the latest, journalistic topicality. In any case one would have the right to speak of the theological context if one pursued this doubledness; but certainly not if one only adopted the first of these two elements. Incidentally this double layering is likewise present in his writerly demeanour, which, in the style of the popular almanac, pursues epic characters with a simplicity that borders on artlessness, such as only Expressionism could detect.[54]

For Brecht, Kafka was 'the only authentic Bolshevist writer', because of his evocation of permanent astonishment tinged with panic-stricken horror in relation to the deformations of life.[55]

Benjamin returned to a deformed life in Germany. On 5 June the second emergency decree was carried for protection of the

KLEINE GESCHICHTE DER PHOTOGRAPHIE
Von Walter Benjamin
(Fortsetzung)

Man muß im übrigen, um sich die gewaltige Wirkung der Daguerreotypie im Zeitalter ihrer Entdeckung ganz gegenwärtig zu machen, bedenken, daß die Pleinairmalerei damals den vorgeschrittensten unter den Malern ganz neue Perspektiven zu entdecken begonnen hatte. Im Bewußtsein, daß gerade in dieser Sache die Photographie von der Malerei die Staffette zu übernehmen habe, heißt es denn auch bei Arago im historischen Rückblick auf die frühen Versuche Giovanni Battista Portas ausdrücklich: „Was die Wirkung betrifft, welche von der unvollkommenen Durchsichtigkeit unserer Atmosphäre abhängt (und welche man durch den uneigentlichen Ausdruck ‚Luftperspektive‘ charakterisiert hat), so hoffen selbst die geübten Maler nicht, daß die camera obscura" — will sagen das Kopieren der in ihr erscheinenden Bilder — „ihnen dazu behilflich sein könnte, dieselben mit Genauigkeit hervorzubringen." Im Augenblick, da es Daguerre geglückt war, die Bilder der camera obscura zu fixieren, waren die Maler an diesem Punkte vom Techniker verabschiedet worden. Das eigentliche Opfer der Photographie aber wurde nicht die Landschaftsmalerei, sondern die Porträtminiatur. Die Dinge entwickelten sich so schnell, daß schon um 1840 die meisten unter den zahllosen Miniaturmalern Berufsphotographen wurden, zunächst nur nebenher, bald aber ausschließlich. Dabei kamen ihnen die Erfahrungen ihrer ursprünglichen Brotarbeit zustatten und nicht ihre künstlerische, sondern ihre handwerkliche Vorbildung ist es, der man das hohe Niveau ihrer photographischen Leistungen zu verdanken hat. Sehr allmählich verschwand diese Generation des Uebergangs; ja es scheint eine Art von biblischem Segen auf jenen ersten Photographen geruht zu haben; die Nadar, Stelzner, Pierson, Bayard sind alle an die Neunzig oder Hundert herangerückt. Schließlich aber drangen von überallher Geschäftsleute in den Stand der Berufsphotographen ein, und als dann späterhin die Negativretusche, mit welcher der schlechte Maler sich an der Photographie rächte, allge-

Photo Germaine Krull

mein üblich wurde, setzte ein jäher Verfall des Geschmacks ein. Das war die Zeit, da die Photographiealben sich zu füllen begannen. An den frostigsten Stellen der Wohnung, auf Konsolen oder Gueridons im Besuchszimmer, fanden sie sich am liebsten: Lederschwarten mit abstoßenden Metallbeschlägen und den fingerdicken goldumrandeten Blättern, auf denen närrisch drapierte oder verschnürte Figuren — Onkel Alex und Tante Riekchen, Trudchen wie sie noch klein war, Papa im ersten Semester — verteilt waren und endlich, um die Schande voll zu machen, wir selbst: als Salontiroler, jodelnd, den Hut gegen gepinselte Firnen schwingend, oder als adretter Matrose, Standbein und Spielbein wie es sich gehört, gegen einen polierten Pfosten gelehnt. Noch erinnert die Staffage solcher Porträts mit ihren Postamenten, Balustraden und ovalen Tischchen an die Zeit, da man der langen Expositionsdauer wegen den Modellen Stützpunkte geben mußte, damit sie fixiert blieben. Hatte man anfangs mit „Kopfhalter" oder „Kniebrille" sich begnügt, so folgte bald weiteres Beiwerk wie es in berühmten Gemälden

'Little History of Photography' appeared in instalments in *Die literarische Welt*, on 18 and 25 September and 2 October 1931 (no. 39). This image shows an extract from the instalment in the issue published on 25 September.

economy and finances. Wages, pensions and benefits were cut and a crisis tax introduced. The government ruled only through emergency decrees from then on. Rowohlt went bankrupt, eliminating some of Benjamin's publishing possibilities. Benjamin recorded his personal despair in a diary, ominously titled 'Diary from August 7 1931 to the Day of My Death'. It began: 'This diary does not promise to be very long.'[56] He resolved to put to good use his final few days or weeks, having wasted many days wondering whether to kill himself in his studio flat or in a hotel. The rest of the diary reflected on the imbrication of literature, journalism, popularity, expertise and class.

The diary ended and Benjamin did not kill himself. September and October saw the appearance, in instalments in *Die literarische Welt*, of his essay 'Little History of Photography'. At issue were technology, the social world and the image. Benjamin considered a photograph of the philosopher Schelling who, sitting in his home and sunk into his creased clothes, exuded duration and familiarity. Each crease in his garments recorded his longevity at the same time as it recorded photography's long duration of exposure, which was technically necessary at the time. In contrast was a photograph of Kafka as a little boy. Displaced from the home, he sat adrift and alienated in a photographer's studio. Sharper lenses captured the scene more quickly, as befitted an age that ran at a swifter tempo.

In this essay too Benjamin outlined his concept of aura:

What is aura actually? A strange weave of space and time: the unique appearance or semblance of distance, no matter how close it may be. While at rest on a summer's noon, to trace a range of mountains on the horizon, or a branch that throws its shadow on the observer, until the moment or the hour become part of their appearance – this is what it means to breathe the aura of those mountains, that branch.[57]

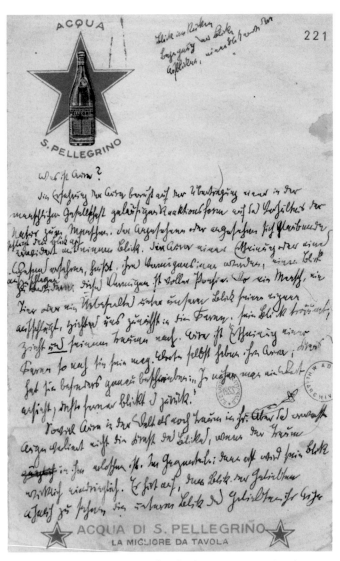

What is Aura? – manuscript. Benjamin's undated notes on aura were jotted on a café receipt advertising S. Pellegrino water. 'When a person, an animal or something inanimate returns our glance with its own, we are drawn initially into the distance, its glance is dreaming, draws *us* after its dream.'

Aura was given to those who sink into a panorama, forgetting activity and adopting a contemplative attitude to nature. Auratic perception was the vision of someone ensconced in a halcyon world. Early photography captured the closing auratic days of the nineteenth century in the long exposures of portrait photography of a rising bourgeoisie. Efforts to recreate the fuzz and wistfulness of aura – in dreamy portrait photography or compositions that mimicked oil paintings – were false, throwbacks that could not acknowledge contemporary technical – and correspondingly, social – standards.

Photographers such as August Sander and Germaine Krull had found new ways of using the contemporary state of photography to express something truthful and necessary about the epoch. Benjamin insisted, as did Moholy-Nagy, that contemporary literacy has less to do with the ability to read words and more to do with reading images.[58] Benjamin quoted Goethe in connection with August Sander's social typological images that are gleaned 'from direct observation': 'There is a delicate empiricism which so intimately involves itself with the object that it becomes true theory.'[59] The empiricism of indexical, chemical photography could unveil physiognomic, political and historical aspects in the material. Sander soberly photographed a gallery of representative contemporary types. In an age in which people were increasingly judged according to what role they adopted or had thrust upon them, a photography book such as Sander's *Face of Our Time* (1929) acted as a training manual or guide of the current moment.

Germaine Krull, whose photographs of arcades, shop frontages and neglected city niches Benjamin collected, documented the odd life of the commodity as revealed by the strange liveliness of shop windows and the deadliness of evacuated corners. She captured the poetry of advertising and all the suggestive clutter of the arcades, where large looming clocks arrested time for ever. In one photograph a set of identical dolls' heads gazed out blankly, their faces excessively painted with blusher and their hair a dark blob of glossy perm-like waves. In another, flattened cut-outs of various mannequin heads jostled for attention in the window, again their dark wavy hair like a helmet issued by the forces of modernity. These images recalled Surrealism's fascination with the inanimate beautiful dummy woman. For Benjamin that was a reference point – summoning up the context of sexual fetishism as much as commodity fetishism. But they also added another layer to his modern mythology. The photograph of the once-fashionable heads froze a moment in time – itself a kind of permanent wave – that was then cast into the past. Even the modern was always becoming yesterday.

At the beginning of October Benjamin told Scholem that the economic situation in Germany offered 'as much firm ground as the high seas and the emergency decrees collide with each other like the crest of waves'.[60] Unemployment was pushing the working class towards the National Socialist party. The Communists lacked contact with the masses. Anyone with a job was regarded as part of the labour aristocracy. Benjamin's own situation struck him as ironic. Even when wages fell, he still remained as busy as ever. His time was occupied by editing the letter series for the *Frankfurter Zeitung*; attempting to show the links between Kant's stupidity in old age and his philosophy; writing a devastating review of Theodor Haecker's *Vergil*; composing a short study of Paul Valéry and judging film scripts for a sound film prize. He had also secured a contract with *Die literarische Welt* to deliver four instalments of his autobiographical writings, *Berlin Chronicle*, each of 200–300 lines, at a line price of 25 pfennigs.[61] With his flat and his library he felt grown up for the first time in his life. But his study had no table, so he wrote lying down on a comfortable sofa that once belonged to a paralysed woman.[62]

Never to be demoralized, to aim for a constantly cheerful attitude: these were the qualities of the 'destructive character', a figure depicted by Benjamin in a short sketch published in the *Frankfurter*

Zeitung in November 1931. The figure, who, 'because he sees ways everywhere', he 'always stands at a crossroads',[63] was based on Gustav Glück, director of the Foreign Section of the State Bank and a friend. The destructive character was the enemy of the comfort-seeking 'étui-man', who looked for velvet-lined cases, the uphol-stered coffins that harbour his traces in the world. The destructive character left no traces, liquidating situations with the conscious-ness of an historical man who 'sees nothing permanent' – and reduced what existed to rubble – in order to find ways through. The destructive character wanted to make possible the formulation of experience according to revised and appropriate tenets. He pro-posed a grand Futurist vacuum-cleaner to suck up the dust of ages in a streamlined, techno-modernist age.

Benjamin's own most up-to-date practice of radio work continued in the winter and the spring of the following year. Brecht's dramatic practice provided a good model for the future development of culture in a media age. At the same time Benjamin was interested in Brecht's theoretical analyses. In 1932 Brecht wrote an essay called 'The Radio as an Apparatus of Communication'. In this essay Brecht railed against the way in which the radio, originally designed as a two-way instrument of communication, became, because of the pressing inter-ests of power, a one-way instrument of promulgation. Radio, claimed Brecht, 'is one-sided when it should be two-. It is purely an apparatus for distribution, for mere sharing out. So here is a positive sugges-tion: Change this apparatus over from distribution to communica-tion.'[64] Brecht insisted that this 'vast network of pipes' be turned into something that lets the listener speak as well as hear, and brings listeners into a relationship instead of isolating them. The task was to innovate radio – while recognizing the limitations to this process within the current socio-economic order – and to make innovations that press for revolution in the wider social and economic system.

Benjamin's own efforts to increase the interactive aspects of radio resulted in the programme *Radio Games: Poets by Keywords*, a 'not-unprofitable psychological and pedagogical experiment' broadcast in January 1932.[65] Benjamin adapted a parlour game from the Baroque period. A child, a woman, a poet, a journalist and a businessman were given a list of unrelated words. Each person had to thread the words together to tell a short and coherent story. Listeners were asked to rate the various attempts and to participate themselves. Listeners' results were published subsequently in the radio station's journal.[66] The participants began from a given set of words that are all at least double in meaning: *Kiefer; Ball; Strauss; Kamm; Bauer; Atlas* – pine/jaw; ball(toy)/ball(dance); bouquet/ostrich/struggle; comb/ridge/neck; farmer/cage; atlas/satin. The first reader's effort brought out the curious slipperiness of language, mutating each word through its various meanings. The second was more straightforward, fastening through context the words into singular meanings.

> Under the pine tree/with trembling jaw/in pink satin/Gretchen leafs through the atlas/and then hurries to the ball/the ball is made of snow/Oh woe, my bouquet/there is a struggle!/She threatens with the comb/her neck bristles/If you were only in a cage/you good-for-nothing farmer!

> Under the pine tree an atlas lay open, and next to it was a ball and a bouquet of flowers, which had not yet been bound. This was proof that father and mother and child were disturbed when the farmer called for help from the ridge of the mountains.

Creativity, popular surrealism and a pedagogic reflection on language were introduced in this way into radio culture.

In February, a radio lecture on the collapse of the bridge across the River Tay in Scotland in 1878 related the dramatic story of a Victorian disaster, as well as a miniaturized theory of technology.[67] The bridge's collapse did not mean that technology was a malign force – iron building had simply not been well enough understood at that time. The relationship between humans and technology was that of 'a great struggle from which humans have emerged victorious and shall remain victorious unless they themselves destroy the work of their own hands once more'. Benjamin characterized technological discoveries as either timely or untimely. Untimeliness implied that a certain technology had arrived too early to be properly used or assimilated, or to find its proper form. It arrived amidst an inappropriate organization of production relations, as had, for instance, radio.

Benjamin sought ways to exploit the technical possibilities of radio and, specifically, to encourage audiences to reflect upon the medium to which they were exposed. In March he broadcast a radiophonic work aimed at children, *The Brouhaha Around Little Kasper*.[68] It was an hour-long play and the story was as follows: one foggy day Kasper was sent to the market to buy some fish. On the way, someone from the radio station asked him to come in and do a broadcast. Kasper went to the studio, but had no concept of what radio was and so was nervous. Having established that an acquaintance in Putzingen would be able to hear the show, Kasper let off a torrent of abuse directed at him. Chaos ensued and Kasper had to go on the run. He got into various tangles at the railway station, the fairground and the zoo, where he was finally cornered, and sent home to bed. Unbeknownst to him the bed was miked. His tirades from there upon waking up were cut together and broadcast, and so the radio station won – it got its Kasper material. Kasper received 1000 marks for his unwitting trouble.

The themes of the play were heady. It educated the listeners as to the types of permissible radio discourse. It demonstrated the mobility of radio broadcasting – its omnipresence in the city. It dealt with radio's intrusion into the most intimate space, the bedroom. It reflected on the alienation and commodification of cultural work – and, significantly, it did this by using a folk-theatre figure, Kasper, now resident in a new media space. Radio itself thus became an object of discussion, baring its mechanisms, its means of reproduction. It also used the specific – sonic – capabilities of radio. The dialogue deployed wordgames and dialect. It began in the fog, as if to suggest the demotion of vision and promotion of hearing, and used a myriad of sound effects and noises. Through this sonic aspect Benjamin tried to establish an interactive radio culture, as children were asked to contact the radio station to guess what sounds were heard during the show.

In April 1932 Benjamin boarded a ship in Hamburg. After its arrival in Barcelona he travelled in the post boat to Ibiza. Once there, he shared lodgings with a friend from his Munich days, Felix Noeggerath, and family, in San Antonio, in the shadow of a broken windmill. In Ibiza he might exist on 70 or 80 marks a month, though his situation was complicated by debts in Berlin. There he met the art historian Jean Selz, who recalled the prematurely greying Benjamin's 'physical stoutness and the rather Germanic heaviness he presented', which 'were in strong contrast to the agility of his mind'.[69]

In May it was clear to Benjamin that the National Socialists would attain power and the Third Reich would be proclaimed in Germany.[70] He wished never to return. He established a routine of rising at 7 am each morning, bathing in the sea and the sun. There was much enforced abstinence: no butter, electric light, brandy or running water, no flirting or newspapers.[71] Stimulation came from reading Trotsky.[72] He was writing more, too, occupied by the auto-biographical sketches for *Berlin Chronicle*. He wrote of his aunt in her cluttered interior like a goldfinch in a cage. He wrote of prosti-tutes in back rooms and attics, who lifted their skirts for rich Americans in the inflation years, and one who gave herself to him when his 'legs had become entangled in the ribbons of the streets'.[73] He wrote of linguistic reinventions and mishearings by children, and the words that retain for ever an 'unfathomable

This image of a windmill in Ibiza is amongst those in Benjamin's postcard collection. 'I had just spent another hour poring over my maps, when an acquaintance, a local, invited me on an evening walk. He wanted to take me to the hill just outside the town, from where the windmills that had long been still had so often greeted me above the tops of the pine trees.' From Benjamin's vignette *The Wall*, *GS*, IV:2, pp. 755–56.

mystery', existing on the frontier between the language of adults and children, a straddling that he saw echoed in the words of Mallarmé's poems.[74] He wrote of cafés where bohemians and intellectuals met and where he composed his Baroque book, while a jazz band played. He wrote of parks and zoos filled with music, and benches for adults only and sandpits for children. He wrote of the nursemaid who entered his room at half-past six on cold winter mornings, her lamp casting her shadow on the ceiling as she lit the fire in the stove. He wrote of shopping expeditions to stores for the wealthy and his father's antiquities and business concerns. He wrote of postcards of far away places and noisy 'matter-of-fact Berlin, the city of work'.[75] Benjamin's cynosure was thresholds, crossable and uncrossable – between social strata, between males and females, between adults and children, between the world of fairytales and that of commerce, between consciousness and the unconscious.

It was not autobiography that Benjamin wrote. Autobiography implied sequence, a continuity of events. This was instead a number of scenes, a recall of 'a space, of moments, of discontinuities'.[76] In *Berlin Chronicle*, Benjamin announced that those who wish to approach their own past must be prepared to dig, unafraid to return again and again to the same matter, turning the soil, like an archaeologist. Such sifting excavated ever-deeper, unsuspected layers, ever-new recollections. The booty was comprised of disconnected images, encountered in the sober rooms of our later insights.[77] Remembering was not simply an inventorying of the past. Memory's significance depended on the strata that smothered it, right up to the present, the moment and place of their re-discovery. Memory actualizes in the present.

Benjamin gestured at uncanny moments of recognition through 'entranced removal'.[78] Twice in *Berlin Chronicle* he reflected on the irruption of the forgotten past into the present. The first reflection described those peculiar moments when something akin to a magnesium flare indelibly seared on to memory an image or circumstance – in Benjamin's example, a room – as if memory were a photographic plate. Some time later that image flashed again into consciousness' view.[79] These thoughts led Benjamin into an anecdote involving uncanny knowledge of a repressed past returning in the present. He revealed how, one night, when he was five or six, his father entered his bedroom to wish him goodnight, but lingered to report a relative's death. The little boy was indifferent to the news concerning his older relation. Unable to assimilate the facts his father relayed about heart attacks, instead, as his father spoke, he imprinted onto his memory all the details of his room – because he felt 'dimly' that he would one day have to return to search for something 'forgotten' there. This he does, some years later, when he finds out the repressed (because scandalous) truth: the real cause of his relative's death was, in fact, syphilis.[80]

Benjamin's second reflection on temporal displacement involved *déjà vu* – or what Benjamin preferred to imagine as the 'already-heard', noting how some events seem to reach us like an echo awakened by a call from the past: 'It is a word, a tapping, or a rustling that is endowed with the magic power to transport us into the cool tomb of long ago, from the vault of which the present seems to return only as an echo.'[81] A wayward segue of past and present produced a 'shock'. Or, contrarily, a 'forgotten glove or reticule' once stumbled upon caused a word or gesture to suddenly return. Montaging past and present, telescoping one through the other, Benjamin mapped a city of irrevocable transformations, but, by invoking a child's perception, suggested a repeatability, an inkling that each new generation experienced the same wonder, curiosity and hopefulness. Even as the days darkened, Benjamin cast his glance across the historical field, disinterring utopian possibilities of the past that might yet motivate change in the future. The chronicle was dedicated to his child, 'dear Stefan', a replacement for his initial urge to offer it to 'his dear friends', Sasha Stone, Scholem, Asja Lacis and Fritz Heinle.

In June 1932 Benjamin alluded to Scholem that he might take his life in Nice soon.[82] He left Ibiza in July and booked into the Hotel du Petit Parc in Nice. From there he wrote to Scholem on 26 July about future plans, including the four books he intended to write: on the Paris Arcades, collected essays on literature, the selected letters of German humanists and 'a highly significant book about hashish' that had to remain a secret.[83] His assessment of his work to date was that there were many or some small victories, but to these corresponded the large defeats.[84] His main source of income, radio work, ended that summer when Chancellor Franz von Papen installed the NSDAP-member Erich Scholz as Radio

Commissar, in charge of a 'radio reform' that dismissed the Left and the experimentalists. From Nice, Benjamin wrote short farewell letters to Franz Hessel, Jula Radt and Ernst Schoen. A long letter to the Wissings outlined his situation on the cusp of forty. He was tired of chasing money by telegram. The likelihood of existing in Germany as a writer with his attitude and education was rapidly diminishing. He worried that his work was too attuned to journalistic needs to be of lasting significance. Only something definite to work on, or a woman with whom to live, would give him impetus. He had asked Ola Parem, a woman he met at the Hessels in 1928, to marry him, but she refused. Like a plant, in the mornings he wanted to live, by evening he wanted to die. The energies he summoned lasted only a day, but they were the best energies he had ever possessed.[85]

The main business of the letter made plans in the event of his death. He named Egon Wissing as his executor and suggested arrangements for the deposit of his papers. His handwritten papers were to go to Scholem and the university library in Jerusalem, excepting a small blue leather-bound book – presumably *Berlin Chronicle* – that was to go to Hessel and, after his death, Stefan. He also entrusted Scholem with the rights to any edition of his selected writings and requested that royalties therefrom go partly to Stefan. Scholem was also to receive the correspondence. Benjamin possessed the archives of his boyhood friends, the brothers Fritz and Wolf Heinle. He entrusted them to Scholem, amused by the idea of two Jews passing on the work of two non-Jews to a Jerusalem library. Stefan was to inherit his books, though friends were offered quantities up to a specific value. Klee's *Angelus Novus* was destined for Scholem and his *Introducing the Miracle* was for Schoen. Bloch was to receive a religious image and a decal image. Childhood drawings by Wolf Heinle were for Stefan or Dora. Elisabeth Hauptmann was to receive a silver Soviet-Russian dagger, Lacis a first edition of Goethe's play *The Natural Daughter*, Jula Radt a small Delft bowl, Gretel Karplus an ashtray, Gert Wissing a bureau and Alfred Cohn a carpet.[86]

He did not kill himself. Scholem received a letter on 7 August from Poveromo, where Benjamin was living on credit and pocket money for cigarettes lent him by Speyer, with whom he was planning trips in Italy and working on a detective play. The play was about a lawyer, his estranged wife and her lover who purchase in a department store a hat, a coat and gloves, objects which come to play a crucial part in a subsequent murder trial.

Benjamin wrote to Adorno about his reading Arthur Rosenberg's *History of Bolshevism*, a book that Benjamin thought no one should ignore. It had, he claimed, illuminated the ways in which the political impinges on private destiny.[87] He intended to stay in Italy for some weeks – he could not afford to return until Speyer was ready to drive him back. He would not see Adorno – who had been offering a course on Benjamin's Baroque book at Frankfurt University[88] – for Benjamin no longer had reason to visit Frankfurt, as the radio work appeared definitely over. Flesch was dismissed from Berlin radio on 13 August. Benjamin heard no word from Schoen and wondered about his fate. His second source of income, articles in the *Frankfurter Zeitung*, was also diminishing. In October he complained that articles and letters sent to the *Frankfurter Zeitung* had not been acknowledged for the last few months. He thought that his work was subject to a boycott as well organized as that against a 'small Jewish clothes dealer in Neustettin', the location of a synagogue burning and anti-Semitic riots in 1881.[89] *Die literarische Welt* informed him that they no longer needed his co-operation.[90]

Benjamin consoled himself in memories. He worked on the vignettes of *Berlin Chronicle*, refining and developing them for a book titled *Berlin Childhood around 1900*, which he hoped Rowohlt would publish. The redrafting sifted people from the scenes. Objects and spaces loomed ever larger in the re-imagined world.

He returned to Berlin in November, where he worked further on a first draft.

Adorno, in later reflections, revealed that Benjamin was most enamoured of those glass baubles enclosing a snow-blanketed landscape, which, on being shaken, awakened to new life.[91] Such were the experiences fixed in *Berlin Childhood around 1900* – miniature exposures of significant experiences, shaken from memory back to life. Their manuscript was an attempt to hold onto possibilities, lives, promises, that were losing currency. Details of his past life were captured once more in memory, as if experience itself were to be rescued. An early version of one of the thirty-odd vignettes rendered experience under threat. 'The Little Hunchback' detailed the cliché of a rapid film of a 'whole life' streaming past the mind's eye at the moment of death.[92] Benjamin's vignettes evoked climacteric nodes in past time – portmanteaux of pressures and tendencies, hopes and omens – that came to shape collective social futures. Imprints of the past allowed the possibility of grasping unripened hopes as well as the ominous fruits of actuality. A place or a moment might not be fully apprehended in its own time, but later study of its graphic rendition laid bare the dense web of connections that had produced the future. When Theodor and Gretel Adorno collated Benjamin's writings for Suhrkamp in 1955, they lodged *Berlin Childhood around 1900* in a section called 'Picture-Puzzles and Miniatures'. Benjamin cherished these two things: rebuses, because they demanded to be solved and the clues were contained in the image, and miniatures, because they condensed the world into handleable, studiable form. He hoped to parallel their trickery verbally.

The child-Benjamin remembered the spaces of Berlin. His spaces – for instance, balconies, which generated from early on a desire for the air of the courtyards – were situated on the edges between two worlds or in none. Unexplored places attracted him, such as little-used rooms, a rarely visited part of the zoo, or a garden's edge. He wished to break free from the old West End, where his family kept him as 'prisoner'.[93] But he was also drawn to comforting interiors, such as the home in Blumeshof, abode of Benjamin's maternal grandmother, where the heavy furniture of the 1870s emanated a faith in an eternity that hoped to exclude misery and death.[94] Benjamin's remembered Berlin is a series of significant spaces, scenes of vivid sensation. In such places he found objects charged with meaning, prompts to fantasy: the telephone, the strip of light under his bedroom door when his parents were entertaining, Christmas dolls and lambkins.

His mother and father are glimpsed, in *Berlin Childhood around 1900*, but there is more substance in their objects: her sewing box, his walking stick, her medicine spoon, his breastplate-like dress shirt, her sparkling belt brooch. This child harboured no prejudice about the inferiority of objects. As Benjamin observed in 'Doctrine of the Similar', written at the beginning of 1933, the child identified so much with objects that he imitated things – windmills, trains – as much as he aped other people.[95] On being photographed as a child in a studio, with a painted Alpine scene or in the shadow of a small palm tree, clutching a straw hat, Benjamin recalled an inability to resemble himself and a desire to be identical with the embroidered cushion or the ball handed him as props.[96] Benjamin's recall outlined the displacement, alienation and crushing domination by an objective world ushered in by industrial capitalism, but it also conjured up the utopian 'sense for all that was kindred in the world'.

He noted, in a letter to Scholem on 28 February, that he had composed four small handwritten sides that represented a new theory of language, which had germinated under the most unfavourable living and working conditions as he 'fixed' the first pieces for *Berlin Childhood around 1900*.[97] In the vignette 'Mummerehlen', where he mentioned his identification with the Chinese porcelain of the family home, Benjamin wrote: 'The gift of perceiving similarities is, in fact, nothing but a weak remnant of the old compulsion to become similar and to behave mimetically.'[98] This 'mimetic faculty' was increasingly fragile, for the perceptual world of modern humans contained fewer magical correspondences than those of the ancients or primitive peoples, who lived with astrology, divination from entrails and coincidences – the reading matter of a pre-scriptural world. But other than in the world of children, it still existed, even if its form had mutated. In 'Doctrine of the Similar' Benjamin detailed the concept of 'nonsensuous similarity', whose workings were made clear in onomatopoeia, but also graphology, for the mimetic faculty was an aspect of language and inscription:

> The most recent graphology has taught us to recognize in handwriting images – or, more precisely, picture puzzles – what the unconscious of the writer conceals in his writing. It may be supposed that the mimetic process which expresses itself in this way in the activity of the writer was, in the very distant times in which script originated, of utmost importance for writing. Script has thus become, like language, an archive of nonsensuous similarities, of nonsensuous correspondences.[99]

Language's mimetic capability described writing's alignment with the microcosm of the body, and through it, alignment with the macrocosm of the stars and the whole span of human and non-human history.

'Doctrine of the Similar' was not destined for publication, but Benjamin was not completely voiceless. The *Frankfurter Zeitung* had not severed all links. One piece from long ago suddenly appeared: a Marseilles hashish protocol from 29/30 September 1928 was published in December. Vignettes from *Berlin Childhood around 1900* appeared in the coming months, pseudonyms replacing his name. These were memoirs of nobody and everybody. A few short reviews found a home that spring in the literary supplement of the *Frankfurter Zeitung* and in the *Vossische Zeitung*. But a radio play on Lichtenberg that he wrote at the beginning of 1933 was not broadcast.

Germany was under National Socialist rule. Hitler was made Chancellor on 30 January 1933. Many of Benjamin's acquaintances made preparations to leave Germany. Benjamin told Scholem that there were places where he could earn a minimum of money and places where he could exist on a minimal amount, but the two did not coincide.[100] The Reichstag fire on 27 February was a glaring signal to leave the city, whatever might come. Brecht and Kracauer left the next day. Bloch left a few days later. Brecht's swift departure had scuppered his arrest. Ernst Schoen had been less lucky. Benjamin's homeland was turning into the land of blankings, where those deemed undesirable were blanked, or worse, blanked out. Felix Noeggerath wrote to Jean Selz about their friend: Benjamin barely dared to step outside the door.[101]

Benjamin left on 17 March 1933 for Paris.

6

Noms de Plume, 1933–7

Paris offered a temporary home with Jean Selz. In pursuit of a
cheaper destination, Benjamin returned with Selz in early April to
Ibiza, via Barcelona and the bars of the Barrio Chino with their
naked dancers.[1] He took up residence in a house in San Antonio
with the Noeggeraths, informing Gretel Karplus on 30 April that he
had few opportunities to exchange words with anyone.[2] He told his
friend Kitty Marx-Steinschneider on 1 May that, apart from walks,
his only entertainment was reading the second volume of Trotsky's
History of the Russian Revolution. He also read detective novels by the
fairy light of a few candles once darkness set in and occasionally
wrote in cafés, just to hear the bustling sounds of life.[3] On one occasion in June Selz procured opium and the two experimented,
entranced by the extraordinary conceptual and linguistic formulations that curled with the smoke from their lips: the city was made
of fabric to enable their 'curtainology'; Benjamin's Russian skullcap
became 'a hat fashioned in trombone marmalade'; it was a starting
point for 'entry of ideas into the chamber of meanders' where
Castilian Spanish words became visible 'in the form of dogs'.[4]

   Benjamin scraped together an existence on 'the European minimum' of about 60 or 70 Marks a month, through writings, selling
books from his collection, donations from Gretel Karplus, Adorno
and the Radts and whoever else could be persuaded. He worried
about the fate of the Jews in Germany and specifically Stefan, who
was still in Berlin, and he attempted unsuccessfully to persuade

Dora to send him to her brother, Victor Kellner, who had settled in Palestine.[5] Conscious of spies everywhere in Germany, Dora used her middle name to speak of her movements in her letters to Benjamin.[6] Any exchange of information about the course of events in Germany was seriously impeded. Rumours of his brother's capture by the NSDAP's Sturmabteilung reached him – on 12 March Georg had been re-elected as local councillor for the German Communist Party. He had been beaten and taken to the prison at Plötzensee.[7] The new Press Legislation, presented by Goebbels, threatened to remove Benjamin's few remaining publishing opportunities.[8] Benjamin complained that, despite never 'stepping forwards politically', his radius of action as a writer had shrunk to a minimum and, worse, his enforced existence in Ibiza cut him off from the basis of his production, for he could cultivate no contacts nor purchase any books in instalments.[9] The pseudonymous Detlef Holz was building a greater profile than the vanishing Walter Benjamin – he signed off his letters to Gretel Karplus with this impostor's name. Under his own signature he worked on his first commissioned submission to the *Zeitschrift für Sozialforschung*, the journal of Max Horkheimer's Institute for Social Research: 'The Present Social Situation of the French Writer'.

He moved to more convivial quarters in June and found a young man to act as his secretary.[10] He returned to the theme of Stefan George for the *Frankfurter Zeitung*: 'The generation for whom George's most beautiful and perfect poems provided something of a refuge was doomed.'[11] In his retrospective, Benjamin condemned George's idealism, his impotence and ability 'to prescribe only feeble rules or courses of action, remote from the realities of life' in the face of catastrophe. He criticized too the narrow frameworks – literary, religious, spiritual – of those who analysed him. Only an historical view, a placement of George within the matrix of war, could bring insights. Through such an approach, the critic might realize how historically determined was George's motivating force

Walter Benjamin at Palma di Mallorca, 1933. Benjamin visited the island in July 1933, while staying in Ibiza. He described the photo to Gretel Karplus: 'It is, you see, a passport photograph, which I had made in Mallorca. It is not too bad, but it has not yet reached its destination, as there has been no response to date from the Berlin office.' (*GB*, IV, p. 257).

of chaotic nature. Benjamin sent a copy to Karplus in August but, underscoring his difficult living and working conditions, he had to request its return as he had no duplicate.[12] He also relied on money from Karplus – who considered Benjamin her 'adopted son', a sibling to her other child, Adorno.[13]

Whenever possible Benjamin slipped back into his memories, encouraged by their appearance in the *Vossische Zeitung*, under Detlef Holz's by-line, and in the *Frankfurter Zeitung* anonymously or by 'C. Conrad'. He was also buoyed by Selz's plans to co-translate some vignettes into French. During a bout of illness in July – unable to walk, his legs assaulted by inflamed wounds from the heat or poor nutrition, and sleeping away from home on 'the worst mattress in the world'[14] – he wrote 'Loggias', his 'self-portrait'.[15] Loggias, small balcony-like rooms at least partly open to the air, are presented as cribs for his first recollections of the city.[16] As these memories, and their nourishing fantasies of Sunday contentment, fade or are disabused, the loggias become the tomb of an entire bourgeois class, condemned, 'in panicked horror' (according to Adorno's subsequent afterword) to witness its 'disintegrating aura', and to come to 'awareness of itself: as illusion'.[17] The ring of the telephone, instrument of his father's business transactions, was an 'alarm signal' that menaced not only his parents' midday nap but also 'the historical era that underwrote and enveloped this siesta'.[18]

Sometime between the spring and the autumn of 1933 Benjamin wrote a short reflection titled 'Experience and Poverty', which considered the world of the next historical era, the shocking world of war. Twentieth-century warfare had unleashed a 'new barbarism' in which a generation that went to school in horse-drawn trams stood exposed in a transformed landscape, caught in the crossfire of explosions and destructive torrents.[19] This was no lament for the old days, for those were unliveable for the propertyless, and the habits engendered by the cluttered and smothered interiors were unsustainable.[20] 'Erase the traces!' Benjamin repeated, echoing Brecht, and invent a 'new, positive concept of barbarism'. Benjamin heralded the honest recorders of this newly devalued, technologized, impoverished experience: Paul Klee, Adolf Loos, and the utopians Paul Scheerbart and Mickey Mouse. By all of these the brutality and dynamism of contemporary technology was used, abused, mocked and harnessed.

In Ibiza he fell in love again, with a Dutch painter, Anna Maria Blaupot ten Cate. In a draft of a letter he wrote: 'From your features rises everything that makes the woman into a guardian, a mother, a whore. You transform each into the other and give each a thousand forms.'[21] Benjamin composed two versions of a cryptic autobiographical sketch, perhaps for his new love, on 12 and 13 August. Both were titled 'Agesilaus Santander', and one copy was presented to Blaupot ten Cate on her thirty-first birthday. He identified the

Dutch woman as the female counterpart to his cherished *Angelus Novus*. He told of how he had held up the New Angel from his task of singing his praises to God, and so God, taking advantage of Benjamin's birth 'under the sign of Saturn – the planet of the slowest revolution, the star of hesitation and delay' – sent a feminine angel, but via the 'most circuitous, most fatal detour', even though the two had once unknowingly been close neighbours. Still, Benjamin had learnt patience, and observed that he could wait until she whom he loved fell into his hands, 'ill, aged, and in ragged clothes'. He would wait for happiness – 'that is to say, the conflict in which the rapture of the unique, the new, the yet unborn is combined with the bliss of experiencing something once more, of possessing once again, of having lived'.[22]

His illness abated slowly. In September he was still feverish: a letter from Dora observed that she could tell from his handwriting that something was still wrong.[23] He spent time with a book on Luther and discovered for the fifth or sixth time in his life the meaning of justification from the position of faith. But, as with calculus, he understood it for a few hours and then it disappeared again for years.[24] A letter from Speyer on 12 September 1933 noted the progress of the detective play, *A Hat, A Coat, A Glove*, on which they had worked together. It was to be performed in New York the following month.[25] As a result, money would accrue to Benjamin – 10 per cent of the theatre takings to a maximum of 5000 reichsmarks, according to a contract with Speyer – but Speyer proposed giving it to Benjamin directly, as the man responsible for payment at the publisher's was a 'disgusting anti-Semite'.[26]

By October 1933 Benjamin was back in Paris, where he was diagnosed with malaria and had to take quinine, having spurned Dora's offer of respite in Berlin where she would take care of him. Dora thought that attacks on the Jews had ceased, or were at least restricted to those who were politically active. But still there were worries. She wrote her thoughts to Benjamin in code, as if writing about a third party of quite different political stripe: 'He [Benjamin] has never personally done anything to oppose the Revolutionaries [National Socialists], but he does have so many friends amongst the aristocracy [political opposition], that one cannot, of course, be sure.'[27]

In Paris Benjamin enjoyed access to a library for the first time in months. The love affair with Blaupot ten Cate was over, but they remained friendly, and he met her in Paris in the company of her lover Louis Sellier. In November Brecht arrived, and the two of them, together with Margarete Steffin, lived at the Palace Hotel in the Rue du Four. Benjamin planned a series of detective stories with Brecht, and Steffin helped him to prepare his manuscript of German humanist letters, to be published under the title *German Men and Women*. The seven weeks that Brecht spent in Paris were lively. There were encounters with Klaus Mann, Kracauer, Lotte Lenya, Kurt Weill and Hanns Eisler. Once Brecht left on 19 December the city seemed dead.[28] There was work to occupy Benjamin, which was his salvation, for life amongst the emigrants was unbearable, life alone no better and life amongst the French impossible to achieve. The Institute for Social Research commissioned a study of the aged Marxist writer and collector Eduard Fuchs, as well as a review of publications on the philosophy and sociology of language.

Brecht invited Benjamin for an extended visit to Denmark at the end of the winter. Life could be lived cheaply there. It was warmer than Paris, he assured Benjamin, who feared the cold, and Brecht's wife, Helene Weigel, calculated that it was possible to survive on 100 kroner (60 reichsmarks, or 360 francs) a month. In addition the library in Svendborg could obtain any book, and there were numerous temptations and benefits – radio, newspapers, playing cards, cooking stoves, small coffee houses, an easily understandable language and, crucially, a number of Benjamin's books would be sent there. In Denmark the 'world perished more quietly'.[29]

On 14 December newspaper laws came into force in Germany, compelling all journalists to join the Reichsschriftumskammer, the Reich Chamber of Writers. Benjamin considered joining, so that he might continue to publish.[30] He searched for outlets. In January he sent the manuscript of *Berlin Childhood around 1900* to Hermann Hesse, who had been one of the few to express interest in *One-way Street*, in case the author could help him to find a publisher. Hesse replied that unfortunately his influence was waning.[31]

Another solution was to forge a career in France. At the beginning of January 1934 Benjamin told Gretel Karplus that he had written his first article in French and a French reader had found just one mistake. He had a commission to write an article on Baron Haussmann, the redeveloper of Paris, for Alfred Kurella's weekly journal *Monde*, and this was appealing for two reasons: Brecht was impressed by the theme, and it brought Benjamin back to the ambit of his *Arcades Project*, after a long pause. The Bibliothèque nationale was not a lending library, so Benjamin spent long days in one of the reading rooms.[32] It was, he noted, 'one of the most remarkable' on Earth. To work there was like working amidst an opera's scenery. His only regret was that it closed at 6 pm – an arrangement dating back, he claimed, to the days when theatre performances began at that hour.[33] In January he requested help from Gretel Karplus:

> Now I have a small and bizarre request regarding the arcades papers. Since the first setting up of the numerous sheets on which the notes are to reside, I have always used one and the same type of paper, namely a normal letter pad of white MK [Max Krause] paper. Now my supplies of this are exhausted and I would very much like to preserve the external uniformity of this bulky and thorough manuscript. Would it be possible for you to arrange for one of those pads to be sent to me?[34]

Evenings were long and spent alone or reading Somerset Maugham in a variety of hotel rooms or short-term lets.[35]

He enjoyed a certain solvency. In February 1934 he received a payment from the Institute for Social Research, 120 Swiss francs for his essay 'On The Present Social Situation of the French Writer' and for reviews of books on Fourier and Haussmann. This was supplemented by monthly payments of 700 francs from the Alliance Israélite Universelle for a short period. In March he received 450 francs, a communal contribution from Adorno, Adorno's aunt Agathe and a business acquaintance of Adorno, Else Herzberger.[36] That month he also made an agreement with Max Horkheimer for a monthly stipend of 100 Swiss francs. In addition, the Institute paid for the most important half of Benjamin's library to be shipped to Brecht's Danish retreat, awaiting Benjamin's sojourn in the coming months.

Life, he reported, had returned to the arcades work – the weak sparks 'that could not be more lively than myself' had been blown on by Adorno, who showed interest.[37] Indeed by the end of March Benjamin declared that he had conceived a provisional division of the material into chapters. To raise his profile he announced a series of five lectures on 'The German Avant-garde', whereby tickets would need to be purchased for the full series. Beginning with a lecture on the German audience, the rest of the series was to consider an exemplary individual in each genre: Kafka and the novel, Bloch and the essay, Brecht and theatre, Kraus and journalism.[38] He turned his attention to the first lecture – its theme now changed to 'Political Currents in Contemporary German Literature'. The lecture was to be held before invited guests in a private, rather respectable, house belonging to a gynaecologist called Jean Dalsace, but the host fell suddenly gravely ill and the lecture was cancelled.

On 28 April Benjamin reported to Klaus Mann, for whose journal *Die Sammlung* he hoped to write, that he had delivered a lecture titled 'The Author as Producer' at the Institute for the Study of Fascism.[39] Benjamin conceived of it as a counterpart to his work on Brecht's epic theatre, noting those forces – Brecht, Tretyakov – who altered the forms of art such that revolutionary authors became 'engineers' of a production apparatus, rather than suppliers. This apparatus was then *used* by its public, rather than consumed.[40] It was not a question of art expressing revolutionary themes, but rather an effort to persuade revolutionary authors that formal questions of production and reception were the crucial political questions. He requested of Mann that any work published by him be attributed to O. E. Tal, reversal of the Latin *lateo*. Mann rejected the lecture, and the pseudonym resumed its meaning, 'I am hidden'.

That month a letter to Karl Thieme, who had made reference to Benjamin's writings in an article, articulated the gratitude of someone who felt quite obscured.

> For someone whose writings are as dispersed as mine, and for whom the conditions of the day no longer allow the illusion that they will be gathered together again one day, it is a genuine acknowledgement to hear of a reader here and there, who has been able to make himself at home in my scraps of writings, in some way or another.[41]

Benjamin's work continued to provoke criticism from Scholem, who reacted to Benjamin's essay on the social situation of French writers with the query – 'is that meant to be Communist credo?' Benjamin replied that his Communism was not a credo, but rather nothing other than the 'expression of certain experiences' in his thinking and his existence. It was a 'drastic and not fruitless expression of the impossibility of the present-day pursuit of knowledge to offer existence and space'. It was, he claimed, a 'rational attempt' of someone expropriated from his means of production to proclaim his rights. And though it was the 'lesser evil', it was 'a so much lesser evil' compared to that which surrounded them.[42]

He directed Scholem to Karl Kraus's ironic retort to a female landowner in November 1920. She had mocked and criticized Kraus' positive attitude towards the Communist Rosa Luxemburg, who was murdered in January 1919. Kraus proclaimed, in a bitter reply in his journal *Der Fackel*, that Communist praxis could go to hell, but God should preserve its 'purer ideal purpose' as a 'constant threat above the heads of those who possess property' and who preach morality to their 'victims' while giving them syphilis and sending them to war. Communism's existence might at least give them nightmares, ruin their impudence and shatter their confidence. For Benjamin the Communist credo – if this is what it had to be called – left room for manoeuvre in terms of theory. Brecht was significant, noted Benjamin, but Kafka was of no less import, for he did not occupy any one of the positions against which Communism justifiably fought. He instructed Scholem to push for a commission from the Jewish *Rundschau* to write on Kafka, on the occasion of the tenth anniversary of his death.[43] Scholem was successful. He could be helpful in other ways as well. In a letter at the beginning of June Benjamin requested he find out how much the university in Jerusalem would offer for his prized antique edition of Franz Xaver Baader's collected works.

Work for the essay on Kafka kept Benjamin from Brecht until the middle of June. Looking forward to the evenings to be spent playing chess, he told Brecht about the Chinese board game Go. Stones are not moved but rather fill up an initially empty board. It was comparable to Brecht's play *The Round Heads and the Pointed Heads* – each figure and formulation was placed on the right spot, from where it exercised its strategic function.[44] Gretel Karplus voiced concerns about Brecht's influence on Benjamin. Benjamin agreed that in the 'economy' of his existence a few relationships had indeed played the role of transforming him into the opposite of himself, and his friends had always protested. He could ask only that, despite the dangers, his friends should realise how fertile are these relations. Karplus of all people, he remonstrated, should know that his life as much as his thinking 'moves in extreme positions'.[45] The letter also reported on falling under another type of influence: he had tried the drug mescaline, with the Communist neurologist Fritz Fränkel, which brought about a night of 'highly important insights, and in particular a psychological explanation of catatonia'.[46] Catatonic loss of external stimulation was one aspect. Sensory excess to the point of takeover was another. Benjamin observed how: 'In shuddering, the skin imitates the meshwork of a net. But the net is the world net: the whole universe is caught in it.'[47]

A letter from Blaupot ten Cate, who sent gossip regularly from Provence where she then lived with her husband Sellier, reacted with some vehemence against Benjamin's suggestion that they reanimate their love affair.[48] In the middle of June he set off for Skovsbostrand in Denmark. He took a room in a house close to Brecht's in isolated countryside and prepared to spend time there with his books and his friend. There was a complete collection of the Social Democratic journal *Die neue Zeit* at Brecht's, and its study allowed Benjamin to make an analysis of the cultural politics and cultural direction of this most important journal of old-style social democracy, in whose milieu was Eduard Fuchs. In a letter to a Danish committee that offered financial support to refugee intellectuals, he outlined his publications; he mentioned how he had tried to make a living in Paris, but France was too expensive, and he was no longer published in Germany, despite his membership of no party; he mentioned his brother's arrest, abuse and detention from April till December 1933 in the concentration camp Sonnenburg. Benjamin was without any property, apart from a small working library.[49]

To Scholem he complained that, having spent his last reserves to ship his Paris library to Denmark, he was penniless and dependent on the hospitality of Brecht.[50] But Denmark offered a good place to work – an essay for the *Nouvelle Revue Française* on Johann Jakob Bachofen, theorist of matriarchy, was one focus. There was also more work on Kafka, in response to comments on a first type-written version by Werner Kraft, Scholem and Adorno. World politics was 'at the forefront of interests' at Brecht's.[51] Benjamin's 'modest optimism' about improvements in Germany was dashed as the summer progressed.[52] The northern silence was disturbed by radio broadcasts from Germany. In July 1934 Benjamin heard Hitler's voice for the first time, delivering a speech justifying the putting down of the Röhm Putsch and the 'law for new measures of state defence'. Radio made world history present in 'one of the most remote regions imaginable': Benjamin followed the putsch in Austria in July from the very first moment, having tuned into a Viennese radio station by coincidence.[53] He was relieved to hear that Dora was about to leave Germany for Italy – and she invited him to spend some time at a hotel in San Remo, where she was to take a job. The South was a prospect once again. The usual summer activities of walks and bathing were not part of the Brecht-Weigel itinerary, and Benjamin missed them. In August he told Anna Maria Blaupot ten Cate that he slept late in the northern climate and his dreams were stronger, more affecting and recurrent. He dreamt of Brecht and Weigel in the form of two towers or gate-like buildings swaying through a town.[54]

In September he reported to Horkheimer that he was writing a 'cultural-scientific and cultural-political inventory' of the *Neue Zeit*. He was keen to show how 'collective literary products especially lend themselves to materialist treatment and analysis, indeed can only be made accessible to rational evaluation'.[55] He needed to stay longer in Denmark to finish the piece. But Brecht – his chess adversary – left for a long stay in London to work with Hanns Eisler on a play and to plan some theatrical productions, and so it was time to move on. Alarmingly Benjamin's receipt of donations from bene-factors, such as Else Herzberger, was threatened. New German currency laws, effective from 24 September, meant that no payments could be made to Germans living abroad unless they were approved by a specific government office. With the Kafka essay finished – or at least suspended so that the results might be published, before he began the usual task of annotating and revising his own work – his series of literary essays was concluded, as Benjamin told Alfred Cohn, in October 1934. There was little chance of publishing these smaller works, and so he decided to turn his attention to larger projects. The large project he wanted most to work on was Baudelaire and the arcades, but for that he had no choice but to be in Paris, which he could not afford for very long.[56] He left his 'ice-cold room' in Denmark for only a brief stay in Paris on 17 October.[57]

That month Horkheimer dangled the possibility of a research post for one or two years in the United States, under the auspices of an Institute for Social Research, then situated in New York. Benjamin agreed. He preferred to stay in Paris to carry out his researches, but complained to Horkheimer that his poverty made this impossible. He moved to Dora's guesthouse on the Côte d'Azur in the quiet winter season.[58] He saw Stefan, who visited for a few days before returning to school in Berlin, but otherwise it was lonely and dull – a peaceful harbour, he told Kracauer, from whence there was nothing to report.[59] Bedtime came each night at 9.30 and he amused himself with detective novels. To escape the dullness of San Remo he travelled to Nice, where the cafés, bookshops and newspaper stands were better. Friends who were now flung far and wide fell out of touch. Brecht and Bloch were silent. Lack of money prevented him from encouraging the contacts who could lead him to more commissions. He complained to Horkheimer that, despite the Institute's regular payments, he could not afford a trip to a nearby town to meet with an editor of the journal *Cahier de Sud*, where a ('profoundly sketchy')[60] translation by Blaupot ten Cate and Sellier of his 'Hashish in Marseilles' was to appear in January 1935.[61] Benjamin later reported to Alfred Cohn that the previous winter he had unsuccessfully attempted to get aid from Jewish welfare groups. Their efforts, he complained, are the continuation of fascist – Streicher-ish – policies by other means. 'If the Jews are dependent only on their own kind and anti-Semites, not many of them will survive', he declared.[62]

In Germany Benjamin's writings made their final pseudonymous appearances. On 6 December 'On the Minute' appeared in the *Frankfurter Zeitung*. In it, Benjamin recalled his first radio lecture. He had prepared and practised a twenty-minute text. The necessity of adhering rigidly to the allotted time could not have been more forcefully presented. He began to read in 'this chamber designed for

San Remo provided
a refuge in the
winter months of
1934/35.

technology and the humanity who has control over it'.[63] At a certain point in the recital he glanced at the clock, and to his horror and surprise he found he had slipped behind. In the most modern of rooms Benjamin was gripped by a 'new terror that was related to the oldest one, which is already known to us'. He skipped pages, gabbled to a close, glanced at the clock only to realize that there were still four minutes yet to go. He had mistaken the minute and the second hand. Deadly silence enveloped him, until he managed to grab from his coat pocket the same manuscript, select a page and begin to read. The text was short, so he drew out each syllable, rolled his Rs and left ponderous pauses between sentences. The next day a friend responded that the broadcast was 'nice' but the radio receivers were still dodgy, as his lost reception for at least a minute. The relationship between humans and their technologies, the new terrors and the new possibilities, were themes that would come to the fore late in 1935, when Benjamin would turn his attention to 'the work of art in the age of its technological reproducibility'.

In the meantime Benjamin hammered out commissions on all manner of subjects. The essay on Bachofen was his first work written directly in French, in February 1935. He wrote on Brecht's *Threepenny Novel* for Klaus Mann's *Die Sammlung*. He wrote on the sociology of language for the Institute for Social Research. This survey of contemporary trends in linguistics – Bühler, Piaget, Paget, Vygotsky, Marr, Carnap and others – considered the merits of onomatopoeia and primitive language acquisition; the language of gesture; the meaning of whispers; the connections of language and material culture; the social context of children's language acquisition and the precession of grammar before logic.

San Remo offered space for reflection on the recent past. The first years of emigration in Ibiza seemed all the more glorious the further away they slipped, he wrote to Alfred Cohn.[64] There, he recalled, he rose at 7.30, bathed in the sea and found an inaccessible spot of forest, where he would sit on a cushion of moss and read

Lucretius until breakfast appeared. But a passion for travel had become enforced exile in a place of survival. He passed the time by writing a list of mistakes and failures of the last two years: 'The weak consolation' was that the first were not always the preconditions of the last.[65] He had achieved very good things in those two years, but he felt that the moment could easily arrive when nobody was interested in those achievements. Indeed, as he told Lacis, who had been in contact again since learning he was at Brecht's, even he was certainly no longer interested.[66] Alongside those achievements, there was hackwork. In March, 'Detlef Holz' published a sketch on the Nice carnival in the *Frankfurter Zeitung*. It was 'a dubious piece', barely excusable as part of a 'struggle for existence'.[67]

Plans to continue existing in San Remo until May were scuppered when Dora's mother appeared. He had to leave suddenly for a hotel in Monaco at the end of February. A letter from Lacis informed him that she had been unsuccessful in an attempt to find Benjamin a position in Russia. He was grateful to find out after the fact, because he thought there were people who enjoyed raising his hopes, only then to dash them.[68] He played with the idea of moving to Moscow and walking through the streets beside Lacis, who would be draped in reindeer fur. Egon Wissing, then a prominent radiologist, had taken a post there at a cancer research institute. Benjamin joked that if he did not find him a job within six months he would never speak to him again.

In February Horkheimer promised to raise his monthly stipend from the Institute for Social Research to 500 francs. In April a letter from Nice, written in the hotel where he was to have killed himself three years earlier, emphasized to Horkheimer that he wished his work to be as tightly and productively connected to the Institute as possible.[69] Benjamin needed to cultivate relationships. The review of Brecht's *Threepenny Novel* had been returned, after he requested a higher writing fee from Klaus Mann. The essay on Bachofen was rejected the following month.

Benjamin longed to be in Paris. Only from there could he work further on the essay on Fuchs for the Institute's journal. He had hoped to live with his sister, but she was ill, lived in one room and earned money by caring for five children there during the day. He took a room in the Hotel Floridor on Place Denfert-Rochereau in Montparnasse. Soon after arrival he met with Friedrich Pollock, one of the Institute's directors, and this led to a doubling of that month's stipend and the impulse to fix some of the themes of the *Arcades Project*, for possible publication by the Institute.[70] He informed Adorno of his plan to compose an exposé of the whole.[71] In May he told Alfred Cohn in a letter that, after an interruption of several years, he was returning to the project, the 'Paris Arcades', which, since its beginnings seven or eight years earlier had never yet been so keenly pursued.

> There now exists a comprehensive exposé of this work, which allows traits of the actual book to be perceived. Whether this will ever get written is, of course, more doubtful than ever before. The only thing that is fairly certain is that to a much greater degree than I might have suspected earlier, it will become a counterpart to the baroque book. The old title 'Paris Arcades' is discarded. The book is now called: Paris, The Capital of the Nineteenth Century.[72]

The 1935 Exposé careered between urban architectural structures and the figures associated with them: Fourier or the Arcades; Daguerre or the Panoramas; Grandville or the World Exhibitions; Louis-Philippe or the Interieur; Baudelaire or the Streets of Paris; Haussmann or the Barricades. Other polar tensions motivating the project included commodity fetishism versus the collector who emancipates things from the 'drudgery of being useful'; the obsolescence of art versus the promotion of *l'art pour l'art* as reaction to technology; the interior as the private universe of the bourgeoisie versus the streets where the flâneur and the prostitute pace; Haussmann's city planning versus its burning negation, the Paris Commune. Enmeshed in the historical data, which Benjamin had distilled from hundreds of books, were methodological impulses.

He concluded the Exposé with the comment that it was Balzac who first spoke of the ruins of the bourgeoisie, but it was Surrealism that allowed its gaze to wander uninhibitedly across the field of rubble that capitalist development of productive forces had left in its wake. This ruined matter was confronted by dialectical thinking, which was, for Benjamin, a name for 'historical awakening'. An awakened consciousness scrutinized the 'residues of a dream world', in the form of the arcades and *intérieurs*, exhibition halls and panoramas.[73] Imaginatively, the emancipation of matter, nature, art and humanity jostled alongside enslavement in the commodity form. These spaces, these things were riven with contradiction, as was too 'the collective consciousness', which in its wishful response to all that has been socially produced 'seeks both to overcome and to transfigure the immaturity of the social product and the inadequacies in the social organization of production'.[74] The utopia of the classless society, traces of which were stored in the unconscious of the collective, in memories of a primal past, left deposits 'in a thousand configurations of life, from enduring edifices to passing fashions'.[75]

At first Adorno was surprised that Benjamin regarded the material in the Exposé as a possible Institute publication. The Institute's work was historical and sociological. Benjamin's project, he assumed, as Gretel Karplus had insisted, would be 'the great philosophical work' for which all Benjamin's 'true friends' had long waited.[76] In addition, Adorno feared the influence that Brecht might exercise on the work. On 31 May Benjamin related, in response, how once he could only ever read two or three pages of Louis Aragon's *Paris Peasant* at a time, because his heart would beat so much that he had to put the book down. The first notes on the arcades stemmed from that time. Then there came the Berlin years when his many conversations with Hessel nourished the project – that was when the subtitle 'a dialectical fairy spectacle' arose. The project, conceived as a newspaper article, was rhapsodic at that time. After that came the Frankfurt discussions with Adorno, and, in particular, an 'historical' one in the 'little Swiss house' in the park. He also recalled an important one where Lacis, Karplus and Horkheimer were all present. 'Rhapsodic naïvety' was over, but a new shape had not yet been found by that point. It was then that Benjamin's 'external difficulties' began, which turned out to be providential as a tarrying, dilatory method was the one he preferred. The 'decisive meeting with Brecht followed – and with that the highpoint of all the aporias of this work'.[77] It was another stage of the work, the latest of several, and he was certain he would accept no 'directives' from Brecht. He enclosed the Exposé in the letter.

Benjamin received the doubled stipend from the Institute until the end of the summer, so that he might work on the *Arcades Project*, before completing the long-outstanding essay on Fuchs. He hoped the Paris studies could find a 'place in the intellectual and material economy of the Institute', because then he could argue for an extension of the increased stipend as he developed it into 'the grand work'.[78] He implored Adorno to support him in this. After reading the Exposé, Adorno was very favourable, responding promptly on 5 June, but he revealed some methodological reservations. First, he thought that Benjamin's definition of the commodity was not attuned to the differences between different historical epochs. Second, he objected to the concept of the 'collective unconscious' as it did not incorporate an awareness of class. Benjamin left these issues to one side for the moment, but he insisted that, while the project must be secured against Marxist objections, it attempted something new, namely the 'genuine abandonment of the idealist image of history with its harmonising perspective'. Such an effort could benefit Marxist historiography too, and that was why he had incorporated into his notes Adorno's comment, in a letter from 16 August 1932, on the 'catastrophic destruction of the recently past'.[79] Benjamin's was a history told from the perspective of ruination, including the ruination of old models. Refinement of his Marxist understanding was also a task for the summer. He informed Adorno that he had begun to read the 'alp grey' mass of Marx's *Capital*, volume one.[80]

June 21–25 brought the International Writers' Congress for the Defence of Culture to Paris, organized by André Malraux, Louis Aragon, André Gide and Jean-Richard Bloch. Hundreds of intellectuals, writers and artists collected together to discuss the cultural front against fascism. Benjamin attended and saw Brecht, 'the most enjoyable – almost the only enjoyable – element of the event'.[81] Benjamin relished making the 'physiognomic acquaintance' of various writers. The cultural-political value appeared to be negligible. Lacis turned Benjamin's criticism against him, in a clumsy and ill-spelt German. Even Bloch, she grumbled, had written a book against fascism, albeit a bad one. She had heard nothing of Benjamin at the Congress, and mocked his 'isolation': 'Not even fascism can rouse you to life, even though it has given some deaf people hearing – against misticism [*sic*].'[82]

On 30 June the last article by Detlef Holz or any other of Benjamin's pseudonymous characters appeared in Germany. 'The Common Touch as Problem', published in the literary supplement of the *Frankfurter Zeitung*, was a critique of a study of Schiller by Hermann Schneider. Schneider wanted to make popular once more a writer who had become to modern readers a stranger, boring and pale. In Benjamin's estimation, he failed. Popular science worked, claimed Benjamin, when it offered readers a glimpse of revolutionary, 'avant-garde' positions. In the jubilee year of 1859 the German bourgeoisie had discovered Schiller as their own – separating him from the court at Weimar – and had been able to produce a genuinely popular figure.[83] There was no revolutionary reception awaiting Schiller in the Germany of the Third Reich.

In July Benjamin was able to move into his sister's Paris lodgings while she was away. After two years of living in hotels and furnished rooms, he enjoyed the sense of being in 'secluded rooms'.[84] He devoted his time in the main to working intensively in the library for several weeks, until he had no option but to complete the Fuchs essay.[85] There were few friends in Paris that summer. Even many emigrants had scraped together a few pennies and taken off on holiday. And there were those from whom he preferred to keep his distance. Benjamin suspected Bloch and Kracauer of stealing his ideas and was disinclined to voice his thoughts in front of them.[86] But there were some pleasant diversions. For example, he enthused over the appearance of Jean de Brunhoff's elephant Babar, he recommended a study by the fashion journalist at the *Frankfurter Zeitung*, Helen Hessel, on the Paris fashion industry, and he planned to attend some fashion shows.[87]

On 2 August Adorno's detailed critique of Benjamin's Exposé arrived.[88] From the Black Forest, Adorno expanded on the criticisms that he had already made and questioned Benjamin's historical accuracy on various points. One of Benjamin's mottos, 'Every epoch dreams its successor', was a crystallisation of all that was wrong. The 'undialectical' sentence implied that Benjamin's crucial methodological figure of the dialectical image was simply a product of consciousness, a dream image in an unclassed collective consciousness, which imagined utopias to come. The dark sides of modernity had been lost. The theological vision of Heaven as well as Hell, Arcadia and Underworld, was compromised. Adorno suggested the addition: 'Every epoch dreams that it has been destroyed by catastrophes'. But, noted Adorno, the force of the dialectical image was too much to remain a dream figure. The dialectical image – for example, as fetish commodity – produced consciousness rather than being 'a fact of consciousness'. Adorno objected to

Benjamin's use of a utopian image from Grandville, whereby a cast-iron balcony surrounds the planet Saturn, perfectly placed for night-time gallivanting. Benjamin presented this as an image of the commodification of the universe in utopian form. Nature, cosmic nature beyond human scale, apparently partook no less of fashion.

Adorno reminded Benjamin of his rather different recollections of the moon in his autobiographical writings. The moon's light displaced the child-Benjamin, transposing him to an alternative reality. It made his room unfamiliar and alienated his self. It made him anxious, and the strangeness that the moon evoked made it impossible for him to 'think the world'. In his Berlin memoirs Benjamin related a dream that he had at the close of his childhood. The moon appeared one day above the streets of Berlin. He stood with members of his family on an iron balcony. The full moon suddenly expanded, hurtling towards Earth, until it tore the planet asunder. The iron balcony on which the family stood shattered into a thousand pieces, their bodies pulverized. This was a crossing point for Benjamin. When he woke from this, everything was changed, and the horror of the moon gripped him from then on for the rest of his life.[89] The world had absorbed the moon and its energy, its sovereignty was smashed. This was the planetary balcony Adorno wanted, the one that forced its gazers to participate in cosmic shudder and black realization. The cast-iron balcony was to become a ring of Saturn, not the other way round, which amounted to a banalization of cosmic experience.

Benjamin postponed a detailed response to the criticisms, noting that there would need to be a series of letters and a meeting in the not-too-distant future. But he argued that the Exposé was not a second draft of the project. Rather it was 'another' draft of the project: its ideas of modernity as hell remained operative, for the first version, presented in conversations and letters, formed the thesis to the Exposé's antithesis. Gretel Karplus was reassured, for she had worried that she could not find the hand of wb in the Exposé.

Benjamin's retort was that he had two hands. He told her how, as a fourteen-year-old at the school in Haubinda, for hour after hour he had practised writing with his left hand.[90] He also told Karplus of impending changes. His sister was returning and he needed new accommodation.

On 1 October he took up lodgings in the 14th arrondissement with Ursel Bud, a young female Berliner working in Paris as a secretary. On 9 October he hinted to Karplus about new investigations into the contemporary situation of art, thoughts occasioned by his studies of the nineteenth century. He told her he had found that aspect of nineteenth-century art that was only 'now perceivable'.[91] The past laid spores that certain moments in the present can discover as their own. This was the first reference to his theses on 'The Work of Art in the Age of its Technological Reproducibility'. He also enthused about an essay by Freud on telepathy and psychoanalysis. It was accessible, but more importantly it substantiated Benjamin's thesis in 'On the Mimetic Capability' that language was preceded by telepathic forms of communication.[92] Discussing the common purpose that arises in 'great insect communities', Freud noted that their communication occurs without language or speech. Such a non-linguistic mode of communication, Freud suggested, may well be 'the original archaic method of communication between individuals'. Human language replaced this 'in the course of phylogenetic evolution', but 'the older method might have persisted in the background and still may be able to put itself into effect under certain conditions'.[93]

On 16 October Benjamin wrote to Horkheimer, who had commented encouragingly on the Exposé, about his miserable situation living as a subletter with emigrants. Benjamin managed to stake a claim to a free lunch normally reserved for French intellectuals, but could take it only on those days when he was not at the library, as it was located too far from there. He had no funds to renew his Carte d'Identité nor to join the foreign press organization. But he reported excitedly on his new production. He was developing 'materialist art theory', locating 'the precise place in the present' where his historical construction found its 'vanishing point'. Art's fateful hour had arrived, and his new work attempted to outline the significance of this 'immanently, avoiding all *abrupt* reference to politics'.[94] In November he wrote to Blaupot ten Cate that his room was small but comfortable and he even enjoyed a bath and a telephone, rare treats for emigrant life. It was this room that had exerted a force on his studies and shifted his interest. If the *Arcades Project* was comprised of endless details and facts gleaned from the past, the thoughts on art in the age of mechanical reproduction represented the other side of the scale, the setting out of a few 'heavy and massive weights' that freighted the present.[95] He spent the rest of the year writing a first version.

Benjamin understood technological reproduction in culture in two ways. First, it referred to the easy accessibility of postcard representations of 'great art', illustrations in books and magazines, posters: copies that could be acquired, held in the hand, cut out and incorporated into a viewer's environment. Some sort of experience of artworks, previously available only to those who could travel to the place of deposit, could now be had by all – in copy form. It was as if art had undergone the type of evolution that the printing press had brought about for the written word. Second, technological reproduction was an aspect of relatively new cultural forms: film and photography. These were mechanical forms of cultural production in their own right, and their appearance bore important implications for concepts such as originality and uniqueness, key concepts of traditional art understanding. Photography and film possessed no original. Each print from the negative was as 'original' as the next or the one before it. Each filmstrip was as authoritative as all other versions of the same film. Each recording from a master was of equal validity. The unique original object either tended towards irrelevance or disappeared.

These developments, Benjamin insisted, brought about the decline of what he termed art's 'aura'. He observed how unique, authored works of art exuded a special presence and effect, akin to magical or mystical experience. Art's aura was a sort of glow that adhered to products of high art, making them untouchable, unapproachable, immensely valuable artefacts of geniuses. Auratic artworks disenfranchised the spectator, who became an individual privileged enough to enjoy unique communion with the art object. They compelled the spectator into the position of a passive beholder who consumed the vision of genius. Benjamin argued that the decline of this 'aura' – the happy by-product of mass reproduction – opened the way to a new appropriation of art by the masses.

A technologically prompted process of breaching distance, of bringing art, data and materials within the ambit of the masses – to be used and manipulated by the masses – is the paramount promise outlined in 'The Work of Art in the Age of its Technological Reproducibility'. The new art forms met the viewer 'halfway', exiting from darkened niches, out of the gallery, from the captivity of singular time and space. In the age of technological reproducibility, art was, at least potentially, removed from its traditional spaces; indeed, art disintegrated and multiplied all at once. As Benjamin's tale of the fate of art goes, by 1900 or thereabouts, art had the opportunity to break away from or be broken from magic, ritual and religion and their modern analogues. By 1900 photomechanical reproduction was perfected, swallowing up the images of all previous art and generating its own inimitable forms. By that time too the French photographer Atget had formulated a desolate subject for photography, breaking with the sentimentalism of portraiture to document spaces of the objective world. Technological art forms surfaced because they were demanded by the matrixed masses inhabiting a technologized world.

A demystified appropriation of culture by audiences was best witnessed in the cinema, a collectively produced and consumed cultural form. In perceiving artworks in a more casual fashion, in different environments, and in perceiving more and more of them through the organs of the press, audiences learnt to manipulate them, to criticize and evaluate. This was not without contradiction. Benjamin was keenly aware of the ways in which the production of culture within the property relations of capitalism acted to constrain the progressive, democratic potential of culture. The Hollywood star system, for example, attempted to reinstate an awe before the product. And Benjamin concluded that it was the counter-revolutionaries, the Nazis, who were able to make excellent use of modern mass media forms, such as radio and film. The star system and capital accumulation reestablished barriers between audience and film, and Nazi propaganda films tried to illuminate Hitler and friends with a flattering 'auratic' charismatic glow. In radio and film, as in politics, a new selection by the apparatus was underway – those with the right voice, the good looks and skilled exhibitionism were favoured. The beneficiaries of this were the champion, the star and the dictator. But, at the same time, procedures such as Sergei Eisenstein's workers' cinema or Charlie Chaplin's battles with technology and authority showed that cinema had at least the potential to generate a critical, politically based culture.

The acknowledgment of Chaplin and popular cinema – as in the references in the first drafts of the essay to Mickey Mouse – was crucial. Benjamin's was no manifesto for self-proclaimed avant-garde art. One of the films Benjamin recalled in a letter to Karplus while working on the 'Work of Art' essay was a 1933 film version of *Alice in Wonderland*, one of the few books he had managed to read in part in English, as well as in French and German.[96] The film, which he called 'an extraordinary thing', starred Gary Cooper as the White Knight, Cary Grant as the Mock Turtle and W. C. Fields as Humpty Dumpty. It was rich with special and optical effects, and the Walrus and the Carpenter sequence was animated by Max Fleischer. This was the type of film that attracted Surrealists and mass audiences alike. It proposed alternative, disfiguring and analytical vistas on the real.

The epilogue of Benjamin's essay reversed the optimistic current – all the potential credited to art in the age of technology evaporated before the techno-mysticism and class-violence of the National Socialists. In the essay's coda, Benjamin determined that fascists mirrored mass society in representations without substance; they too participated in technological modernity. But, as he stated in the opening thesis, fascists and reactionaries could not participate in his discussion of technological modernity. In Nazi film culture, the masses came to their expression but not to their rights. Effectively, the masses expressed themselves – they left an imprint of their presence, but they were not present. They were 'represented' formally, but not represented politically in any meaningful way. Their image was appropriated by film.

Under reactionary uses, film was no longer the product of a camera operator as dissector, as surgeon cutting into and reconstructing the real for purposes of analysis and recombination. No more did the segmenting, annihilative effect of film slice through the natural appearance of everyday life, contravening the tendency of film to mirror the surface. For Benjamin, such dissection – an investigation of the world in close-up, the production of links between things through montage, the analysis of movement through slow motion and so on – was part of a critical, scientific approach to the world, where the image becomes 'a multiply fragmented thing, whose parts reassemble themselves according to new laws'. Instead, under fascism's 'rape of the machine', film represented at best an accurate rendition of a wrong state of affairs.

'Aestheticization' is the appeal to the eye. Politics, under the sway of aestheticization, was a passive matter. Masses were represented from the outside, as masses in rallies or war. The fascist camera gobbled up passive masses as the raw material for an awe-inspiring fascist ornamentalism. Having infiltrated a medium that came to meet its viewers halfway, the fascist camera reestablished distance. Halfway came to seem a long way again. It was the same sort of gesture as that made visible by John Heartfield in his photomontage of Goebbels hanging a Marx beard on Hitler. The Nazis moved halfway towards acknowledging the political desires and 'rights' of the masses to democratize property relations and be politically represented, but transmuted it craftily into an illusion, a deception, a surface. Film gripped the masses and yet, in this case, there was nothing for them to grip hold of in return, just a shiny surface with twitching flat ghosts that were supposed to be them. They were represented only superficially. In contrast the masses who were genuinely gripped by liberatory politics became self-active, loosened up, got aerated in their self-activity. Such dissolution demanded the skills of the modernist camera, tracing motility, mobility, transformation, speed and simultaneity through film's arsenal of montage, superimposition and time effects.

Benjamin worked on the essay through the autumn and winter of 1935 under difficult circumstances. In the winter he received a large packet of provisions from Vladimir Kirschon, paid for by donations from Soviet Russian writers in support of their German colleagues.[97] In December Horkheimer visited Europe and met Benjamin, who was given assurances of further money from the Institute. The essay would be published in French in the Institute's journal, translated by Pierre Klossowski. But first there would be a long and difficult struggle, as Brecht's influence was yet again at issue. Horkheimer wrote to Adorno about his discussions with Benjamin on the essay's weaknesses. Benjamin, he noted, had rejected the suggestion of influence by Brecht. Horkheimer blamed the shortcomings on Benjamin's situation of 'material need' and pledged to aid him. Adorno reminded him that they had agreed to pay a stipend of 1000 francs.[98] Before the translation could go ahead revisions had to be done.

Benjamin expanded the essay in the first two months of 1936 by seven manuscript pages. He added extensive footnotes and shifted materials around. He developed new concepts such as semblance and play. Film, Benjamin insisted, related more to play, manoeuvrability and experiment than to the cult of illusion represented by semblance. These insights were not just applied to film, though film might act as their training ground. The play-form of technology, of which film was an instance, allowed a new, non-abusive accord between humans and nature. Released from drudgery by new technology – a 'second technology' – human room for play expanded considerably. Film was interpreted from the perspective of social liberation. Revolution was a game with consequences.

The second version of the essay retained its references to Marx, but they did not survive the editor. While Benjamin accepted that all occurrences of the word 'fascism' would be changed to 'totalitarian doctrine', he was angry that all references to socialism were cut in the edited version of the French translation. He told Horkheimer that a mockery had been made of his main thesis.[99] At the end of March he conceded to some of Horkheimer's changes, but he continued to insist on the reinstatement of the opening thesis with its references to Marx.[100] The following day, in response to a letter from Horkheimer, he wrote again, conceding the changes and expressing the desire to do everything in his powers 'to restore the old trust of the Institute' in him.[101] Benjamin hoped simply for the essay to be read by French and Soviet intellectuals. He doubted he would see its appearance in German. His wish that the French intelligentsia take note was granted when André Malraux made reference to it at a conference on 'cultural heritage' in London in the summer of 1936.[102]

In April Wieland Herzfelde wrote to Benjamin asking him to work on the new Moscow-based journal *Das Wort*, with Brecht, Willi Bredel and Feuchtwanger. Benjamin had not failed to notice a turn in Communist politics. The Popular Front policy, which saw

Communist Parties entering into alliances with almost any party that was willing to repudiate fascism, struck Benjamin through visual means – he observed the 'sentimentalism' of an election poster in which were portrayed a woman beaming with a mother's happiness, a healthy baby and a cheerful, well-heeled man with a determined look. It was, in short, a glorious vision of the French family, which eliminated all reference to the working class.[103]

Benjamin wrote to his son about the year's two main essays. He had decided that the 'Work of Art' essay would not be comprehensible to Stefan for a few years, but he was confident that his essay on the nineteenth-century Russian writer Nikolai Leskov, a reluctantly accepted commission from *Orient und Occident*, was accessible.[104] Ostensibly its subject matter was a storyteller who belonged to a very different and distant world. But Benjamin used the essay to reflect on current forms of industrial labour and mass communication. Leskov, Benjamin revealed, felt bonds with craftsmanship and he faced industrial technology as a stranger. Often Leskov's stories featured craftsmen, such as the silversmiths of Tula, whose expertise exceeded the most technologically advanced nation of the time, England.[105] His story 'The Alexandrite' presented another craftsman, the skilful gem engraver Wenzel. Benjamin described Wenzel as a perfect artisan with 'access to the innermost chamber of the creaturely realm'.[106] Craft and craftsmen did not just provide subject matter and characters for Leskov's stories. The very act of storytelling itself he declared to be a craft.[107]

Benjamin's own braiding of craft and narration in 'The Storyteller' went further to illuminate an historical, practical affinity between craft skills and storytelling. The ability to tell stories was rooted in two factors: travel to faraway places and knowledge of past local lore.

The resident master craftsman and the itinerant journeymen worked together in the same rooms; and every master had been an itinerant journeyman before he settled down in his home-town or somewhere else. If peasants and seamen were past masters of storytelling, the artisan class was its university. There the lore of faraway places, such as a much-travelled man brings home, was combined with the lore of the past, such as is manifested most clearly to the native inhabitants of a place.[108]

The habitat of the storyteller was the craft milieu, in which resident master craftsmen – who knew the past, who knew time – exchanged experiences with travelling journeymen – who knew distance, space. The wayfarer's imported ken was the key to Benjamin's notion of experience. The German word for handed-down experience, that is, experience born of wisdom, a practical knowledge – *Erfahrung* – finds its root meaning in the word for travel – *Fahren*. Through travel, craftsmen had experience of the world, and this melded with the native's world of past experience.

Thus these journeymen gained audiences, lured into workshops to graft with their hands while absorbing experiences transmitted from mouth to ear to mouth. The best listeners were the ones who forgot themselves, and while their half-conscious minds were engaged in pot-throwing, spinning and weaving, and their bodies were seized by the rhythm of work, the stories they heard forwent an existence on paper, imprinting themselves into fantasy, awaiting the after-lives of retransmissions.[109] The storyteller took what he told from experience, his own or others, and made it the experience of those hearing the tale. True experience was conceived as close and practised knowledge of whatever was at hand. Recurrent in Benjamin's delineations of experience were the words tactile, tactics and the tactical, entering German as it entered English via the Latin *tangere*, touch. To touch the world was to know the world. Pottery featured here – as model and as metaphor – naturally enough, as it was a form of *Handwerk*, handiwork or artisan labour. Storytelling 'submerges the thing into the life of the storyteller, in order to bring it out of him again. Thus, traces of the storyteller cling to a story the way the handprints of the potter cling to a clay vessel.'[110] Touch fingered the world's textures in its offering-up of knowledge. But it did not function alone. Intrinsic to the craftsman, and the gesticulating storyteller too, was the accord of soul, eye and hand.[111]

> After all, storytelling, in its sensory aspect, is by no means a job for the voice alone. Rather, in genuine storytelling what is expressed gains support in a hundred ways from the work-seasoned gestures of the hand.[112]

Thinking, seeing and handling in tandem granted praxis. The storyteller, fashioning his material – human life – and the craftsman fashioning his, moulded their raw matter in a solid, useful and unique way. The aesthetics of the useful and unique story or the crafted pot were far removed from the attributes of cheap mass reproduction or from those of fine art. The story and the pot were formed by a life that had something to tell. Good stories related a practical knowledge; good potters related wisdom based on praxis. In outlining wisdom, Benjamin's metaphorical language picked up another type of craft labour, weaving: 'Counsel woven into the fabric of real life is wisdom.'[113] It was such woven wisdom that the storyteller handed on.

The hand – so crucial to the *Handwerker*, artisan or craftsman – was retired by technological advance. The role of the hand in production shrunk. Stories were lost. Textured, graspable experience was lost, because of the loss of the weaving and spinning activities that went on while the stories were heard. The web that cradled storytelling unravelled at all its ends. Benjamin cited Paul Valéry on how, once upon a time, the artisan had imitated the patient processes of nature, but so it was no longer. Valéry noted:

Miniatures, ivory carvings, elaborated to the point of greatest perfection, stones that are perfect in polish and engraving, lacquer work or paintings in which a series of thin, transparent layers are placed one on top of the others – all these products of sustained, sacrificing effort are vanishing, and the time is past in which time did not matter. Modern man no longer works at what cannot be abbreviated.[114]

Industrial speed-up transformed conditions of production and standardized what was produced. The mode of repetition of the artisan's story as it was passed on from mouth to mouth, reworked through the unique experience of listeners, degraded into a mechanical, dead reiteration, just as labour degraded into the unskilled re-performance of simplified and multiply divided gestures. The body acceded to machinery. The themes of 'The Storyteller' segued with those of 'The Work of Art in the Age of Its Technological Reproducibility'. Both essays, Benjamin told Adorno, concerned the 'decline of aura'.[115] The 'Work of Art' essay outlined how, until the arrival of mechanical reproduction, pictures had been made by hand, parallel to the manufacture of goods before the development of industrial machinery. Mechanical reproduction in art, beginning with woodcut technology, advanced sporadically, until it attained a qualitatively new stage in lithographic reproduction. Lithographic duplication permitted mass quantities and speedily changing forms. The invention of photography and film provoked a further speed-up effect, basing reproduction not on the pace of a hand that drew, but on the seeing eye in conjunction with the machinery of the lens. Culture's co-ordination with the body transformed. The time of the machine, not the time of the hand, determined production.

And yet, in relation to mass-reproduced art, the same qualities resurfaced in 'The Storyteller'. Tactility, closeness and indexicality were also qualities of modernity: the mass appropriation of technologically reproducible art was a manhandling of cultural products;

the mass-reproduced copy could be manipulated; tactility, the ability to touch, was a sensuous concept that related the new art to the physical presence of the collectively receiving mass body. Tactility and shock – forces that acted on the body – negated the ideal of artistic autonomy. Aesthetics and art were annexed to the development of the human sensorium. For Adorno, such a move was characteristic of what he labelled Benjamin's positivism, that took its measure from the human body.[116]

On 4 June Benjamin wrote a letter of apology to Adorno. He had complained about his situation to one of Adorno's wealthy friends; she had reported back to Adorno, who was shocked and embarrassed. Benjamin's stipend had recently increased to 1300 francs, which Adorno had trusted was at least sufficient. Benjamin blamed his outburst on the pressure that his financial situation put on him, which, once it had relaxed a little, resulted in a nervous collapse. An unbroken year in Paris under harsh circumstances was tough, and he needed to do something for his 'intellectual/mental economy'.[117] He could not afford to travel and he had tried to secure funds from elsewhere, which had delivered the impression of poor treatment by the Institute.

There were other pressures. His work suffered because he could not make copies of it to give to people. In some cases he had to request originals be sent back. In addition his brother had been arrested again in Berlin in May for treason, and there were concerns over Stefan's schooling. Stefan had left Germany in 1935 to study in Italy. There, without his consent, he had been signed up to the Young Fascists and had to purchase his uniform.[118] Where to spend the decisive final years of his schooling had not been decided. There was talk of sending him to relatives in Austria, but Stefan feared the levels of anti-Semitism in Innsbruck and Vienna.[119]

Summer offered the chance of a break from Paris: a trip to Denmark to Brecht's exile home. Brecht had become an editor of *Das Wort*, together with Lion Feuchtwanger and Willi Bredel, and

Benjamin hoped that his 'Work of Art' essay might find a home there, in German. Another outlet of interest had collapsed before it had even started. He had some contact with the circle around Breton and Bataille called Contre-attaque, an anti-Fascist group that brought together Surrealists and the Cercle Communiste-democratique around Boris Souvarine. By June 1936 arguments had riven the group – Bataille had announced a strategy of 'surfascism' that would beat fascism at its own game. The appearance of a publication seemed improbable. Likewise, the anti-Breton Popular Front journal, *Inquisitions*, established by Caillois, Tristan Tzara, Louis Aragon, Gaston Bachelard and Jules Monnerot, was fractious – it managed one issue.[120]

Having sublet his room, Benjamin left Parisian arguments behind in August to spend some time with Brecht in sunless Skovsbostrand. There were daily chess games. The radio played its role. Benjamin followed with interest the events of the civil war in Spain, the bombing of Ibiza being of particular concern. He was comforted by the stamp of the 'antifascist control committee' on an envelope from Alfred Cohn, evidence of the 'good, necessary vigilance of the new Spain'.[121] News arrived too of the first Moscow show trials of the 'Trotskyite-Zinovievite terror centre' from 19 to 24 August.[122] Benjamin's own thoughts were turning to violence. He sought a 'crucial' text, Johannes Most's *Revolutionary Science of War*, an anarchist terrorist handbook on the use and manufacture of nitroglycerine, dynamite bombs, poisons and so on from 1885.[123] It was essential for his *Arcades Project*, but he could not find a copy.

Benjamin's long-practised art of letter writing resulted in a letter on André Gide and literary and political debates to be published in *Das Wort* under the title 'Letter from Paris'. Brecht hoped that Benjamin's 'Letters' might make a regular appearance. The first analysed Fascist art, and its 'consumers' who were 'duped'.[124] A week after its receipt by Willi Bredel, Benjamin sent an urgent request for payment.[125] A follow-up letter four days later stressed how desperate he was. A third letter gave careful details for payment. Benjamin could not afford for the payment to go awry. He also continued with his project of selecting and introducing letters of German humanism. He sent Bredel letters by Johann Gottfried Seume, Georg Forster and Hölderlin. Upon hearing that the letter by Seume would appear in *Das Wort*, he panicked. His book of letters from the epoch of German humanism was to appear in the autumn, and its title – *German Men and Women*, written in a carefully chosen Gothic script – was designed to encourage its distribution in Germany. Detlef Holz's public profile was to be raised a notch – until the book was properly noticed and banned. Benjamin worried because, though the letter by Seume in that volume was different from the one in *Das Wort*, his introductory words overlapped. The connection of the author to a Moscow-based journal might emerge, hindering the passage of the book in Germany. He requested it be published without commentary.

Benjamin left Denmark in the middle of September. He passed through Paris on his way to San Remo for two weeks. On his return, he spent several days with Horkheimer and Adorno, engendering a closeness with the latter resulting in them calling each other by first names. The Germany of the imminent *German Men and Women* was ever more distant – Benjamin's brother was sentenced to six years in prison at Brandenburg-Görden in October. Writing to Scholem brought up questions of the past, of Jewishness and old arguments. He had noticed some quotations from Martin Buber in a philosophical magazine. These introduced 'the terminology of National Socialism into the debate of Jewish questions without rupture'.[126] Benjamin began a second 'Letter from Paris' for *Das Wort*. He reported on the writings of the photographer Gisèle Freund, who detailed the battle between painting and photography, and how the latter 'bouleversé' the other when it achieved effortlessly the former's ultimate aim of representing realistically the scales of a fish.[127]

In November 1936 Benjamin was about to rush to Vienna to locate Stefan, who had refused all contact for a month. Dora was unable to go, as she owed tax in Germany and feared the Austrians would report her presence to the Germans. Benjamin skirted Germany but tracked Stefan down to Venice. On the way there he visited Ravenna, where he had wanted to go for twenty years, to see the Byzantine mosaics, photographs of which had been stuck on the walls of his student digs. He was also struck by the churches there: serious, fortress-like, unornamented façades, fronting massive chapels and basilicas which were sunk into the ground and entered by steps, tracing a descent that doubled the consciousness of broaching the past.[128]

Stefan was ill, mentally, disturbed by his expatriation. Benjamin diagnosed this not least from a reading of his handwriting – the verdict of Paris graphologist Anja Mendelssohn was that Stefan felt neglected and lonely.[129] He was in need of a doctor, and Benjamin, having returned him to San Remo, was keen to send him to Siegfried Bernfeld, an Austrian psychoanalyst who had been a leading member of Wyneken's youth movement and was presently practising in Menton, near Nice. Such treatment had a practical aim: Benjamin was very keen for Stefan to complete his *Abitur* exams. Psychoanalysis was also a theoretical issue for Benjamin. Adorno was pressing him to write something against Jung in order to inoculate his *Arcades Project* from the universalising horrors of the 'collective unconscious'.[130] The Institute's stipend rose in December to 1500 francs. Benjamin sent off his second 'Letter from Paris' with a request for prompt payment.

At the end of January 1937 Benjamin wrote to Horkheimer. He reflected on his writing, for Horkheimer had queried his philosophical method. Benjamin stated that he was determined to find a mode of expression that was not technical. Some used philosophical terminology uncritically, even deceptively, as a stand-in for thought. For Benjamin 'the concrete-dialectical analysis of each object under examination includes criticism of categories in which it was apprehended at an earlier level of reality and thought'.[131] But general accessibility was not at this moment a criterion of writing. Small groups would, for the time being and for a long time to come, shelter and transmit knowledge: 'It is indeed not the time to exhibit in kiosks what we believe to hold in our hands. Rather it seems to be time to think about bomb-proof storage for it. Maybe this is where dialectics lies: finding for a truth that is nothing less than evenly worked, a safekeeping that is as evenly worked as a steel cassette.'[132]

There were practical matters concerning the storage and distribution of knowledge. Jay Leyda from the Film Section of the New York Museum of Modern Art had called Horkheimer requesting the German version of the 'Work of Art' essay, so that he might translate it into English for the library. The question of versions and political terminology opened up again. Horkheimer asked Benjamin not to provide a German manuscript, in order to obscure the discrepancies.[133] Other old disputes rumbled on. In February Benjamin reminded Bredel that he had not acknowledged the second 'Letter from Paris', nor had he sent him the requested few copies of *Das Wort* with his first Letter in it. In the middle of March it was still unclear if the second 'Letter from Paris' would appear and if he would be paid for it. *Das Wort* also received the 'Work of Art' essay, but gave no signal as to whether publication might be expected. He was also owed payment for the Seume letter. Benjamin spent the whole year repeating his various requests. The letter never appeared, nor apparently did any money.

The essay on Fuchs was finally finished in the spring of 1937. Benjamin was glad to be rid of it. The more he read of Fuchs the more contemptuous he grew. He compared the essay's writing to the task of a man who turns up in a place of ill repute, finding a sad old acquaintance who has come down in the world and is struck by palsy. His last wish is to be buried in a hillside cemetery. Transporting the corpse is no pleasure, and the hope is that the mourning guests can edify themselves on the view from the mountain.[134]

Fuchs was a collector and a historian. Through these aspects of his activity, Benjamin reflected on historical materialism as method, and on the legacy and discontinuity in Social Democracy of the Marxist founding fathers' thought. Engels was evoked as a critic of idealist histories of progress and the passive contemplative attitude towards the past: 'Historical materialism conceives historical understanding as an afterlife of that which has been understood and whose pulse can be felt in the present.'[135] History was incomplete. Fuchs had glimpsed this, but he also carried traces of the 'old dogmatic and naïve idea of reception', assuming that the meaning of a work was the meaning attributed by its contemporaries. However, Fuchs' practical passion for collecting caricatures and pornographic imagery proposed a different relationship to historical work. Fuchs rejected culture as a marker of value, and a locus of classical beauty; his practical activity in the field of reproduced imagery destroyed traditional conceptions of art; his materials were destined for a mass audience, and his anti-classicism led him to seek truth in the extremes of expression, such as the grotesque.

Through Fuchs, Benjamin gestured at the negative side of historical movement, its anti-progress: 'There is no document of culture which is not at the same time a document of barbarism.'[136] Cultural history was unable to take note of this state of affairs, for it regarded culture as a booty that dropped into the lap of mankind, a bonus, an eternal good – and a commodity, detached from the wider social conditions of its production. The Marxists-turned-Positivists had been unable to recognize technology as an historical, and not just scientific, development. Positivists saw only 'the progress of natural science, not the concomitant retrogression of society'. Capitalism shaped technology, and illusions of neutral technological progress made proletarian efforts to seize it under its control ever more unthinkable. Benjamin argued against such illusions for the return of the 'destructive side of dialectics'.[137] Fuchs approved the essay.

His thoughts on Fuchs chimed with the work of an obscure writer from the Baltic, Carl Gustav Jochmann, whom he came across unexpectedly in March. Jochmann, he claimed, was 'one of the greatest revolutionary authors of the German-speaking realm'.[138] In his lifetime only one book appeared, *On Language*, published anonymously in 1828. Jochmann's essay in this volume, 'On the Regression of Poetry', which propounded the thesis that the retreat of poetry was the progress of culture, struck Benjamin as 'a meteorite from the twentieth century sent back to the nine-teenth'.[139] Citing his 'Work of Art' essay, Benjamin appeared to identify with this revolutionary from the advanced guard of the bourgeoisie, forgotten, ignored and isolated. His reading of 'On the Regression of Poetry' echoed ideas in the 'Work of Art' essay: poetry was degraded; such loss of imaginative faculties and influence was to be applauded and not deplored; the finest products of higher culture were crutches for a crippled society; poetry must end in order for humanity to progress; only when the value of peripheral things ceased to be inflated by their rarity would true value emerge in a 'truly human society'. Jochmann closed with a twist. Poetry would return, after social revolution, but it would be unlike what came before, and would be available to all.[140]

In March Adorno arrived in Paris. He was planning a book on mass art under monopoly capitalism, which was to include Benjamin's 'Work of Art' essay and other essays on popular culture. Together they visited a Constantin Guys exhibition and spent an evening with the epistemologist and economist Alfred Sohn-Rethel. After his departure Benjamin reported to Horkheimer on his new plans regarding the *Arcades Project*. He planned to develop a critique of cultural history and 'pragmatic history' in relation to materialism, and he wished to follow Adorno's sugges-tion that he investigate the significance of psychoanalysis for materialist history writing.[141] He waited for Horkheimer's go-ahead, and in the meantime completed some reviews. He also pushed for an improvement in his finances, outlining his budget to Friedrich Pollock: 480 francs went to rent; 720 francs for food; 120 francs for clothes repair; and stamps, cafés and travel came to 440 francs. In all it amounted to 1760 francs – and he needed another 150 francs for a new suit, two pairs of shoes a year (accoutrements of the flâneur or tramp), laundry, cinema, exhibitions, theatre and medical treatment. He also needed money for two new pairs of glasses and dental treatment that could no longer be postponed. He reported on his earnings for the year (in addition to the Institute's stipend) – 1200 francs for *German Men and Women*, 250 francs for the first 'Letter from Paris' and 150 francs for the essay on Leskov.[142]

A letter to Bredel expressed his frustration at the paradox of industrial reproduction in publishing: 'The route from manuscript to published text is longer than it ever has been before and, with that, also the span of time, after whose expiry the effort of work discovers its reward, is stretched to breaking.'[143] Bredel rejected the 'Work of Art' essay for *Das Wort*. It was, he said, too long. Benjamin was alarmed by Kracauer's book on Offenbach, arguably a social history of nineteenth-century Paris comparable to Benjamin's own researches. The book, Adorno and Benjamin agreed, was crass and poorly written and it had the character of an apology – Offenbach's Jewishness was expunged from the work. And the concept of 'intoxication', one dear to Benjamin, was 'nothing but dingy confectionery'.[144] In May he made efforts to speed the passage of his 'Work of Art' essay into English. He wrote to Leyda that he would be very glad to see what he called his 'work of art in the age of its capacity of technical reproduction' appear in English, based on the French or, preferably, the German version with its numerous additional paragraphs. Indeed, he thought it worthy of publication as a book.[145] Another possible English outlet was Bryher's journal *Close Up*.

Late May brought more conflict with the Institute. The first paragraph of his Fuchs essay was cut. Benjamin requested that, instead, the word 'Marxist' be replaced by 'materialist', 'Marxism' by 'materialism'; he was unsuccessful.[146] He left for San Remo in late June, reflecting in a letter to Scholem on the recent 'turbulent months' in Paris with its worsening economic climate – the franc was devalued in June – and his persistently uncertain situation. He blamed his failure to visit the Paris World Exposition on this state of affairs.[147] He wanted to devote the weeks in San Remo to a study of Jung and a confrontation with Adorno's queries about the archaic image and the collective unconscious, but Horkheimer's request that he work on the Baudelaire chapter of his proposed book took precedence.[148] There were methodological reasons to undertake the study of Jung, but there were also political ones. Jung had set about helping only the 'Aryan soul'. National Socialism had been long prepared. Benjamin intended to investigate the nihilism of the doctor-writers Gottfried Benn, Céline and Jung.[149]

On 9 July he wrote to his friend Fritz Lieb that whatever window one looked through the view was always gloomy. His suspicions about the Popular Front government were confirmed. The French Left were 'clinging to the fetish of the Left majority', ignoring the fact that the policies carried out by the supposedly Leftist government would provoke riots had they been implemented under the banner of the Right. Benjamin had read the Communist review *Vendredi* every week for two years, but by mid-1937 thought its dislocation from the masses and its sinking intellectual level were apparent.[150] Benjamin returned to Paris for an International Congress of Philosophy. A brief trip back to San Remo allowed him to observe a welcome improvement in Stefan's condition.

In September Benjamin lost his room in the Rue Bénard in Paris to another emigrant who had received an expulsion order: in his desperation, the other emigrant had apparently been willing to pay any price and grabbed Benjamin's room at a higher rent.[151] Efforts to get compensation so that Benjamin might stay in a decent hotel were ineffective, despite promises. Luckily he received an offer to stay short-term in the maid's quarters of Else Herzberger's home at Boulogne sur Seine, as Herzberger was spending some time in the United States; unluckily, however, it was located on one of the main roads out of Paris, and the noise of lorries passing along the 'narrow asphalt strip' by his bed disturbed his work and sleep.[152] He turned to Horkheimer once more for help and a new accord was reached, which would help Benjamin to secure a studio or one-room flat. Beginning in October he received a stipend of $80 a month, in an effort to minimize the effects of an unstable franc.

Seeking new accommodation further interrupted his work and the plans he had agreed upon with the Institute. He spent some time in the library, but progress was slow. He did, however, compose a 'literature letter' for Horkheimer on 3 November, a form agreed to by both of them, in which Benjamin presented a round-up of cultural events, debates and publications in Paris. The Fuchs essay finally appeared in October in the *Zeitschrift für Sozialforschung*. The delay was the result of an attempt not to prejudice Fuchs's efforts to persuade the German authorities to return his collection. The collection was auctioned off regardless.

In November Benjamin signed a rental agreement for a flat on the top floor of a seven-storey house at 10 Rue Dombasle, available as of the following January. It did not have enough room for the entire 'saved portion' of his library.[153] But it made possible what he had desired for so long – the possibility of entertaining French friends. His address book from this period, with its 310 names with addresses and phone numbers, showed his connections to French intellectual circles as well as around 80 German émigrés. A displaced Germany made its mark on Paris's cultural front. In November Brecht's *Senora Carrar's Rifles* was performed with Weigel in the main role. It was Brecht's first realist play, and for Benjamin it provided proof of his prognoses in the 'Work of Art' essay.[154] On 6

December Benjamin reported on cultural matters in France and the ways in which Stalinism muddled thought. He criticized Alexandre Kojève, who had delivered a lecture on Hegelian thought in sociology: Benjamin dismissed Kojève's dialectic as idealist. Gide, for his part, had turned against both Stalinism and dialectical materialism.[155]

At the close of the year, Benjamin returned to San Remo until his new residence became available. He saw Adorno and Gretel Karplus, who got married in London that summer, for the last time before their exile in the United States. Benjamin was anxious about Stefan's future: he was helping out in his mother's pension.[156] About wider political futures Benjamin felt hopeless, writing a balance sheet on the Popular Front government to Lieb: 'The leadership has managed within two years to rob their workers of the elementary basis of their instinctive activity: that infallible sense of when and under what circumstances a legal action must turn into an illegal, an illegal into a violent one.'[157] The December strike wave produced fear in the hearts of the bourgeoisie, but in reality there was no will and no power to terrorize.

Benjamin published a review that considered the black arts of politics and the instincts of the masses. Grete de Francesco's *The Power of the Charlatan* was the pretext for an investigation of the methods of fraudsters, swindlers and counterfeiters, such as Bragadino the 'pretend' alchemist or quack doctors Mondor and Cagliostro, in the context of technological and economic advance. Such charlatanry revealed to Benjamin much about the original essence of advertising, a contemporary form of influencing the masses, and inevitably it resonated with the current situation in Germany. Benjamin's class politics emerged, even in this little review. He noted how Francesco assumes that those 'duped' are the masses, the 'half-educated', and that those immune to the fraudster are an 'elite', 'the small minority of the immune'.[158] Benjamin commented that 'influencing of the masses is not a black art that one must ward off by appealing to the white art of the elites'. That an idea reached and motivated the masses could be progressive, he still insisted, and could, as in the case of Cagliostro and Saint-Germain, enact 'revenge against the ruling caste on behalf of the Third Estate'.

Dark arts and dark thoughts were the order of the day. Benjamin was occupied by 'a strange find' that would influence his Baudelaire work 'decisively': he had come across the final 'infernal' piece of writing by Louis-Auguste Blanqui, a 'cosmological speculation' titled 'Eternity through the Stars', written in 1872. The French revolutionary activist, who had been imprisoned time after time for his political exploits, reflected on humanity's unstinting subjection to a mechanistic universe, in the most terrible vision of a society that projected just such an image on the heavens.[159] In Blanqui's cosmology, everything that happened from birth to death on our planet occurred identically on a myriad of brother-stars. Humanity lived in a prison as if it were an immense globe, and the universe, with vulgar re-editions of mankind, reiterated endlessly the same monotony and same immobility on foreign stars. On millions of earths the future witnessed repeated ignorance, stupidity and the cruelty of former ages. Progress was a myth. Benjamin aligned the bleak thoughts with Baudelaire's – though where Blanqui's cosmos had become an abyss, in Baudelaire the abyss was bleaker, for it was starless. Indeed, it was not even a cosmic space.[160]

Benjamin's thoughts descended on the image of progress over the coming months.

7

Writer's Block, 1938–40

Benjamin began the year in San Remo, where a wave of icy coldness
had set in. On 15 January he was able to move into the one-room flat
at 10 Rue Dombasle, the same day as the publication of his review, in
the French journal *Europe*, of an exhibition of Chinese paintings at
the Bibliothèque nationale. The lift rattled ceaselessly through each
day, and he hoped, as wry compensation, it might weave its noise
into his work.[1] He hoped too for a way to reclaim his books from
Brecht's, as his sister, Dora, posted much of the remainder of his
Berlin library to him.[2] *Angelus Novus* took up its place on the wall.
One day he listed the addresses he had occupied since 1933. This was
the thirteenth and, apart from the displacement of internment,
it would be his last. He was happy to have gathered together some
of his papers, inasmuch as they had been 'saved',[3] and he was glad
to be able to receive friends. Scholem visited on his way to New York.
Much of Benjamin's time was devoted to completing a study of
Baudelaire, piling 'books upon books and excerpts upon excerpts'.[4]

Benjamin also composed an essay on the Institute for Social
Research, 'A German Institute for Free Research', for Thomas Mann's
journal *Mass und Wert*. He feared 'sabotage' by editor Ferdinand
Lion, and wrote the essay avoiding the terms 'materialism' and
'dialectic'. The eleven manuscript pages were, in any case, reduced
to four upon publication in April.

There was fruitful intellectual exchange with Adorno. Benjamin
read Adorno's manuscript on Wagner and especially enjoyed

Adorno's 'Radio Exposé', written as part of the Princeton Radio Research Project.[5] As a smoker, Benjamin found himself addressed in the essay, when Adorno described the 'gesture of smoking' as the opposite of the 'gesture of concert listening': smoking directed itself against 'the aura of the artwork, the noise has smoke blown in its face'. The smoker escaped the magic of the piece, and yet smoking allowed a certain concentration. 'The smoker isolated himself and made himself accessible at the same time'.[6]

In March and April Benjamin devoted time to revising the vignettes in *Berlin Childhood around 1900*. These reflections on Berlin were a definitive leave-taking. On 9 March he submitted a formal request for French citizenship, with signatures from Gide, Valèry and Jules Romains, yet it was not acted on until spring 1940. A letter to Ferdinand Lion revealed that the writing of the childhood memoirs was a way of inoculating himself in exile. In summoning memories of childhood, he evoked those images that most awaken homesickness. The feelings of desire should not overcome the intellect, just as a healthy body did not succumb to a vaccine. And in any case, this work was not to be seen as biographical reflection, but rather an effort to conjure up something socially irretrievable from the past.[7] Benjamin wanted *Berlin Childhood around 1900* published above everything else. He told the theologist Karl Thieme that the book had 'something to say to thousands of expelled Germans'.[8] The possibility of a private printing by Heidi Hey brought temporarily cheering news.

In April he updated Horkheimer on the progress of his Baudelaire essay. It constituted a miniature model of the *Arcades Project* and revolved around three themes: idea and image, antiquity and modernity and the new and ever-same.[9] Baudelaire was presented as an associate of Blanqui, with his forlorn starry eternity, and Nietzsche, with his eternal recurrence. Baudelaire's allegorical writing made this ceaselessness legible as the flip side of capitalism's fashionability. Baudelaire was a poet of alienation and reification, a commentator on a commodity-producing society, in which the new was shown to be the return of the ever-same, the mass a seductive veil for the lonely flâneur.

By May the relationship with Hey had soured. The two had an unpleasant conversation on the telephone – Benjamin accused her of not being serious about the book publication. By subsequent letter, she proposed one final meeting, when Benjamin was to give her the manuscript in the form he wished to see it appear. She would decide on the paper, format and typeface and would publish it in a numbered limited edition for bibliophiles – her interest was in publishing something quite on her own. The proposal came to nothing.[10]

Benjamin's former wife had been making efforts to obtain a new passport for Benjamin by striking up good relations with a German diplomat in San Remo. She reported her telephone conservation to Benjamin:

Consul: Does Dr Benjamin still require his passport actually?

Dora: Oh yes, certainly Sir.

Consul: But he is no longer here?

Dora: No, through an acquaintance at the French embassy in Rome he managed to get permission to enter France using his *carte d'identité*, but now he is there with no German documents at all and so he can't budge. Has the passport arrived?

Consul: Hmm, yes but . . . can you tell me how long he has been working for that magazine?

Dora: I don't know what you are referring to, Sir, he isn't working for any magazine. As far as I know he delivers scientific lectures on the radio.

Consul: No, no, he worked for a magazine.

Dora: Which one?

Consul: He worked for the Moscow magazine *Das Wort*.

Dora (immediately): Oh Sir, that was years and years ago. Back then they asked him to write an article or rework something on the philosopher Green, an English philosopher from the 19th century. He has had nothing to do with those people since then.

Consul: Are you certain?

Dora: Absolutely, Sir, we often talked about what a good thing it was that that he completely distanced himself from those people back then, because it would be rather dangerous for him now if he had worked for Moscow!

Consul: Well, I would not say that quite so absolutely. It would only be the case if he had acted to subvert the state.

Dora: (laughing) Perhaps you remember him Sir, he is really such an unworldly, apolitical person, who lives solely for his philosophical work. He has never had anything to do with such things. So has the passport arrived?[11]

Yes, said the consul, but insisted that Benjamin pick it up at the German Embassy in Paris. Benjamin was intimidated. He had heard that he had to declare under oath that he had not sought refugee status in France. To do so would constitute fraud.[12] The German regime cast its shadow far. It also made its appearance in Benjamin's writings, even if only in incidental asides. Mass society and fascism were addressed in his review of Anna Seghers' novel *The Rescue*, for *Die neue Weltbühne*. Titled 'A Chronicle of Germany's Unemployed', the review defended the viewpoint of the proletarian, arguing that intellectuals are 'hindered by prejudices impossible to overcome in a day':

> According to one of the most persistent of them, the proletarian is a 'simple man of the people', contrasted not so much with the educated man as with the individuated member of a higher class. To see in the oppressed person a child of nature was the stock reaction of the rising bourgeoisie in the eighteenth century. After

that class had triumphed, it ceased to contrast the oppressed, whose place it had now ceded to the proletariat, with feudal degeneracy, and henceforth set them in opposition to its own finely shaded bourgeois individuality. The form in which this was manifest was the bourgeois novel; its subject was the incalculable 'fate' of the individual, for whom any enlightenment was to prove inadequate.[13]

The remainder of the review considered the fate of the 'simple man' in novels. This developed into an analysis of the rise of the Nazi 'national comrade', a figure who emerged from the shattered psyche of war and the erosion of class-consciousness by unemployment. Benjamin carefully outlined how Seghers's novel charted the tensions in working-class existence in the years of the Nazi ascendancy. He observed how Seghers's prose allowed the reader to 'gain access to forgotten chambers of the everyday world through slight shifts in the commonplace'.[14] Benjamin crept inside Seghers's narrative style in order to bring out her – and his – subtle revolutionary politics of hope in the midst of despair. In the course of the review, sharp criticisms of the contemporary situation burst out. Just as the coming of the Antichrist mimics the blessing promised by the coming of the Messiah, so too

the Third Reich mimics socialism. Unemployment comes to an end because forced labour is made legal. The book devotes only a few pages to the 'awakening of the nation'. But they evoke the horror of the Nazi dungeons better than almost any other text has done, though they reveal no more about what goes on there than a girl can learn when she asks at an SA barracks after her boyfriend, who was a Communist.[15]

In late May Benjamin and Stefan exchanged letters, and these revealed something of the difficulties of lives bureaucratized and monitored. Stefan wrote from San Remo about photocopying Benjamin's birth certificate because, at the muster for the military, it had been noted that he was a foreigner and various documentary proofs were needed of this, in order to exempt him from national service for a while. Benjamin, in turn, wrote of how glad he was to have his 'refugee papers' in his hands, giving him a 'modest chance' in the present political situation. There were problems with his naturalization. He had found out that he was illegally subletting and so could not obtain the necessary prerequisite, a *certificat de domicile*. Benjamin commented: 'One loses the ability to be surprised.'[16] A supporter in the naturalization office, André Rolland de Renéville, recommended substituting the residence certificate with a work certificate. He had to prove three years of work in France and required documentary evidence of this from the Institute. While obtaining the evidence, he also requested that the Institute pay for his library to be shipped from Denmark to Paris.

He continued to brief Horkheimer on cultural and political events in Paris, reporting on a recent essay by Bataille in *Mesures*. Benjamin, who encountered Georges Bataille frequently, for he was a librarian at the Bibliothèque nationale, noted that the essay presented different stages in a 'secret history of humanity', illustrated by views of the Place de la Concorde. At work in this, Bataille claimed, was the struggle of the monarchist, static, Egyptian principle against the anarchist, dynamic, destructive, liberating passage of time. Bataille and Roger Caillois had formed a college of sacred sociology in an effort to attract young people to a secret society. 'The secret', joked Benjamin, 'is what connects the two founders!'[17] Later, in August, Benjamin requested that Horkheimer remove the paragraph with these remarks from the published version of his letter in the pages of the Institute's journal. It was expedient to remain on good terms with Bataille because of his role at the library, as well as any influence he might exert on Benjamin's naturalization bid.[18]

Walter Benjamin at Skovsbostrand in Denmark, 1938.

A letter to Theodor and Gretel Adorno on 19 June made several references to America, where the two had relocated. He tipped them off about a collection of primitive pictures by unknown artists from 1800–40, which stemmed mainly from the American Folk Art Gallery and had been shown in Europe. He recommended

Herman Melville's writings. Scholem was in the United States and met with Adorno. Bloch was preparing his move to the US.[19] Since April of the previous year Benjamin had been jotting down thoughts on Baudelaire and related themes, and the title of those notes, 'Central Park', voiced Benjamin's own half-hearted hope that he might resettle in New York.

Benjamin left for Denmark once more on 21 June. He had suffered weeks of headaches in Paris and needed a change of air.[20] He would be reunited with his books, and had the money – 800 francs donated by the Institute for Social Research – to ship them back to Paris as well.[21] In Skovsbostrand, discussions of Soviet politics and aesthetics were frequent. He reported Brecht's opinion that terrible cultural politics were a result of national politics' needs. It represented catastrophe for everything they had supported for twenty years. For example, Brecht's friend and translator Sergei Tretyakov, who had been arrested by the Soviet secret police in July 1937 and accused of espionage, was presumed dead.[22] In Denmark Benjamin was exposed to more 'party line faithful' literature than in Paris, and it irked him to see himself labelled in *Internationale Literatur*, on the basis of a fragment of his essay on Goethe's *Elective Affinities*, as an acolyte of Heidegger.[23] *Das Wort* was crammed with Russian poetry in translation; it was seen as a provocation, Brecht observed, if the name Stalin did not appear.[24] The days did not pass easily: Benjamin noted that Brecht felt increasingly isolated and his enjoyment of provocative feints in conversation was diminished.[25]

Benjamin's aim was to complete the work on Baudelaire while staying at the home of Brecht's neighbour, a policeman. He lived like a monk in Denmark. Despite the friendship with Brecht, he thought that he had to keep his work strictly isolated from him, 'for it contains certain moments that he cannot assimilate'.[26] Yet again he suffered from interruptions – this time it was the noisy children in the policeman's house. Convinced Europe was in its 'provisional dénouement', he spent much time listening to the radio. After ten days in Copenhagen dictating the work to a typist, the essay was completed at the end of September, 'in a race against war'.[27] He felt triumphant once the 'flâneur' who had been planned for fifteen years was 'sewn up' prior to 'the end of the world'. On 4 October a letter from Benjamin to Adorno pondered how long the air in Europe would remain breathable – materially. Spiritually it was already no longer so, after the events of the past weeks.[28] These events included the Munich Accord of 29 September and the first stages of the invasion of the Sudetenland by German troops. Stefan at least was out of any immediate danger – he arrived in London in September to stay with a Dr Warren in Enfield Lock.

Benjamin left Denmark in the middle of October. His sister was very ill with arteriosclerosis. His brother was in a labour camp, building roads. Benjamin noted to Gretel Adorno that life in prison or labour camp was at least bearable: 'The nightmare that hangs over people in his situation is, as I frequently hear from Germany, not so much the coming day in prison, as the threat, after years of confinement, of transfer to a concentration camp.'[29]

Non-publication was Benjamin's immediate fear. He had heard nothing from Horkheimer about the fate of the Baudelaire piece, 'The Paris of the Second Empire in Baudelaire'. Adorno delivered a devastating verdict.[30] He was disappointed to see in the essay not a model of the *Arcades Project* but a prelude. Motifs were assembled but not developed. There was no theoretical interpretation of the various motifs of trace, flâneur, panorama, arcades, modernity and the ever-same. Ideas were 'blockaded' behind 'impenetrable walls of material'. It lacked 'mediation', and Adorno suggested that there was a crude determinism at work, linking the content of Baudelaire's poems 'directly to adjacent features of the social history of his time, especially economic ones'. Benjamin had failed to properly analyse commodity form in Baudelaire's period. His gestures towards Marxism omitted 'the mediation by the total societal process', and so deprived objects of 'their true historico-philosophical weight'. Benjamin's Marxism was better evinced in his essay on 'Elective Affinities' and his book on the Baroque, because these mobilised theoretical dialectics. Adorno did not recommend publication, and requested a new version.

It took Benjamin a month to reply to the 'blow' he had been dealt. His letter from 9 December revealed something of the melancholy and anxiety that saturated his life. While anxious about the long delay in Adorno's response, he had come across a passage in Horkheimer's book *Twilight*:

> Under the title 'Waiting' it reads as follows: 'Most people wait for a letter every morning. That no letter arrives – or, if one does arrive, it contains only a rejection of some kind – generally holds true for those who are sad already'. When I came across this passage, I already felt sad enough to take it as a foretaste or presentiment of your own letter. If, ultimately, there was something encouraging for me in the letter (I say nothing about the unchanged perspective it expresses) then it is in the fact that your objections, however staunchly they may be shared by other friends, should not be interpreted as a rejection.[31]

He attempted to justify his method. He did not wish to engage in esoteric speculation but rather to work philologically in 'The Paris of the Second Empire in Baudelaire', the second section of a larger book, specifically chosen because it could stand alone in the journal. His philological work examined the text detail by detail, 'leading the reader to fixate magically on the text'. Everything rested on the third section of the book, when philosophy would 'exorcise' such 'magic'. The pile-up of themes would be 'illumined' later 'as by a lightning flash'.[32] He argued that in his work 'theory comes into its own in an *undistorted* way', 'like a single ray of light breaking into an artificially darkened room'.[33] It is enough to 'give an idea of the composition of the light that comes to a focus in the third part of the book'. Benjamin rejected the claim that his Marxism was to please the Institute, citing method as emerging 'out of solidarity with the experiences we have all shared over the last fifteen years'.[34] Most important of all, he pleaded for publication of revised parts of it. He needed to hear discussion of it in order to combat his isolation. He agreed to reconsider the entire construction of the book, and thereby clarify his method and intentions, but did not concede to the specificity of Adorno's criticisms.

The year ended desperately. The rapprochement between France and Germany, formalised in the Franco-German Declaration of 6 December – which made their current frontiers inviolate and agreed to consultation on affairs of mutual concern – made Benjamin gloomy about his prospects for naturalization, and rendered them of little use anyway. On 24 January he sent Horkheimer another political round-up of literary affairs in Paris.[35] His analyses were aided by the regular discussion circle on current ideas and books that he attended with Hannah Arendt, her communist husband Heinrich Blücher and Fritz Fraenkel. Surrealism's influence and mutation was a particular concern. He delivered a long discussion of Paul Nizan's novel *The Conspiracy* about a circle of super-intelligent young bourgeois men, attracted to revolutionary thought in a posture of rejection of their philistine families. 'Traitors' to their class, they conspired to force the pace of change, only to then betray their chosen cause. Benjamin saw something of Surrealist Louis Aragon's trajectory in the novel. His cool verdict was that Nizan presented the isolation of the working class accurately in the novel, but he was incapable of analysing its cause.

French literature was in 'a process of decomposition'. Raymond Queneau was described as a lesser Apollinaire. Bataille, Michel Leiris and Caillois were still promoting the Collège de Sociologie. Leiris was writing childhood memoirs under the title 'The Sacred in Everyday Life'. Caillois was splashing about in ambiguities, far from reality. Benjamin voiced criticisms of the 'measured' and 'precisely done' efforts to counter anti-Semitism on the part of Adrienne Monnier and the 'Gazette des Amis du Livre'. The intelligentsia had no contact with the masses. The working class had no voice in the French political system. There were too many compromises with fascism – Benjamin, citing *Vendredi* journalist Jacques Madaule, speculated that if in the coming months those who know what they want, and more importantly what they do not want, do not muster their energies, France, 'the last refuge for people in continental Europe', might collapse. As final evidence of France's decomposition, Benjamin mocked an advertising brochure for the jewellers Cartier penned by the poet Paul Claudel, a beatitude to gemstones.

More personally, the appearance of a book on panoramas in the nineteenth century riled him. It was by a student of Adorno, Dolf Sternberger, and Benjamin considered it plagiaristic of his own work. It was doubly filtered, through Sternberger's skull and through the Reich's censorship office. Its 'indescribably feeble' conceptual apparatus was a degeneration of one 'stolen' from him, Bloch and Adorno. Benjamin's favoured term 'allegory' appeared on every other page.[36] In a draft of a letter to the author, in April 1938, Benjamin claimed that the book represented a revolting hybrid of Hitler's thought and Sternberger's.[37] His full 'denunciation' was completed at the end of January 1939. The existence of personal animus against someone who had usurped his area of study did not obscure the real political disagreements. Sternberger seemed to Benjamin an apolitical and conformist dilettante, dressed in the garb of the avant-garde, and employing such a 'pretentious' German argot that his 'language is a vehicle of regression'.[38] Politics for Benjamin resided in the very smallest of articulations: even a sub-clause could betray regressive political positions. But Sternberger's greatest mistake was to have isolated the nineteenth from the twentieth century, making his work of 'history' useless in the present.

Benjamin proceeded otherwise. He pointed out continuities between the late-nineteenth century of Bismarckian reaction and the present, in an effort to reveal an economic and class analysis of National Socialism:

> The barbarism of the present was already germinating in that period, whose concept of beauty showed the same devotion to the licked-clean which the carnivore displays toward his prey. With the advent of National Socialism, a bright light is cast on the second half of the nineteenth century. Those years marked the first attempts to turn the petty bourgeoisie into a party and harness it to precise political purposes. This was done by Stoecker, in the interest of the big landowners. Hitler's mandate came from a different group. Nevertheless, his ideological nucleus remained that of Stoecker's movement fifty years earlier. In the struggle against an internally colonized people, the Jews, the fawning petty bourgeois came to see himself as a member of a ruling caste and unleashed his imperial instincts. With National Socialism, a program came into force which imposed the ideals of the Gründerzeit – glowing warmly in the light of world conflagration – on the German domestic sphere, especially that of women.[39]

He observed how a late-nineteenth-century petty bourgeoisie 'entered into an apprenticeship to the powers-that-be, one which has been revived and extended under National Socialism', and he noted how the 'middle bourgeois strata' relinquished political power, so that the 'way was cleared for monopoly capitalism, and with it the national renewal'.[40] Benjamin set out from the present, Hitlerism, to comment on the past, and that analysis was significant because it showed the roots of the current situation. Past and present mutually illuminated.

Reflection on the direction of history had come to the fore in his researches into Baudelaire and the *Arcades Project*. He told

Horkheimer on 1 February that he was on the trail of the concept of progress and the idea of history.[41] This left its mark on File N of the *Arcades Project*, 'On the theory of knowledge, theory of progress'. Benjamin confronted the bourgeois idea of progress in its historical unfolding. Where it had once evinced a critical function, 'as the bourgeoisie consolidated its positions of power, the concept of progress would increasingly have forfeited the critical functions it originally possessed'.[42] Various ideologues had assumed the automatically guaranteed nature of progress, from Darwinists to Social Democrats. Progress's actual, present stakes were social regress, accompanied by technological advancement. Progress was adjoined to catastrophe;[43] precisely, the capitalist technological idea of progress ushered in catastrophe. The optical bedazzlements of the nineteenth century – new gas lighting, new colour dyes, new modes of harnessing energy – turned into the colourful infernos of the First World War, which would intensify in the fire terror of the Second World War. The ruins of the twentieth century were the part-ruins of the nineteenth century, detonated once again by technology gone crazy. Technological advance was not progress but a wheel without beginning and end, whose fateful destructive/productive dynamic could ultimately only be ripped apart – ruined again. Progress has two faces, facing in two directions at once. Benjamin was scathing about bourgeois and social democratic notions of social progress, formulating a critique in order to theorize the conditions and measure of actual social progress. But he was not sceptical about progress per se: 'Definitions of basic historical concepts: Catastrophe – to have missed the opportunity. Critical moment – the status quo threatens to be preserved. Progress – the first revolutionary measure taken.'[44] Benjamin set about a struggle over terminology and definition, questioning the content of phrases. The calamitous concepts of the past, which led to the present, had to be challenged by a recovery of the content of terms. Progress needed to find genuine content.

On 23 February Benjamin responded to Adorno's prescriptive set of directions for revision from 1 February. The Institute had agreed to the publication of a revised middle section of 'The Paris of the Second Empire in Baudelaire', on the flâneur. Benjamin pursued the reveries of mid-nineteenth-century Paris, which constructed the city as a succession of glass galleries and winter gardens. Paris was a 'dream city'. Amidst such a dreamscape, the flâneur perceived his environment in a state of intoxication, a perception analogous to that experienced during Baudelaire's experiments with narcotics. Analogousness – a term Benjamin had previously explored in relation to drugs and Surrealism – came to the fore in his studies. Socially interpreted, Baudelaire rendered the historical hallucination of alikeness, which had lodged itself in commodity-producing society. Commodity society reinforced the phantasmagoria of analogousness: the price label made the commodity analogous to all others at the same price. The commodity empathized with its own saleability. Likewise, the flâneur made himself at home in his own purchasability.[45]

If the flâneur put himself on display like commodities on a shelf, Benjamin was compelled to do the opposite. His tracks were disappearing. He relinquished any hold he still had on Berlin, selling in February the remaining items that were left there: some books, a rug, a secretary desk. At the same time, the Gestapo began the process of revoking Benjamin's citizenship – their aim was achieved on 25 March. The reason was likely to have been the publication of his 'Letter from Paris', in *Das Wort* in November 1936. 'Verwisch die Spuren!', 'Erase the traces!', Brecht insisted in one poem in his 1926 lyric cycle 'Reader for City-dwellers'.[46] For those traces – the monograms, screens, knick-knacks on mantelpieces – were also tied up with possession, and so signalled class society. Brecht's poetic sentiment detailed the issue of autonomy at stake: efface the traces, rather than have someone else efface them for you.[47] Benjamin implored 'erase the traces' in February 1933's 'Live

Without Traces', a tiny fragment presenting a horror-vision of the cluttered bourgeois parlour, which detailed the new potential lives to be led within shiny, translucent steel and glass.[48] In his commentary on Brecht's poem, written over the autumn of 1938 and spring of 1939, Benjamin noted that the phrase 'erase the traces' ultimately seems to have been a secret indication of the strategy of crypto-emigration by Communist activists and their thrust into illegality.[49] By then it had long been obvious to Benjamin and others that the powers that be were sweeping out Communist and Jewish 'trash', and whoever else might be deemed social refuse.

Benjamin effaced himself. He wrote a critical piece about Caillois for the Institute's journal but found out that Caillois was very close to his contact in the Naturalization Office and feared a negative review might prejudice his case. He asked for it to be published under the name of Hans Fellner. It appeared under another pseudonym, the anagram J. E. Mabinn, because Horkheimer found it so 'loose' that its appearance could only be justified if those in the know could decipher that it was by a close member of the Institute.[50] The pressure of invisibility increased. To Benjamin's great consternation, in March Horkheimer wrote that the Institute was in financial crisis and might not be able to continue funding him, at least temporarily. The Institute's wealth was largely in property, and the market was not favourable for selling at this time. Horkheimer requested Benjamin report on his efforts to find substitute sources, and suggested that collaborations with academics might be a possibility.

Benjamin admitted that events had conspired to make things difficult in that regard. One supporter at the Sorbonne, the anthropologist Lucien Lévy-Bruhl, was dying. In any case the academics were slipping into apathy, 'probably because any type of intervention would only have to resuscitate their bad conscience'.[51] Benjamin also reported that he had pushed Scholem to secure a contract for a book on Kafka with Schocken Press in Jerusalem. But Salman

Schocken was a 'gloomy autocrat' – the power of his wealth had 'grown immeasurably through the misery of Jews and his sympathies lay with national-Jewish production'.[52] Benjamin reminded Horkheimer of his wish one day to gather together the most important members of the Institute in one town, and noted that he should not be surprised if that day appeared as the peg on which he had flung the cable of his hope. Were it to be in America, there were passport problems. Because of the German quota – 27,230 Germans admitted each year since 1933 with a waiting period of two years in March 1939 – it was necessary to place one's name on a list at the closest American consulate. However, once on the list, a person stayed on the list, relinquishing the possibility of special treatment, such as gaining entry through a professional appointment.

He enclosed with his letter to Horkheimer a new Exposé of the *Arcades Project*, 'Paris, Capitale du XIXeme siècle'. The project's central concern was described as the 'confrontation of appearance and reality'. Each chapter suggested a 'phantasmagoria', a dreamy melding of reality and illusion, 'consequence of the reifying representation of civilization'.[53] There were phantasmagoria of the marketplace, where people appear only as types; of the interior, where men leave the imprint of private individual existence on the rooms they inhabit, and civilization itself, which found its champion in Baron Haussmann and his broad boulevards that changed the face of Paris. All this built up to the 'great phantasmagoria of the universe in Blanqui', a terrifying damnation in which all newness is exposed as re-edition, and revolution a turning on one spot: 'Blanqui's cosmic speculation conveys this lesson: that humanity will be prey to a mythic anguish so long as phantasmagoria occupies a place in it'.[54] The 'facts of class struggle' were largely expunged.[55] But echoes of other more explicitly political formulations could be heard:

The riches thus amassed in the aerarium of civilization henceforth appear as though identified for all time. This conception of history minimizes the fact that such riches owe not only their existence but also their transmission to a constant effort of society – an effort, moreover, by which these riches are strangely altered.[56]

The following day Benjamin wrote to Scholem with redoubled urgency regarding the Kafka contract. He feared losing an existence that was at least 'halfway fit for humans', and hoped to bridge what should be a temporary cessation of income with other sources. He contemplated leaving France: 'amongst the various danger zones into which the earth is divided for Jews, for me presently France is the most threatening, because I stand here economically *completely* isolated'. Once more Benjamin raised the possibility of spending a few months in Palestine.[57] Scholem responded with the news that even a tourist visit to Palestine was difficult of late, given political developments. Many refugees were arriving from Czechoslovakia after the German invasion; finding material support for Benjamin would be very hard. There was further bad news from Palestine. Schocken had decided not to publish in German anymore – a short encyclopaedia entry by Scholem on Jewish mysticism and messianism was the final output in that language.[58]

On 20 March Benjamin observed in a letter to Margarete Steffin that 'of course' he was also considering emigration to the United States, for Europe had become 'uninhabitable'. But the closest he had got to date was a visit to a 'pretty half-Surrealist exposition' in which there were several Mexican images.[59] At the beginning of April 1939 Benjamin observed to Gretel Adorno that all movable goods, material and intellectual, were being speeded to the US. Every poor wretch was trying to find a route there. Benjamin's wealthy Parisian contact, Sigmund Morgenroth, a collector of Renaissance medals, was in the process of emigrating together with his wife Lucie, and his son, Benjamin's friend Stephan Lackner.

Benjamin hoped the family might later help him to find a way there, and perhaps also aid the Institute.

There were compelling reasons to leave France. A new series of decrees concerning foreigners had been issued.[60] Furthermore, there were rumours of a mobilisation of all foreigners up to the age of 52 – in fact, Daladier's decree of 12 to 16 April required all male refugees from 18 years to 48 years of age spending more than two months in France to undergo military service. A few weeks later, obligatory hard labour was imposed in an effort to deter immigrants. Benjamin continued to press Scholem on the possibility of visiting Palestine.[61] He wrote a short résumé of the Institute's history and structure for Morgenroth, identifying himself as the only regular contributor left in Europe. He also admitted that his newfound eagerness to migrate to America stemmed directly from 'the growing danger of war and increasing anti-Semitism'.[62] He hoped that Morgenroth would sponsor his trip, as recompense for earlier efforts helping his son in his literary career.[63] Pursuing funds, he asked Lackner to find out what Klee's *Angelus Novus* might raise if sold in the US. On 18 April he informed Horkheimer of a lack of progress in finding other income. The naturalization attempt looked bleak. Ninety thousand dossiers were piled up at the Préfecture. Benjamin's contacts could exert little influence.

In May he went to Pontigny, where the philosopher Paul Desjardins held an annual ten-day conference called the 'Decades of Pontigny'. Benjamin hoped to meet useful French contacts, but he was shocked by how broken Desjardins appeared. The food, in addition, was miserable, and the library was full of young Scandinavians taking courses, placing it out of bounds. There were pianos everywhere on which people tinkled their finger exercises constantly. Benjamin witnessed a dreadful lecture by Emilie Lefranc of the Confédération Générale du Travail, an example of vulgar Marxism effortlessly serving counter-revolutionary ends. The main theme of the lecture was that the workers should not nourish their spirit of revenge, but rather simply be inspirited by the struggle for social justice.[64] Benjamin gave a talk on Baudelaire. It galvanized the broken Desjardins, for a moment.[65] But Benjamin could not escape the future there. Thoughts of a passage to America plagued him, and he wrote to Horkheimer from Pontigny about his various options – the quota, a sponsored post, a visitor's visa. He was one of more than three million foreigners in France, and information was emerging about the construction of concentration camps for all foreigners, without exception.[66]

Benjamin returned to Paris in late May. In June he reported on the progress of the Baudelaire study to Margarete Steffin, who kept him in tobacco supplies. 'The newyorkers' had demanded a rewrite, and this would have been long done were it not for the noise from the lift that made it impossible for him to work. It was summer and he could work on the balcony, but across the narrow street on the facing balcony a bad painter whistled all day. Benjamin plugged his ears with 'truckloads' of wax, paraffin, concrete, but it did not help.[67] He related a sick anecdote that Karl Kraus would have relished: the gas supply had been cut off from Jews in Vienna because they were using it to commit suicide and not paying their bills.[68]

On 24 June Benjamin reported to Horkheimer on the latest developments in his researches into the flâneur. The figure was to be addressed in three chapters: one on the arcades, one on crowds and one on the intoxication produced by the commodity market.[69] Benjamin had recently read Karl Korsch's *Karl Marx*, which 'gripped' him. Practical politics was more disappointing. The fissures amongst anti-fascists in Paris, both cause and consequence of defeat, dismayed him.[70] Confusion reigned amongst the émigrés. He had witnessed Alfred Döblin's report on his PEN Club-sponsored America trip to the World Congress of Writers. Apparently on board the transatlantic vessel were a number of bourgeois émigrés, who expressed no criticisms of Hitler. But Benjamin was little impressed with Döblin's analysis. Döblin had abandoned any interest in Marxism – which he had never understood anyway – and retreated into the ivory tower. That was all well and good, but Benjamin thought it a mistake to lure such people out to verbalize their nonsense. Döblin met Roosevelt for a few moments and, as a consequence of this, painted the future of America as the apotheosis of freedom, a big brother up to whom Europe should look with confidence.

Benjamin was not so sure. In the United States a decree had been issued against the publication of anti-Semitic propaganda, but Benjamin saw fascist ideology at work in more subtle forms. He told Horkheimer about a film he had seen, Frank Capra's *You Can't Take it With You*, an Academy Award-winning film that demonstrated how far 'the film industry's complicity with fascism' could go in the US. Lenin's line – he meant Marx's – about religion as the opium of the people was proven obsolete:

> The best opium for the *Volk* today is a certain type of inoffen-siveness, that narcotic, in which 'heart-warming' and 'silliness' are the most important ingredients. This Capra film proves how reactionary the slogan 'against plutocracy' can be.[71]

There was brighter news about his move to the US. At the American Consulate he was told that he could obtain a visitor's visa at any time, provided he had a Paris rental contract and funds for the journey. His réfugié-passport turned out to be one of the rarer and better authenticating documents.[72] Stefan wrote to him from London, requesting he visit. It was hard, he said, to find English friends, but London was full of immigrants, and he lived in an interesting, if ugly, area, close to Hyde Park and swarming with fencers of stolen goods and second-hand shops.[73]

At the end of July Benjamin sent a new version of the second part of the second chapter of the Baudelaire book, 'On Some

Motifs in Baudelaire', to Horkheimer. Some smaller projects came to fruition while he awaited Horkheimer's response. 'What is the Epic Theatre?' from 1929, rejected from the *Frankfurter Zeitung*, was published anonymously in the summer of 1939 with a few alterations in *Mass und Wert*. In *Europe* he placed 'Germans of 1789', an essay on the French Revolution's reverberations in Germany. This essay, together with 'The Regression of Poetry' on Jochmann, which he completed in the summer of 1939, interrogated European history and the ways in which Germans received French ideas. The most progressive Germans fled Germany in order to pursue research in more democratic circumstances. Justus von Liebig, Karl Gutzkow, Heinrich Heine and Alexander von Humboldt perceived Paris as the metropolis of world citizenship.[74] When the class that had spawned those progressive Germans bound their fate with the Prussian Reich, the link to Paris was severed, as was any sense of world citizenship. Germans entered Paris as military conquerors in 1871. So began an epoch of militarism, culminating in the imperialist and racist Nazi Reich, which forced Benjamin to seek refuge in Paris until it fell again.

The backdrop to Benjamin's continued writing and reviewing was a desperate situation in Europe: the build-up to war, the news of oppression at home, the loss of stable networks of communication and outlets. Who was the audience for which he wrote these messages of hope amidst despair? It was others in exile, trying to maintain discussions in journals run by exiles. Benjamin insisted on reviewing European literary and cultural histories, endeavouring to hold Europe open as a place of progressive thought.

On 6 August Benjamin told his former wife that he had scaled back his letter writing for six weeks, in order to finish a chunk of his Baudelaire study. The work had to 'penetrate' because his existence was still under threat. It was likely he would visit the US for a few weeks or months, with an aim to seeing if he could lead a life there.[75] A letter to Stefan the same day congratulated him on passing his university entrance examinations, and expressed concern about Stefan's isolation from his peers:

> This isolation belongs to those plagues, of course, that Hitler, as much as his Social Democratic and Communist midwives, brought into the world. Hopefully and probably fortuity will bring redress one day. For my generation, which was decimated by the last war, something similar is less likely.[76]

He asked Stefan to send him English tobacco – the French stuff was unsmokable. He had to return some tobacco sent by Margarete Steffin, as he could not afford to pay the duty on it. As he reported to her, in an unbearably rainy and cold Paris summer, he felt 'rainy, tired, sad and overworked'. He read English ghost stories in French to recuperate.[77]

Plans to visit the US developed through August. He needed, according to his calculations, 10,000 francs to cover the trip. That was the price to pay in order to be in the same place as 'practically *all* the people who had any concept' of his work.[78] He contemplated sailing on a cargo ship for $60 instead of the usual third-class fare of $90 on the passenger ships. The sale of the Klee painting, were it to go ahead, would cover only part of the cost of the trip.[79]

On 3 September war was declared in Europe. The following day Benjamin informed Horkheimer of his new address at Chauconin, at the home of Mme Betz, wife of the Rilke translator Maurice Betz. The mobilization of all male refugees under 49 had begun. Benjamin was 47. Before leaving Paris, he had handed his writings and notes to an unnamed French female friend. A few days later he joined other German immigrants between the ages of 16 and 50 at the Colombes stadium for ten days, and afterwards he was placed on a train to Nevers. Confusion reigned – Alfred Koestler, for one, managed to flee during the transfer from stadium to internment camp. After an hour and a half of walking, which

Benjamin found difficult,[80] the refugees arrived at the Château de Vernuche.

The building was empty. Only some time later did they receive straw on which to sleep.[81] Benjamin's camp contained 300 people. In time a camp society developed, with cigarettes, nails, buttons and pencils as currency. Benjamin contributed to the cultural life of the camp, offering lectures for tobacco. He planned a regular camp newspaper. While interned he maintained contact with the Institute and his friends – his letters were written in French, to make the censor's work easier. A regiment of supporters, Bryher, Gustav Glück, Gretel Karplus-Adorno, the two Doras, Adrienne Monnier, Sylvia Beach, Gisèle Freund and the secretary of the Institute, Juliane Favez, provided newspapers, books, chocolate, tobacco, pullovers and blankets, and paid his rent. Moral sustenance came from various sources too, and most important was the Institute's approving verdict on the Baudelaire essay. He asked Bernard von Brentano to send him his latest novel, though he was not sure if he was allowed German books. In any case he requested Brentano slip some chocolate in the package too.[82]

Benjamin was released from the camp towards the end of November, after pressure by Adrienne Monnier, the diplomat Henri Hoppenot and the French PEN Club. He was thin and weak. America loomed larger. A second option was to go to London, where his former wife hoped to open a boarding house. Gretel Adorno wrote to him in English emphasizing how essential it was to know the language in the US, as Ernst Bloch had found out to his detriment.[83] Benjamin vowed to learn English. He applied to join the German émigré section of PEN. In possession of a letter from the National Refugee Service containing documents for the visa application submitted by Milton Starr of Nashville, Tennessee, Benjamin hesitated to hand it to the consulate. He was attached to France, socially and – crucially – intellectually: for him, 'nothing in the world could replace the Bibliothèque nationale'.[84] But war was changing Paris and rigid rules were being imposed. He asked for Horkheimer's views on the matter. The reply, on 10 January 1940, counselled that there was a huge backlog of immigration visas to be processed. It could take months, Horkheimer warned. He also made clear that Benjamin's stipend in the US would be no more than in France, which would 'signify considerable privation', though this would be compensated by the existence of his companions and colleagues.[85]

On 11 January 1940 Benjamin's letter to Scholem declared 'Every line that we manage to get into print today – given how uncertain our future is – is a victory wrung from the forces of darkness'.[86] 'On Some Motifs in Baudelaire' and '"The Regression of Poetry"' by Carl Gustav Jochmann' appeared in a double-issue of the *Zeitschrift für Sozialforschung* at the beginning of 1940. Other efforts were lost to the darkness. He wrote a review of Henri-Irénée Marrou's *Saint Augustin and the End of Antique Culture*. The doctoral thesis considered Roman decadence in intellectual matters and Augustine as a *lettré de la decadence*, a theme that had long concerned Benjamin. Marrou made reference to one of Benjamin's earliest mentors, Alois Riegl and his *Late Roman Art Industry* of 1901. Evoking another theme close to Benjamin, Marrou presented St Augustine's allegorical exposition of the Bible, a 'sacral philology', in which the Bible's loci '(like the overdetermined elements of the dream in Freud) were capable of two, three or more interpretations'.[87] The review, which evidenced the consistency of Benjamin's fascinations over twenty years, was not published.

In the letter to Scholem of 11 January, Benjamin noted Scholem's desire to 'preserve what we hold in common', and commented that provisions were better for this than 25 years ago. There was no reason any longer for fiery arguments:[88] those days had passed. The numbers of those, he noted, who could get their bearings in this world was shrinking rapidly. Benjamin was not one.

He was isolated. The times, his state of health, the general state of things meant that he stayed at home. His apartment was heated, though not quite enough to allow him to write if the temperature outside was low. He enjoyed two short meetings with his former wife, whose reports on Stefan's progress were not very favourable, but also not a cause for alarm. He spent time reading – the double-issue from the Institute impressed him. He was especially gripped by Horkheimer's essay 'The Jews and Europe', which presented anti-Semitism in the context of capitalism: 'No one can demand that, in the very countries that have granted them asylum, the émigrés put a mirror to the world that has created fascism. But whoever is not willing to talk about capitalism should also keep quiet about fascism.'[89] Persecution of the Jews was an effort by bureaucratic monopoly capitalism to expunge the sphere of economic circulation in which Jews had been particularly active, Horkheimer argued. Fascism was its current form, and its effects were radical. It had birthed a new obsequious individual from the oppressed nineteenth-century industrial worker. This was its strength, and it left intellectuals at a loss for ideas of what to do once the progressive forces were defeated. The intellectuals deluded themselves by think-ing that anything that actually works is good and that, therefore, fascism could not succeed. This was their error.

In February, living in his now unheated flat in the coldest spell, Benjamin began the process of applying for an American visa at the American Consulate, which had transferred from Paris to Bordeaux. Ten days later he informed Horkheimer that he was writing another lengthy round-up of the literary situation in France, as requested. He also mentioned that he was working on 'a certain number of theses on the concept of history', which were to serve as a 'theoretical armature' for his second essay on Baudelaire and which 'specified an aspect of history that had established an irremediable split between our mode of seeing and the survivals of positivism'.[90] The literary round-up, in French, was sent to Horkheimer on 23 March. Surrealism's mark on French literary culture continued to be a theme. Michel Leiris' Freudian autobiography, *L'Âge d'Homme* had some pages of philosophical interest, including a theory of the orgasm and an erotic theory of suicide. Gaston Bachelard's study of the Surrealist mentor Lautréamont was another focus. Once again, psychoanalysis was at issue. Benjamin was most interested in an aspect of Bachelard's book that entirely escaped the author – its latent content. Its analysis of violence evinced traces of 'Hitlerian domination'.[91] The literary scene in Paris developed in relation to the strange pressure exerted by the agreement of the non-aggression pact between Hitler and Stalin. Benjamin, for his part, was reading material critical of developments in the Soviet Union. He mentioned Victor Serge's *Midnight in the Century*, whose literary value was zero, but it did contain 'picturesque descriptions of Stalinist terror'.[92] It was, however, far less valuable than Panaït Istrati's disenchanted triptych of ten years earlier, *Vers l'autre flame*, *Sovjet* and *La Russie nee*, which had attracted the vicious attentions of Istrati's former Communist friends, such as the Stalinist Henri Barbusse.

The last book in the round-up was Georges Salles' *Le Regard*.[93] This became the subject of Benjamin's final unpublished review and his final published piece of writing in his lifetime – in the form of a letter to Adrienne Monnier in *Gazette des Amis des Livres*, in May 1940. Salles was a curator of oriental antiquities at the Musée du Louvre. Benjamin praised Salles's recognition of how material was perfected by time. The effect of time's passage, the visibility of aging on the object, brought forth the mode of seeing of a 'dreaming eye', 'an eye plunged into the depth of years',[94] which it met in the object, a witness of its epoch and all subsequent ones. This was an eye that opened the object up to historical investigation and imaginative projection. Benjamin quoted Salles's remark: '*Each eye is haunted*, ours as much as those of primitive peoples. In each moment it grasps the world according to the schema of its cosmos.'[95]

This eye, embedded in a historical and social moment of perception, observed objects that have lived and are damaged by fissures, traces of collision in which the dialectical movement of history exposes itself.[96] The eye that gazed at the 'liquidated object', battered by time, greeted once radiant but now deceased works, 'just as we still see the brightness of a long extinguished star'. This is the tender, lover's eye of the collector. The collector's moment, history, stance intersected with the encrypted meanings of the object as historical witness to produce a spark of charged social memory. Benjamin confesses in the review to a particular interest in Salles's topic, noting how he collected for a number of years with an ardent passion. He had been separated from his collection for seven years and so had not experienced since then that 'fog, which, forming in the interior of the beautiful and desired thing, captivates you'.[97] Though he felt nostalgic for such drunkenness, he had, he noted sadly, neither the energy nor the courage to begin such a collection once more.

On 6 April Benjamin detailed his poor state of health to Horkheimer. Hypertension was causing congestive heart failure. A specialist doctor recommended rest in the countryside. Benjamin forwarded the x-ray analysis, in case the Institute could provide money to help in times of illness. Money was provided. He required a commission from the Institute, in case the rumoured revision of conditions for German refugees occurred. He required proof that he had worked for the Institute for seven years, and that his duties involved research into the history of French literature at the Bibliothèque nationale.[98]

A letter to Gretel Adorno at the start of May returned to the theses on history. He evoked happier times, a day in May 1937 when Karplus, Adorno and the economist Alfred Sohn-Rethel ate lunch and Benjamin delivered his thoughts on progress.

> The war and the constellation that it brought with it have led me to jot down some thoughts about which I can say that I have kept them safe for 20 years, indeed I have even kept them safe from myself. This is also the reason why even you two have

barely been allowed a fleeting glimpse of them. Our conversation beneath the chestnut trees was a breech in these 20 years. Even today I hand them to you more as a bouquet of whispering grasses collected on contemplative walks, than as a collection of theses. In more than one sense the text that you shall receive is reduced. I do not know how much reading them will surprise you or, what I do not want, mislead you. In any case I draw your attention in particular to the 17th reflection: this is the one that allows the concealed but conclusive relationship of these considerations to my previous works, in that it succinctly vents the method of the latter.[99]

The theses were not destined for publication. *On the Concept of History* was truly written in the 'midnight of the century'. Benjamin's 'testament' was a reflection on a specific history and its telling, which emerged out of his researches on the previous hundred and fifty years of economic and political development. Benjamin's gnomic meditations took nineteenth-century historians to task for their myth of progress, supposedly guaranteed by technological advance and by the spread of enlightenment ideals. This mythology was broadcast to disastrous effect by the very people – German Social Democrats – who believed that they spoke in the name of popular liberation, but actually only gave a boost to its negation in National Socialism. Still, even at the darkest moment, Benjamin adhered to a commitment to a popular wisdom – a class struggle – conducted with 'confidence, courage, humor, cunning and fortitude'.[100] What else could have saved the day? The theses refused to endorse any idea of progress that avoided the active participation of the working-class in their own emancipation. Some 'paralipomena' to the theses extended Benjamin's attacks on positivism and historicism, likening their methods to those of natural science with its discovery of 'laws'. In their stead Benjamin asserted history as a form of 'remembrance', and the present as a time in which, at any moment, the revolutionary 'chance for a completely new resolution of a completely new problem' might emerge.[101] The theses contained startling images of historical and social process: history as strands of frayed hair to be bundled into a coiffure; historical materialist procedures as spectrum analyses of light; revolutions as the emergency brake on locomotives; and Nietzsche's 'eternal recurrence' as a school detention where 'humanity has to copy out its texts in endless repetitions'.[102]

'On the Concept of History' is Benjamin's reckoning with Social Democracy, Stalinism and bourgeois thought, none of which were able to prevent the disaster of fascism. Social Democracy had engaged in deals with the political establishment and with capital, just as the Communist parties entered into a pact with Hitler. There was reason for despair. But the theses offered hope too, or at least attempted to formulate a way of thinking that might be of use for a revived revolutionary practice. Benjamin was clear: 'The subject of historical knowledge is the struggling, oppressed class itself.'[103] Just as in the analysis of reproducible art, in the theses on history the accent is on the mass as active participants in their culture and history. And he adds that in Marx the last enslaved class is the avenger that completes the task of liberation in the name of generations of the downtrodden.

Throughout the theses the emphasis is on the intimate connection between struggle and historical practice on the one hand, and knowledge and theory on the other. Liberation comes only after breaking with some of the inherited modes of understanding the world in terms of automatic progress, crisis as exception and history as objective unfurling towards an ever-better future that never arrives – modes that could neither foresee nor prevent fascism. Benjamin wished to write history that could conceive revolutionary change. His procedure of 'brushing history against the grain' disturbed conventional ways of presenting what has been, refusing to accept history as something completed or closed. The past built the present, just as our interest in the past is inflected by present concerns. Benjamin's history sought the outflow of the past in the present: As he put it in the notes on knowledge and progress in the *Arcades Project*: 'The materialist presentation of history leads the past to bring the present into a critical state'.[104] Equally, it attempted to open up the possibilities that existed in the past but were yet to be activated.

A letter to Adorno on 7 May 1940 discussed Baudelaire and Proust, Stefan George and Hofmannsthal. The letter was a mix of self-explanation and resilient reflection on a now crumbling European culture, in terms of what it might offer to theories of memory and experience as well as to the notion of 'defiance'.[105] Benjamin wrote of solitude, not as 'the locus of a man's individual fullness', but as 'his historically-determined emptiness, the locus of his persona that is his misfortune'.[106] Benjamin was not fulfilled by solitude – the letter, like all the others, disclosed how much he thrived in dialogue – but it was forced on him by historical determination.

Benjamin left Paris in June, just as the German troops arrived. He headed for Lourdes, where a number of refugees had collected, and found a cheap room. He was carrying a single book, the memoirs of the seventeenth-century agitator Gondi, the Cardinal of Retz.[107] He felt every newspaper to be a personal notification and every radio broadcast the voice of the bearer of bad news. Fearful that an American visa would not arrive in time, he contemplated going to Switzerland until he could obtain a visa for Portugal or a non-European state.[108] In August he headed for Marseilles where refugees applied for visas, planning their methods of escape from a country whose capital had fallen and whose Pétain government in Vichy had made an accord with Hitler. The French slogan 'Liberty, Equality, Brotherhood' was replaced by 'Work, Family, Homeland'. In Marseilles Benjamin encountered Koestler once more and shared with him his means for suicide, morphine pills, carried by Benjamin since the burning of the Reichstag. It was a city full of putative escapees hatching crazy plans. Benjamin's effort to bribe his way onto a freighter, dressed as a French sailor with his friend Fränkel, failed. While in Marseilles Benjamin learnt that he had been awarded a non-quota visa from the National Refugee Service. The US was now a concrete possibility – and if not there, the Institute proposed that a guest lecturership at the University in Havana, Cuba might suit.[109]

At the end of September 1940 Benjamin set out with a small party to cross the mountains into Spain, on route to a passage to America. He carried with him $70 and 500 francs, and a black leather briefcase containing six passport photographs; an x-ray and medical note; a pipe with an amber handle; glasses in a dilapidated case; a pocket watch of gold with a worn nickel chain; an identity card issued in Paris; a passport with a Spanish visa and letters, magazines and papers, some of which may have been a manuscript, contents unknown.[110] The fifteen-mile route took the refugees to high altitudes, along a smugglers' route that the Communist General Lister had used in the Spanish Civil War. It was an arduous journey, especially given Benjamin's weakened state of health.[111] On the test run along the path to explore the terrain, Benjamin refused to turn back and insisted on spending the night without protection against the cold or animals on the mountain. The next day the rest of the party rejoined him. The man who had so enjoyed giving himself up to the chance formations of the city proved to be remarkably adept at reading the basic map of a remote region. They found their way to the border.

The party was held up in the border town of Port Bou. New visa regulations meant Benjamin was refused passage into Spain without a French exit visa. He feared being handed over to the Gestapo. Benjamin must have passed through Port Bou on various occasions through the years before being stopped there forever. He was not alone in his fate. Even the most powerful succumbed, for the President of Catalonia was arrested by German agents at the same time and shot by the Spanish government in October, the month that Hitler and Franco met.

A view of Port Bou. This antique French postcard describes it as a 'small fishing port nestling in a cove'.

On 25 September 1940 one of the fellow travellers with the party, Henny Gurland, was the recipient of Benjamin's final words on a postcard, which she destroyed, committing its contents to memory:

> With no way out, I have no other choice but to end it. It is in a little village in the Pyrenees where no one knows me that my life reaches its conclusion. I ask you to transmit my thoughts to my friend Adorno and to explain to him the situation in which I find myself. There is not enough time for me to write all the letters that I would have wished to have written.[112]

It is assumed that sometime that day or the next, under police guard in the Hôtel de Francia before being compelled to return to France, Benjamin ingested morphine pills and, after four visits by a doctor who administered injections and blood letting and measured his blood pressure, was dead at 10 pm on 26 September 1940.

8

Afterwords

Alternatively, in the autumn of 1940 the portly intellectual Walter
Benjamin arrived in the United States of America, after an arduous
journey through the Pyrenees. He took up a position working on
Theodor Adorno's research project 'The Authoritarian Personality'.
A few years later he met Timothy Leary and participated in Leary's
experiments with drugs in the Harvard Psilocybin Project in 1960.
After this his interest in technological reproduction led to an
involvement in work with the cybernetician Heinz von Foerster on
computer prototypes. The laurels of fame never came to him in the
US. He died a forgotten man in an old people's home in Ann Arbor.

   Not the last years of Benjamin, but rather artist and filmmaker
Lutz Dammbeck's fantasy of what might have happened had he
made it into an American exile. There is something about Walter
Benjamin that draws people into speculation about what he might
have been, could have been and should have been. The appalling
outcome of his biography is subverted in attempts to make incomplete, at least in the imagination, the history that is completed.
He should have gone to Palestine. Had he left a day earlier he
would have entered Spain without query and been able to travel
on to the US. He would have got a professorship there, for sure. Or
had he left for Palestine in the 1920s he might have found a university career, like his friend Scholem. Or might commitment have
secured him a future in Russia, had he become a Communist Party
member or fellow traveller? He should have been more decisive. He

should have been a Zionist. He should have been more Marxist. He should have been a Rabbi. He should have developed immunity to Brecht's 'crude thinking'.

It is as if in the question of his own identity Benjamin was mistaken. He made mistakes, false moves, blunders. He was indeed cursed by that figure of whom he wrote in his Berlin childhood memoirs: the little hunchback 'Mr Clumsy', who turned up every time Benjamin broke something or fell down. This 'gray assessor' barred his way, only had to stare at Benjamin to make him stumble and, as he wrote, exacted 'the half part of oblivion from each thing to which I turned'.[1] When Benjamin wrote of him in the 1930s he thought him long since abdicated. But perhaps he did return once Benjamin himself was broken.

His death, in any case, was a matter of mistaken identity. On 28 September 1940 a funeral following Catholic rites took place in Port Bou for a Dr Benjamin Walter, a name reversed for a man assumed to be of Catholic faith, who while in transit had died, so the doctor concluded, as a result of a cerebral haemorrhage. If his identity was lost, so too were the possessions he had dragged over the mountains – including the briefcase, which, the rumours say, contained a manuscript. Given over to the authorities in Figueres, whatever was there was likely to have been damaged by water and eaten by rats in the intervening years. The only known remainder from the briefcase is the certified letter from Horkheimer that attested Benjamin's useful employ by the Institute. The remains of the Catholic traveller were placed in a niche on the southern side of the chapel of the Catholic graveyard. His dollars and francs paid the rent for five years.[2] Indeed the short time in Port Bou consumed most of his money, with the hotelier taking occupancy fees for four nights, five lemonades, four telephone calls and medicines, and the doctor, the coffin maker, the priest and the judge all receiving their share. Of 971.55 pesetas, only 273.60 remained.[3] After five years in a grave niche, Benjamin's remains were moved to a collective grave.

Conjectures about the death abound. Nothing is settled. Mistaken identity and the loss of possessions are only the beginning. Some suggest that perhaps, fearful of being caught with subversive materials, Henny Gurland took Benjamin's papers and destroyed them, just as she destroyed Benjamin's last postcard, the suicide note. Perhaps she took the remaining morphine tablets – for none were found on Benjamin's person, and he apparently carried with him enough to kill a horse. The accounts of people who were in Port Bou on the day of his death – Gisèle Freund, Henny Gurland, the hotel proprietor Juan Suñer – differ markedly in the details. So many stories, one for each person. Except Benjamin.

Contradiction leads to further speculation. Ingrid Scheurmann, for example, takes seriously the doctor's claim that the cause of death was cerebral haemorrhage, not poisoning, of which the doctor seemed unaware. But the doctor's assessment could have been a cover-up, as suicide was a grave injustice against a Catholic god. If it were true, at least it would be an antidote to the widespread, tragically accented and seductively poignant suicide story, proving the story a confection of assumptions and wish-fulfilment, and part of a mythologization of Benjamin as unlucky melancholic. In the absence of that story, the accent falls less on Benjamin as a particularly hapless individual, and more on Benjamin as representative of a typical fate, that of a refugee, the displaced person, only one of many forced on the run, who may or may not have reached a destination that he was forced to choose. Benjamin comes to stand in as a symbol of emigration at all times – though unusually in his case he is one of the few that are named, a refugee whose name we know.

There are more outlandish claims that refute the suicide story. The one-time Trotskyist turned Neo-Conservative Stephen Schwartz garnered attention in 2001 for his claim in the *Weekly Standard* that Benjamin might have been assassinated. Agents of Stalin might have been responsible, for it is unquestionable that the Soviet secret police operated in the South of France, targeting fleeing exiles for liquidation. That Benjamin had a scant relationship to the Communist Party did not necessarily rule him out.

A film from 2005, *Who Killed Walter Benjamin?*, by David Mauas, fingers a different perpetrator. Mauas returns to the 'scene of the crime' to find that Port Bou was a town crawling with Falangists and Fascists after the Civil War. The hotel proprietor, Juan Suñer, was on friendly terms with the Spanish police and the local representatives of the Gestapo, who ate in his restaurant. Might he have had a hand in the death? Or the doctor, also apparently a supporter of Franco: what role might he have played? Is it conspiracy and not suicide that lies behind Benjamin's death?

This shift from fact to fiction, from certainty to speculation, goes further. Something about Walter Benjamin – the life, his theory – makes him a favoured candidate for representation or fictionalization. He has been the subject of two novels, *Benjamin's Crossing* (1997) by Jay Parini and, a decade later, *The Angel of History* by Bruno Arpaia, and has played a walk-on part in a couple more. He

Benjamin (and his nemesis, a Spanish border-guard) confronting the spectres of Marx and Einstein in the underworld – a scene from the 2004 Munich premiere of Brian Ferneyhough and Charles Bernstein's *Shadowtime*.

is intimated as a presence in the Staatsbibliothek Berlin in Wim Wenders' *Wings of Desire*. Two major pieces of musical theatre refer to him: Claus-Steffen Mahnkopf's *Angelus Novus* (2000) and *Shadowtime* (2004), composed by Brian Ferneyhough, with a libretto by poet Charles Bernstein. Jewlia Eisenberg recorded *Trilectic* in 2002, a setting of texts about the relationship between the two 'lefty nerds' Benjamin and Lacis – with Lacis, a Christian, mistakenly cast at a Jewess (of course, she has to be to strike the right tone): it was released on John Zorn's Tzadik label, in the Radical Jewish Culture series. As object of fiction, Benjamin cuts an incompetent figure, tossed on the waves of history and too uselessly cerebral to manage the business of life.

There is a longer history to Benjamin's traces as culture. Valerio Adami's lithograph *Ritratto di Walter Benjamin*, from 1973, depicts Benjamin faltering on a border. In the same period R. B. Kitaj's *The Autumn of Central Paris (after Walter Benjamin)* appeared, harking back to happier times of intellectual exchange. So began a fetish for Benjamin's moon-glassed face. Paintings and collages using photographs of his face crop up now and again, echoes of the book covers that inevitably use one or another photograph of him. Indeed, there may be more artworks 'inspired' by Benjamin than any other thinker.[4] First his work on mass reproduction and aura filtered into art practice – what art college over the last thirty years has not put his writings on the mass reproducibility of art on the requisite reading list? Generations of students are confused by the idea of aura: taught to them simplistically detached from the axis of revolutionary possibility and capitalist actuality, they believe Benjamin to be the naïf soul, who thought this odd quality really was abolished and photography and film really had instituted democracy, when clearly aura still persists, art has not gone away and photography and film could be put to use by fascists. Art fights back against Benjamin, even with the tools of its mortal enemy, in Timm Ulrichs's wry negation of the

thesis of the 'Work of Art' essay from 1967. Ulrichs photocopied
the front cover of the Suhrkamp edition of 'The Work of Art' essay
multiple times to show that eventually the degradation of each
copy results in illegibility, or perhaps something after legibility,
the beautiful tonal variations of an aura reluctant to abolish itself.
Art believes, in this, it has trumped political theory. It hopes
thereby to keep itself alive.

More recently, as a reflection of the process of Benjamin's
'biographization', Volker März fashioned countless little Benjamin
figurines. In *Aura Transfer*, each little clay statue comes with a
knowing caption or title. We see Benjamin with prostitutes,
Benjamin dreaming, Benjamin and Jews, a Benjamin with holes
through which water streams who pleads with Adorno for help
(Adorno says No). Prices start at a hundred euros. There are plenty
of angels in März's work and elsewhere, such as in Anselm Kiefer's
The Angel of History: Poppy and Memory, from 1989, and in Aura
Rosenberg's digitally manipulated photographs, direct responses
to Benjaminian themes, as angels hurtle across the horizon and
rubbish piles up skywards. Gloom and melancholy pervades much
of this Benjaminian work. Gisèle Freund's series of photographs
staged for an illustrated magazine in 1937, in which Benjamin
posed as what he already was, a reader at the Paris Bibliothèque
nationale, is updated in Candida Höfer's 1998 photograph of the
same library, now superseded by a new development in the east
of the city: this is history cast in the melancholic pall of loss.
GDR artist Werner Mahler's dreary photographs of 1989 of
Port Bou, where Benjamin died, are part of a project on lines
of flight, with special resonance in a world still divided by the
Berlin Wall.

The poetic and fragmentary nature of Benjamin's thought leaves
many crevices and footholds for practitioners. And it might seem as
if the more Benjamin is served up as a document of culture, the less
there need be any specific analysis of the barbarism subtending the

world that needs and tolerates culture. Furthermore, the allusive mode of address in parts of his work encourages thematic rummaging by artists who may not fully grasp his critical thought; this thematic rummaging occurs even for a practice as concrete as restructuring the built environment. At the high-concept end there is Daniel Libeskind's Jewish Museum in Berlin (1998–2001), which claims to pay homage to Benjamin's *One-way Street*. Elsewhere in Berlin a more prosaic project was in train. As a sign of Benjamin's rising market value and brand name recognizability, Walter-Benjamin-Platz was built, reclaimed from a car park in Benjamin's childhood stalking ground of Charlottenburg. An Italian piazza is displaced to the cooler northern clime, surrounded by granite façades and colonnades with art deco lamps that front offices, apartments, restaurants and cafés. In its centre computer-powered fountains and, on weekends, a farmers' market, are designed to make this count as classy modern real estate.

Now that the cultural pulse of Berlin throbs in the shabby area around Mitte, at the newly restored core of a reunited Berlin, an art outing to prim and posh Zehlendorf on the south-eastern edge of the city feels like a quest into some exotic and impenetrable zone, even if its strangeness resides in an un-Berlinerish well-heeled banality. The long-haul feeling is intensified when the destination address is Argentinische Allee, and the tube station Krumme Lanke is one stop beyond Onkel Toms Hütte. This same geographically confusing sense of things struck Susanne Ahner as she walked between the tube station on Argentinische Allee and the s-Bahn on Mexikoplatz, in the months before she participated in an exhibition devoted to Benjamin's traces in art in Haus Am Waldsee, not very far from Benjamin's family home in Delbrückstrasse. Echoes of distant locations in the Berlin suburb reminded her of Benjamin's comments about the Quartier Europe in Paris, where the street names conjure up cities from across half the globe and allow a traveller to journey beyond physical geography imaginatively. Ahner sought further signs of the wider world secreted in the nearby streets and managed to find – and photograph – places and scenes that relate to the many towns and streets in which Benjamin spent his 48 years, from San Remo to Svendborg, Riga to Naples. Ahner's project went further: her photographs grace little tablets of high quality bitter chocolate, and, available at the museum's café for 50 eurocents, they become collectables, evoking Benjamin's drive to collect and his fascination with the postcard and photograph. It evokes also our own fetishization of the man who was dislodged again and again: his collecting passion becomes a psychological symptom.

The wider world of Walter Benjamin reached a limit on the border of France and Spain. In a video made there by Michael Bielicky, a figure picks his way through the mountain paths. He puffs and pants. The image that we see is one mediated by surveillance technologies. This is Benjamin on today's US-Mexican border or the like, visible to power through its technologies of infra-red and global positioning systems. To be a refugee is a high-tech affair these days. Benjamin's walk was a foreshadow of that of nameless refugees who risk all to cross borders, in a world that is economically globalized, and yet whose frontiers are lined with fortresses against people. This walk is nowadays one retraced by countless academics and intellectuals, hoping to understand thereby something of the ordeal to which Benjamin was subjected.[5] It is important that those seekers have something to see once they have endured the gruelling walk: Port Bou obliges. Art segued with memorialization in Dani Karavan's 'Passagen', a conceptual work placed outside the cemetery in Port Bou in 1994. The monument is a cramped iron passageway. This narrow corridor arrests the visitor behind a thick windowpane, enforcing the metaphor and the actuality of the impossibility of passage. The visitor is stranded and directed to feel as Benjamin felt in September 1940, as a tiny and fragile figure suspended above a vision of the perilous swirling of the sea below. Etched on the glass in several

Dani Karavan's 1990–94 memorial *Passages – Homage to Walter Benjamin* in Port Bou.

According to a commentary on the artist's website, the artwork is comprised of whirlpools, rocks, corten steel, glass, olive trees, stones, fence and text. The olive tree, for example, which was already growing there when the memorial was erected, symbolically 'fights for its life'.

languages are some words from notes for *On the Concept of History*:

> It is more arduous to honour the memory of the nameless than that of the renowned. Historical construction is devoted to the memory of the nameless.[6]

Benjamin is, at least, one of the remembered. Indeed, multiply so at this little border town. In 1979 a little plaque in Catalan was set in the cemetery wall. It reads 'A Walter Benjamin – Filòsof alemany – Berlin 1892 Portbou 1940', and in the context of post-Franco Spain it appeared to hint at the possibility and necessary recovery of a non-Fascist tradition in Spain and Germany. Inside the cemetery too another memorial stone was placed, this time from 1990. It bears the much-quoted line in German, Catalan and English: 'There is no document of culture which is not at the same time a document of barbarism.'

Three memorials: so much celebration. Benjamin was not a celebrated figure when alive, and his writing brought him some fame but little fortune. In the years after his death this changed. The Institute for Social Research made the first efforts to bring Benjamin's thought to a wider public. *On the Concept of History* was published in 1942, in a hectographed volume called *Walter Benjamin in Memoriam*. As well as the theses on the philosophy of history, it contained a bibliographic note on Benjamin's writings, two essays by Max Horkheimer and an essay by Adorno. In an introduction to the theses, Adorno noted that, though not intended for publication, 'the text has become a legacy'. Adorno and Horkheimer, joint-editors of the volume, wrote: 'We dedicate these contributions to the memory of Walter Benjamin. The historical philosophical theses at the front are Benjamin's last work.'[7] Published as a special issue of the *Zeitschrift für Sozialforschung*, it reached a relatively select number of readers. Adorno pressed further for an edition of Benjamin's selected writings to appear in

German, while Hannah Arendt was pursuing an English language edition for Schocken in 1946. She wrote to Brecht that October to find out who, if anyone, held the rights to Benjamin's work. Benjamin's sister was dead.[8] His brother, sent to the concentration camp Mauthausen in 1942, died there on 26 August the same year, after, according to the testimony of the camp commandant, touching the power line.

There were French efforts too to raise Benjamin's profile posthumously. Pierre Missac translated *On the Concept of History* in 1947 for *Les Temps Modernes*. This publication garnered no response. Silence greeted the theses again in 1950 when they were published in German in the *Neue Rundschau*. By then Adorno had managed to persuade Suhrkamp to publish some works in Germany. In 1950 *Berlin Childhood around 1900* appeared, and, after long discussions with Suhrkamp, a two-volume selected writings was published. Other collections followed, the most important of which were the cheap paperbacks *Illuminationen* in 1961 and *Angelus Novus* in 1966. The 'Work of Art' essay, the 'Little History of Photography' and the essay on Fuchs appeared in one volume in 1963, as did a collection of city sketches. 'Critique of Violence' came in 1965, and essays on Brecht in 1966, along with two volumes of letters. In a politicized atmosphere in late-1960s Germany, arguments over appropriation and the politics of editing began. From 1972 to 1989 the stakes of Benjamin's legacy were debated thoroughly as volume after volume of the fourteen-part *Gesammelte Schriften* appeared in Germany, replete with expansive scholarly apparatus, omissions, inclusions and editorial steerage by associates of the T. W. Adorno archive.

The question of Benjamin's 'politics'– specifically his relationship to Marxism – has caused much debate and bafflement. In West Germany, following 1968, there was little doubt that Benjamin's work represented a contribution to Marxist scholarship, if an unconventional one. He was called on as a guide to political

Outside the ceme-
tery in Port Bou.

Marking a body
that is not there –
a memorial to
Walter Benjamin
inside the ceme-
tery at Port Bou.

praxis too. The mobilized students of the late 1960s took their lessons from him in pirate editions. The cadres of social revolt imagined him with a photocopier in one hand and a joint in the other.
In a moment of revolutionary upheaval it was a succinct emblem of
Benjamin's outreach (relations of production and distribution in the
media) and inreach (the druggy defamiliarization of experience).
This image might be embellished by a Kalashnikov or bomb –
Andreas Baader of the *Rote Armee Fraktion* would cite Benjamin in
the coming years, for example evoking ideas from *On the Concept
of History*, in his 'Letter to the Prisoners' from 1976.[9] Out of this,
and sometimes in critical dialogue with it, there were significant

neo-Marxist appropriations of him too, perhaps most notably in the work of Jürgen Habermas. Habermas's essay 'Consciousness-Raising or Redemptive Criticism', published first in German in 1972, was an influential statement.[10] It located Benjamin as an exponent of 'redemptive criticism', in contra-distinction to 'ideology critique' or 'consciousness-raising' criticism. Redemptive criticism had no immanent relationship to political praxis. Habermas's was an effort to wrest Benjamin away from any instrumentalist uses to which the student movement might put him.

In the 1970s a new 'materialist' literary theory was proposed on the basis of Benjamin's differences from Lukács.[11] Benjamin provided writers and artists on the Left with a vocabulary that did not share the assumptions of the Socialist Realism with which Lukács was associated. Socialist Realist directives ranked the intelligibility of content above form. Lukács, in line with Socialist Realists, advocated nineteenth-century paragons of realist style such as Balzac and Walter Scott. Socialist Realism recommended the return to traditional forms of oil painting and novel writing. Benjamin by contrast was a theorist of modernity and its new modes and media of representation. He criticized the way that the development of Socialist Realism repressed technological and formal experimentation in art, restoring old models of culture with their disempowering modes of reception, which expected audiences to stand in reverential awe before 'great works'.

Benjamin celebrated, though not without qualification, the progressive function of technical reproducibility in art. Aptly enough, it was the very reproducibility of Benjamin's theses on reproduction that made them subsequently so prevalent. The essay's compression, just a few easily photocopiable pages, its salability or availability in sundry readers or compendia, the limpidity of its argument – a narrative of transpositions that tolerates cursory, boiled-down retransmissions – all these factors have reinforced the omnipresence and unforgoability of the 'Work of Art' essay, which is still the work of Benjamin's best known and most discussed. It is as if the essay about reproduction were designed for reproduction. His work contributed to a burgeoning critical and media theory, as evinced in the writings of Hans Magnus Enzensberger with his advocacy in 1970 of the potentially liberatory uses of the photocopier within the ideologically stultifying and privatized 'consciousness industry'.[12]

There was another German story. In the GDR 'On Some Motives in Baudelaire' was published in 1949, and in 1956 and 1957 some writings on Brecht and an essay on Gottfried Keller appeared. A collection of texts in 1970 challenged the apparently politically determined decisions of the West German editors.[13] 1984 saw the first appearance of *On the Concept of History* in the GDR, in an anthology that acknowledged the 'theological' aspects of Benjamin's work.[14]

As the aftershock of social movements abated, so too did the use of Benjamin as model for Marxist praxis. In English-speaking countries, especially the United States, the relationship of Benjamin to Marxism has been a controversial subject. The publication of Scholem's memoir, *Walter Benjamin: Story of a Friendship* in 1981 significantly influenced the reception.[15] Scholem castigated Benjamin's Marxism as the weakness to which he ultimately lost his life and Zion. Elsewhere he described Benjamin as 'a theologian marooned in the realm of the profane'.[16] In addition, Scholem perceived Benjamin first and foremost as a metaphysician of language, absorbed in mystical accounts of linguistics, in the tradition of Hamann and Humboldt. Dominant streams in Anglophone Humanities scholarship in the 1980s and 1990s seemed able to find links between Benjamin's language theory and poststructuralist thought and, subsequently, merged Benjamin with his adversary, Heidegger.

That Benjamin became identified with the very figure he repudiated is perhaps some sort of supplement to a theory-world that propounds dislocated and schizoid identities. Benjamin as schizoid, though, is not cherished but chastised for inconsistency. From the purview of the secondary literature, Benjamin appears to be a multiple personality, a collation of figures of wildly varying types, convictions, orientations and interests. Benjamin was a Marxist, or a Messianic thinker, or an impossible hybrid of the two. Benjamin's thought was coherent from day one to the end, or fractured in abrupt breaks. He has been read as a Kabbalist, a poststructuralist, a messianist, a theologian and a more or less 'vulgar' materialist. A variety of political positions have been attributed to him, from left-liberal to communist to anarchist, from tragic defeatist to revolutionary optimist. Typically those who attribute such stances to Benjamin cast him as a reflection of their own position, or they condemn him to the shadows that are the underside of their own apparently clarified thought: the genre of Benjamin as failure, as misguided, as naïve. Few take the time to reconstruct historical context or political possibility, or to carefully set Benjamin's action and thinking within the realm of such context and possibility.

Nor indeed is he placed back into the networks that sustained him – even as other collaborations undermined him. Benjamin is ceaselessly presented as lonely. The abiding image is of a lonesome scholar in the Bibliothèque nationale, beneath what he described as the rustling sounds of the painted leaves on the ceiling. But this was a man who lived through his connections to others: from the days with Wyneken and the friendships he established at Haubinda and in the Youth Movement that lasted a life long, to the women he liked and loved, who remained correspondents, friends and supporters, to the intellectual contacts that he made and sustained over the years. He distributed his writings amongst these people and he relished their careful guardianship and their responses. He lived from the pull and persuasion of others, and pulled and persuaded in turn. But he lived in a world turned peculiarly vicious, which separated people from one another and made his existence precarious to the point of death.

The floodgates of criticism are open. Book after book by and about Benjamin appears. The German and French text scraps of the *Arcades Project* were homogenized into English for publication by Harvard University Press in 1999: the thick slab of notes, turned book-like, propelled further waves of interpretation and day-dreams. A substantial portion of Benjamin's output now exists in various languages, including Spanish, French, Italian, English and Japanese. In addition, scores of studies have asserted the value of Benjamin's insights for philosophy, art history, cultural studies, media studies, geography, architecture . . . in short, all the academic disciplines, as well as interdisciplinary approaches.[17] A veritable Benjamin industry exists. A by-product of this industry is the production of biography, a form that proposes to bring the reader closer to the motivations of its subject.

Benjamin eschewed the biographical form, even in his memoirs. These present a type of anti-biography, choosing instead to show the child-Benjamin as a product of his environment, his time, his location and his class. This biography in your hands has adopted a conventional form, but takes at least from Benjamin's procedure the will to set him in relation to the geographies that attracted him and the historical events that impacted him and shaped his thoughts. This book you are reading has told Benjamin's story as a biography – but the intention is to present him, Benjamin-like, as an active symptom of his times.

In one of his final publications, Benjamin praised Georges Salles, because he was a writer 'for whom the dialectic is not a bookish concept but a thing proven in life'.[18] This life that Salles theorized – the life of the 'liquidated' objects rescued in his museum collections – is one 'damaged by fissures, traces of the collisions with which they expose the dialectical movement of history'.[19] This book presented Benjamin's life as just such an object involved in a series of collisions, some of which – personal encounters, places, books – generate his extraordinary thinking, some of which wound him, but are no less generative of his thought. Through his life can be read the violent unfolding of the twentieth century, which destroyed not only him, but millions of others. Yet his writings envision a world not condemned to repeat its mistakes, unlike the defeatist cosmology of a Blanqui; a world in which the political subject still has recourse to revolutionary praxis, unlike the disempowering theory of a Habermas. Benjamin's writings tell of other possibilities, models for future thinking and acting, re-encounters with the past and proposals for what might yet be to come. Such are his important living remains.

In the first thesis of 'The Work of Art in the Age of its Technological Reproducibility' Benjamin stated his intention to coin concepts that, unlike the current ones, were 'completely useless for the purposes of fascism'.[20] Benjamin understood his work on this and many other occasions as a challenge to the prevalent politics and aesthetics. He stood sideways to the dominant streams of the epoch that reinforced privilege, be it the privilege stemming from a conventional and cushioned education or the privilege of possessing expanding capital. His work forced divisions, nailed corrupt lines of enquiry that defend ownership and tradition, and attempted to theorize and galvanize newly forming audiences with new and liberating modes of reading, thinking and acting.

His writings were prophetic, but only in the sense that they took experience seriously and so could recognize, with eyes wide open, both the malign and progressive tendencies of the present issuing from the past and perhaps disbursing in the future. Clearer than many of his generation he perceived the 'suspension of militant communism' in Stalin's Soviet Union.[21] He diagnosed the problem of Stalinism as much from the pitiful imagery thrust on the masses – icon images of Lenin watching over, like policemen, the crevices of daily life – as from its hopeless restoration of pre-revolutionary culture in the theatres. And he predicted the rise of fascism, militarism and nationalism in his homeland earlier than many in his alarmed unpicking of war novels and officer memoirs, burgeoning in the late 1920s, with their aestheticization of violence and longing for annihilation.

Benjamin's writings were able to diagnose alienation and distortion because they possessed a measure of what genuine life might be. This is apparent from the earliest statements of a youthful Romantic rejection of philistinism to the urgent last theses on history, which fulminated against stories in the guise of history told to bolster the ruling classes. In their stead he proposed a 'historical materialist' procedure that accounts for *Erfahrung*, that is, the 'unique experience with the past'.[22] Experience, the subjective sensibility segueing with the objective world, was what Benjamin hunted, in his life and as a quality to be theorized, researched, intensified. Benjamin sought expanded experience in travel, but was compelled to become an exile. Experience as a grasping of life, more life, became the battle to find a place where it might be possible to stay alive. Benjamin's quest was for a life worth living and a fight worth fighting.

He detailed the flaws and contradictions of cultural life in ways that demanded awareness of the conditions of the dispossessed – which, in many ways, became his own conditions. Apathy and delusion – which his aesthetics and his political understanding strove to counter – were responsible for the victory of fascism and his premature death, and not just his. Apathy and delusion remain the proud conclusions of an intelligentsia without hope. The fact of Benjamin's extinction comes to be used as the block on a utopia that is longed for but believed unrealizable. Benjamin's 'failure' – his death – is read as proof of the futility of all desire for change, as change will always be defeated or perverted.

This is what Benjamin as cultural document is made to articulate again and again. But Benjamin (as life and work) is not only a register of horror, but also an index of possibilities yet to be realized – and an instrument towards their realization – once we all begin to truly live.

References

1 Benjamin's Remnants

1 *GB*, III, p. 433.
2 For reproductions of numerous pages see *Walter Benjamins Archive: Bilder, Texte und Zeichen*, ed. Walter Benjamin Archiv (Frankfurt, 2006).
3 *GB,V*, p. 452.
4 *GB*, III, p. 388.
5 *GB*, IV, p. 222.
6 Walter Benjamin, *Das Adressbuch des Exils 1933–1940* (Leipzig, 2006).
7 Ingrid Scheumann, *Neue Dokumente zum Tode Walter Benjamins* (Bonn, 1992).

2 Youth Culture, 1892–1916

1 *SW*, 3, p. 404.
2 *SW*, 3, p. 356.
3 *SW*, 3, p. 349.
4 *SW*, 2:2, p. 621.
5 *SW*, 2:2, p. 630. Also see *SW*, 3, p. 386.
6 *SW*, 3, pp. 383, 406.
7 *SW*, 3, p. 404.
8 *SW*, 3, p. 402.
9 *SW*, 3, pp. 368, 390.
10 *SW*, 2:2, p. 626.
11 *SW*, 2:2, p. 602.
12 In German one word covers both, *geistig*.
13 *GB*, I, p. 263.
14 Benjamin mistakenly recalls the opening year as 1910.
15 *SW*, 2:2, p. 620.
16 *GS*, II:1, pp. 9–12.
17 *GS*, VI, p. 230.
18 *GS*, VI, p. 234.

19 *GS*, VI, p. 235.

20 *GS*, VI, p. 252.

21 *GB*, I, p. 51.

22 *GB*, I, p. 48.

23 *GB*, I, p. 57.

24 *GB*, I, p. 59.

25 *GB*, I, pp. 61–2.

26 *GB*, I, p. 69.

27 *GB*, I, pp. 64–5.

28 *GB*, I, p. 75.

29 *GB*, I, p. 71.

30 *GB*, I, p. 71.

31 *GB*, I, p. 83.

32 *GB*, I, p. 112.

33 *GB*, I, p. 93.

34 *GB*, I, p. 108.

35 *GB*, I, p. 105.

36 *SW*, 1, pp. 3–5.

37 *GS*, II:1, pp. 42–7 and *GS*, II:1, p. 47.

38 *GB*, I, p. 257.

39 *SW*, 1, p. 38.

40 *SW*, 1, p. 43.

41 *SW*, 2:2, p. 606.

42 Uwe Steiner, *Walter Benjamin* (Stuttgart, 2004), p. 28.

43 *GB*, I, p. 263.

44 Gerhard Scholem, *Story of a Friendship* (New York, 2003), p. 10.

45 *GB*, I, p. 271.

46 Scholem, *Story of a Friendship*, p. 12.

47 *GB*, I, p. 262.

48 *GB*, I, pp. 289, 296.

49 *GB*, I, pp. 290–91, 300.

50 *GB*, I, p. 326.

51 *GB*, I, p. 349.

3 Making a Mark, 1917–24

1 *SW*, 1, p. 82.

2 *GS*, II:3, p. 1412.

3 *SW*, 1, pp. 83–6.

4 *GB*, I, p. 394.

5 *GB*, I, p. 422.

6 *GB*, I, p. 390.

7 *SW*, 1, p. 101.

8 *GS*, VI, p. 216.

9 *GB*, II, p. 49.

10 *GB*, I, p. 468.

11 *GB*, I, p. 487.

12 *GB*, II, p. 10.

13 *GB*, II, p. 23.

14 *GB*, II, p. 26.

15 *GB*, I, p. 484.

16 *GB*, II, pp. 34–5.

17 *SW*, 1, p. 206.

18 Ernst Bloch, 'Recollections of Walter Benjamin', in *On Walter Benjamin: Critical Essays and Recollections*, ed. Gary Smith (Cambridge, MA, 1988), p. 339.

19 *GB*, II, p. 47.

20 *GB*, II, p. 66.

21 *GB*, II, p. 52.

22 *GB*, II, p. 68.

23 *GB*, II, p. 84.

24 *GB*, II, pp. 85, 88.

25 *GB*, II, p. 93.

26 *GB*, II, p. 89. In 1922 private lessons in graphology would provide him with a small source of income at 30 Marks an hour.

27 *GB*, II, p. 104.

28 *GB*, II, p. 108.

29 Ernst Bloch, 'Recollections of Walter Benjamin', p. 339.

30 *GB*, II, p. 109.

31 *SW*, 1, pp. 236–52.

32 *SW*, 1, pp. 253–63.

33 *GB*, II, p. 108.

34 *GB*, II, p. 146.

35 *GB*, II, p. 212.

36 *SW*, 1, p. 326.

37 He hoped to rile a number of prominent critics, and eventually the essay was placed in a leading journal, *Neue Deutsche Beiträge*, in 1924–5, but it did not draw any comments.

38 Gerhard Scholem, *Story of a Friendship* (New York, 2003), p. 120.

39 *GB*, II, p. 147.

40 *GB*, II, pp. 182–3.

41 *GB*, II, p. 220.

42 *GB*, II, p. 222.

43 *GB*, II, p. 142.

44 *GB*, II, p. 153.

45 *Walter Benjamins Archive*, pp. 82–3.

46 *Walter Benjamins Archive*, p. 85.

47 *Walter Benjamins Archive*, p. 86.

48 *Walter Benjamins Archive*, p. 89.

49 *Walter Benjamins Archive*, p. 90.

50 *Walter Benjamins Archive*, pp. 89–90.

51 *Walter Benjamins Archive*, p. 92.

52 *Walter Benjamins Archive*, p. 83.

53 *SW*, 2:2, pp. 694–8, 720–22.

54 *Walter Benjamin's Archive*, p. 98.

55 *Walter Benjamin's Archive*, p. 89.

56 *GB*, II, p. 277.

57 *GB*, II, p. 274.

58 *GB*, II, p. 281.

59 *GB*, II, p. 299.

60 *GB*, II, p. 307.

61 *GB*, II, pp. 303–5.

62 *GB*, II, pp. 309–10.

63 *GB*, II, p. 312.

64 *GB*, II, p. 317.

65 *GB*, II, p. 334.

66 *GB*, II, p. 322.

67 *GB*, II, p. 350.

68 *GB*, II, p. 347.

69 *GB*, II, p. 351.

70 *GB*, II, p. 351.

71 *GS*, IV:2, pp. 917–8. A version of the tract found a home in the collection of aphorisms and meditations called *One-way Street* under the title 'A Tour of German Inflation'.

72 *GB*, II, p. 352.

73 *GB*, II, p. 364.

74 *GB*, II, p. 365.

75 *GB*, II, p. 362.

76 *GB*, II, p. 368.

77 *GB*, II, p. 369.

78 *GB*, II, p. 387.

79 *GB*, II, p. 410.

80 *GB*, II, p. 474.

81 *GB*, II, pp. 455–6.

82 *GB*, II, p. 448.

83 *GB*, II, p. 466.

84 *GB*, II, p. 466.

85 *GB*, II, p. 473.

86 *GB*, II, p. 493.

87 *GB*, II, p. 476.

88 *GB*, II, pp. 496–7.

89 *GB*, II, p. 480.

90 *GB*, II, p. 483.

91 *GB*, II, p. 511.

92 *GB*, II, p. 511.

93 *SW*, I, p. 411.

94 *SW*, I, p. 408.

95 *SW*, I, p. 406.

96 *AP*, p. 460. See also p. 860.

97 *GS*, VI, p. 694.

4 Books after Books, 1925–9

1 *GB*, III, p. 9.

2 *GB*, III, p. 14.

3 *GB*, III, p. 15.

4 *GB*, III, p. 15.

5 *GB*, III, p. 61.

6 *GB*, III, p. 31.

7 *GB*, III, p. 50.

8 *GB*, III, p. 39.

9 *GB*, II, p. 482.

10 *GB*, III, pp. 59–60.

11 See Georg Lukács, *A Defence of History and Class Consciousness: Tailism and the Dialectic* (London, 2000).

12 *GB*, III, p. 64.

13 *GB*, III, p. 84.

14 *GB*, III, p. 90.

15 *GB*, III, p. 86.

16 His name means 'unrest'.

17 *GB*, III, p. 25.

18 *SW*, 1, p. 474.

19 *SW*, 1, p. 474.

20 *SW*, 1, p. 474 (translation modified).

21 *SW*, 1, p. 461.

22 *Walter Benjamins Archive*, p. 77. Such a typescript has not been found.

23 *Walter Benjamins Archive*, p. 111. *The Profile* [*Der Querschnitt*] was a magazine of 'art and culture', appearing between 1921 and 1936, edited by Alfred Flechtheim and H. von Wedderkop in Berlin.

24 *Walter Benjamins Archive*, p. 111.

25 *Walter Benjamins Archive*, p. 112.

26 *Walter Benjamins Archive*, p. 112.

27 *SW*, 2:1, pp. 3–5.

28 *GB*, III, p. 126.

29 *GB*, III, p. 133.

30 *GB*, III, p. 134.

31 *GB*, III, p. 133.

32 *GB*, III, p. 137.

33 Bloch, 'Recollections of Walter Benjamin', p. 339.

34 *GB*, III, p. 139.

35 *GB*, III, p. 148. These thoughts were published in the *Frankfurter Zeitung* in July 1926 and found their way later into *One-way Street*.

36 *GB*, III, p. 177.

37 Siegfried Kracauer, 'Two Planes', in *The Mass Ornament: Weimar Essays* (Cambridge, MA, 1995), pp. 37–9.

38 *GB*, III, p. 195.

39 *GB*, III, p. 214.

40 *SW*, I, pp. 435–43.

41 *GS*, IV:1, p. 480.

42 *SW*, I, p. 456.

43 *SW*, I, p. 456.

44 *SW*, I, p. 457.

45 *SW*, I, pp. 456–7.

46 *SW*, I, p. 457.

47 *SW*, 2:1, p. 28.

48 Walter Benjamin, *Moscow Diary* (Cambridge, MA, 1986), p. 53.

49 *GB*, III, p. 221.

50 *SW*, 2:1, p. 23.

51 *SW*, 2:1, p. 24.

52 *SW*, 2:1, p. 24.

53 *SW*, 2:1, p. 32.

54 *SW*, 2:1, p. 23.

55 Benjamin, *Moscow Diary*, p. 35.

56 *GB*, III, p. 222.

57 *GB*, III, p. 237.

58 *GB*, III, p. 223.

59 *GB*, III, p. 232.

60 *GB*, III, p. 248. Kracauer's essay is in Kracauer, *The Mass Ornament*, pp. 291–304.

61 *SW*, 2:1, p. 17.

62 *GB*, III, p. 259.

63 *SW*, 1, 478. It found its way into *One-way Street* in 1928.

64 *AP*, p. 31.

65 *AP*, p. 872.

66 *AP*, p. 872.

67 *AP*, p. 841.

68 *On Hashish* (Cambridge, MA, 2006), p. 20.

69 *On Hashish*, p. 22.

70 *GB*, III, p. 322.

71 See Momme Brodersen, *Walter Benjamin: A Biography* (London, 1995), pp. 99–100.

72 Bloch, 'Recollections of Walter Benjamin', p. 344.

73 Bloch, 'Recollections of Walter Benjamin', pp. 344–5.

74 *GB*, III, p. 322.

75 *GB*, III, p. 375.

76 *GB*, III, p. 392.

77 *SW*, 2:1, p. 134.
78 *SW*, 2:1, pp. 133–4.
79 *SW*, 1, p. 448.
80 *GB*, III, p. 399.
81 *On Hashish*, p. 58.
82 *GS*, VI, p. 416.
83 *GB*, III, p. 418.
84 *SW*, 2:1, p. 146.
85 *GB*, III, p. 420.
86 *GB*, III, p. 420.
87 See Maurice Nadeau, *The History of Surrealism* (Harmondsworth, 1978), p. 115.
88 *SW*, 2:1, p. 216.
89 *SW*, 2:1, p. 215.
90 *SW*, 2:1, p. 216.
91 *SW*, 1, p. 460.
92 *GS*, IV:1, pp. 460–63.
93 *GB*, III, p. 439.
94 *GB*, III, pp. 443–4.
95 *GS*, III, p. 183.
96 *GB*, III, p. 469.
97 *GB*, III, pp. 463–4.
98 *GB*, III, p. 469.
99 *GS*, IV:1, p. 364.
100 *GS*, IV:1, p. 365.
101 *GS*, IV:1, p. 365.
102 *GS*, IV:1, pp. 548–51.
103 *GS*, IV:2, pp. 622–3.
104 *SW*, 2:1, pp. 262–6.
105 *GS*, VII:1, p. 68.
106 *GB*, III, p. 489.
107 *GB*, III, p. 491.
108 *GB*, III, p. 502.

5 Man of Letters, 1930–32

1 *GB*, III, p. 503.
2 *GB*, III, p. 512.
3 Siegfried Kracauer, *Die Angestellten* (Frankfurt, 1930), translated as *The Salaried Masses: Duty and Distraction in Weimar* (London, 1998).
4 *GB*, III, pp. 515–7.
5 *GS*, III, 237.
6 *AP*, p. 205.
7 *AP*, p. 210.
8 *GB*, III, pp. 520–1.

9 *GB*, III, p. 522.

10 *GB*, III, p. 530.

11 *SW*, 2:2, p. 621.

12 *Marbacher Magazin*, 55 (1990), p. 215.

13 *SW*, 2:2, p. 598.

14 *Marbacher Magazin*, 55 (1990), p. 214.

15 *GS*, IV:1, p. 383.

16 *GS*, IV:1, p. 383.

17 For reflection on Benjamin's *Denkbild*, see Adorno's 'Benjamins *Einbahnstraße*', in *Noten zur Literatur* (Frankfurt, 1989), pp. 680–5.

18 *GS*, VI, p. 419. For commentary on the word *overdetermined* see Sigmund Freud and Josef Breuer, *Studies on Hysteria*, Pelican Freud Library, vol. 3 (Harmondsworth, 1974), p. 289.

19 *GS*, VI, p. 421.

20 *SW*, 3, p. 347.

21 *GS*, IV:1, pp. 385–6.

22 *GB*, III, p. 536.

23 *GS*, VI, p. 619.

24 *GS*, V, p. 619.

25 *GB*, III, p. 546.

26 Alfred Rosenberg, 'Aufruf!', *Der Weltkampf*, 5 (May 1928), pp. 210–12.

27 *GB*, III, p. 542.

28 *SW*, 2:1, p. 398.

29 See *SW*, 2:1, pp. 386–93.

30 *GB*, IV, p. 15.

31 *GB*, IV, p. 16.

32 'What is Epic Theatre? (1)', in Walter Benjamin, *Understanding Brecht* (London, 1998), p. 6.

33 *SW*, 2:2, p. 543.

34 *SW*, 2:2, p. 543.

35 *SW*, 2:2, p. 544.

36 *GS*, IV:2, p. 628.

37 *GS*, IV:2, pp. 629–40.

38 *GB*, IV, p. 18.

39 *GB*, IV, p. 19.

40 *GB*, IV, p. 20.

41 *GB*, IV, pp. 19–20.

42 *GB*, IV, p. 25.

43 *GB*, IV, p. 25.

44 *GB*, IV, p. 26.

45 *SW*, 2:2, p. 470.

46 *SW*, 2:2, p. 470.

47 *SW*, 2:2, p. 470. A different special wish – to sleep – is mentioned in *Berlin Chronicle* (1932), *SW*, 2:2, pp. 616–17.

48 *SW*, 2:2, pp. 470–71.

49 *SW*, 2:2, pp. 472–3. See also the discussions with Brecht on Benjamin's 'favourite topic' of dwelling, *SW*, II:2, pp. 479–80.

50 *SW*, 2:2, p. 473.

51 *GB*, IV, pp. 35–6.

52 *GS*, III, p. 295.

53 *SW*, 2:2, p. 482.

54 *GS*, II:3, p. 1198. The note is from a bundle written up until 1931.

55 *SW*, 2:2, pp. 477–8.

56 *SW*, 2:2, p. 501.

57 *SW*, 2:2, pp. 518–19.

58 *SW*, 2:2, p. 527. For Moholy-Nagy's 1932 version of the same sentiment, see 'A New Instrument of Vision', in Richard Kostelanetz, ed., *Moholy-Nagy* (London, 1970), p. 54.

59 *SW*, 2:2, p. 520. Goethe's assertion is in J. W. Goethe, *Maximen und Reflexionen* (Leipzig, 1941), p. 97.

60 *GB*, IV, p. 54.

61 *GB*, IV, p. 58.

62 *GB*, IV, p. 67.

63 *SW*, 2:2, p. 542.

64 *Brecht on Theatre*, trans. and ed. John Willett (London, 1964). ('Der Rundfunk als Kommunikationsapparat', in *Blätter des Hessischen Landestheaters*, 16, Darmstadt, July 1932.) Also see Bertolt Brecht, 'Radio as a Means of Communication', *Screen*, 20, 3–4 (Winter 1979/80), pp. 24–8.

65 As announced and described in the *Südwestdeutsche Rundfunk-Zeitung*, VIII/1 (1932), p. 2.

66 *Südwestdeutsche Rundfunk-Zeitung*, VIII/3 (1932), p. 5.

67 *SW*, 2:2, pp. 563–8.

68 *GS*, IV:2, pp. 674–95.

69 Jean Selz, 'Benjamin in Ibiza', in *On Walter Benjamin: Critical Essays and Recollections*, ed. Gary Smith (Cambridge, MA, 1988), p. 355.

70 *GB*, IV, p. 91.

71 *GB*, IV, p. 95.

72 *GB*, IV, p. 92.

73 *SW*, 2:2, p. 612.

74 *SW*, 2:2, p. 617.

75 *SW*, 2:2, p. 613.

76 *SW*, 2:2, p. 612.

77 *SW*, 2:2, p. 611.

78 *SW*, 2:2, p. 634.

79 *SW*, 2:2, pp. 632–3.

80 In total, Benjamin tells this story four times in *Berlin Chronicle* and the later *Berlin Childhood around 1900*. See *SW*, 2:2, pp. 632–3 and 634–5, and *GS*, IV:1, pp. 251–2 and *GS*, VII:1, pp. 410–11.

81 *SW*, 2:2, p. 634.

82 *GB*, IV, p. 106.

83 *GB*, IV, p. 113.

84 *GB*, IV, p. 112.

85 *GB*, IV, p. 119.

86 *GB*, IV, pp. 119–22.

87 *GB*, IV, p. 127.

88 *GB*, IV, p. 113.

89 *GB*, IV, p. 139.

90 *GB*, IV, p. 140.

91 See Adorno, 'A Portrait of Walter Benjamin', in *Prisms* (Cambridge, MA, 1967), p. 233.

92 *GS*, IV:1, pp. 302–4.

93 *SW*, 3, p. 404.

94 *SW*, 2:2, pp. 621–3.

95 *SW*, 2:2, p. 694.

96 *GS*, VII:2, pp. 794–5.

97 *GB*, IV, p. 163.

98 *SW*, 3, 390.

99 *SW*, 2:2, p. 697.

100 *GB*, IV, p. 163.

101 Jean Selz, 'Benjamin in Ibiza', p. 360.

6 Noms de Plume, 1933–7

1 Selz, 'Benjamin in Ibiza', p. 361.

2 *GB*, IV, p. 193.

3 *GB*, IV, p. 208.

4 Jean Selz, 'An Experiment by Walter Benjamin', in Benjamin, *On Hashish* (Cambridge, MA, 2006), pp. 147–55.

5 *GB*, IV, p. 182.

6 Geret Luhr, ed., *'was noch begraben lag': Zu Walter Benjamins Exil. Briefe und Dokumente* (Berlin, 2000), p. 30.

7 *GB*, IV, p. 202.

8 *GB*, IV, p. 213.

9 *GB*, IV, p. 228.

10 *GB*, IV, p. 247.

11 *SW*, 2:2, p. 710.

12 *GB*, IV, p. 274.

13 *GB*, IV, p. 251.

14 *GB*, IV, p. 291.

15 *GB*, IV, pp. 275, 290.

16 *SW*, 3, pp. 345–6.

17 See Walter Benjamin, *Berliner Kindheit um neunzehnhundert* (Frankfurt, 1950), p. 177.

18 *SW*, 3, p. 350.

19 *SW*, 2:2, p. 732.

20 *SW*, 2:2, p. 734.

21 *GB*, IV, pp. 278–9.

22 *SW*, 2:2, pp. 714–15.

23 Luhr, *'was noch begraben lag'*, p. 35.

24 *GB*, IV, p. 290.

25 In fact it opened in January the following year, but closed after thirteen performances. It was adapted for a film titled *Hat, Coat, Glove*, produced by RKO in 1934, which garnered critical reviews for its contrived nature.

26 Luhr, *'was noch begraben lag'*, pp. 65–6.

27 Luhr, *'was noch begraben lag'*, p. 36.

28 *GB*, IV, p. 327.

29 Erdmut Wizisla, *Benjamin und Brecht. Die Geschichte einer Freundschaft* (Frankfurt, 2004), p. 98.

30 *GB*, IV, p. 403.

31 *GB*, IV, p. 335.

32 *GB*, IV, p. 330.

33 *GB*, IV, p. 365.

34 *GB*, IV, p. 330.

35 *GB*, IV, pp. 375, 377.

36 *GB*, IV, p. 373.

37 *GB*, IV, p. 365.

38 *GB*, IV, p. 362.

39 On the same day Benjamin told Adorno that the lecture was finished but was yet to be delivered. *GB*, IV, p. 402.

40 *SW*, 2:2, pp. 768–9.

41 *GB*, IV, p. 394.

42 *GB*, IV, p. 409.

43 *GB*, IV, p. 410.

44 *GB*, IV, p. 427.

45 *GB*, IV, pp. 440–41.

46 *GB*, IV, p. 442.

47 Benjamin, *On Hashish*, p. 95.

48 Luhr, *'was noch begraben lag'*, pp. 150–52.

49 *GB*, IV, pp. 448–51.

50 *GB*, IV, p. 461.

52 *GB*, IV, p. 466.

52 *GB*, IV, pp. 475–6.

53 *GB*, IV, p. 500.

54 *GB*, IV, p. 482.

55 *GB*, IV, p. 499.

56 *GB*, IV, p. 509.

57 *GB*, IV, p. 516.

58 *GB*, IV, pp. 520–22.

59 *GB*, IV, pp. 530–31.

60 Luhr, *'was noch begraben lag'*, p. 138.

61 *GB*, V, p. 21.

62 *GB*, V, p. 103.

63 *GS*, IV:2, p. 763.

64 *GB*, V, p. 36.

65 *GB*, V, p. 36.

66 *GB*, V, p. 54.

67 *GB*, V, p. 62. In *SW*, III, 25–31.

68 *GB*, V, p. 54.

69 *GB*, V, p. 73.

70 *GB*, V, p. 96.

71 *GB*, V, p. 77.

72 *GB*, V, p. 102

73 *AP*, p. 13.

74 *AP*, p. 4.

75 *AP*, pp. 4–5.

76 *GB*, V, p. 96.

77 *GB*, V, p. 97.

78 *GB*, V, p. 108.

79 *GB*, V, p. 109.

80 *GB*, V, p. 111.

81 *GB*, V, p. 129.

82 Luhr, *'was noch begraben lag'*, p. 209.

83 *GS*, III, p. 451.

84 *GB*, V, p. 132.

85 *GB*, V, p. 136.

86 *GB*, V, p. 138.

87 *GB*, V, p. 133.

88 Reprinted in *SW*, 3, pp. 53–63.

89 *SW*, 3, pp. 406–7.

90 *GB*, V, p. 151.

91 *GB*, V, p. 171.

92 *GB*, V, pp. 171–2.

93 This is in a related piece of work called 'Dreams and Occultism', Lecture 30 of Freud's *New Introductory Lectures on Psychoanalysis*, Pelican Freud Library, vol 2, (Harmondsworth, 1977), p. 86.

94 *GB*, V, p. 179.

95 *GB*, V, p. 199.

96 *GB*, V, pp. 221–2.

97 *GB*, V, p. 255.

98 *GB*, V, p. 225.

99 *GB*, V, pp. 250, 260.

100 *GB*, V, p. 264.

101 *GB*, V, pp. 267–8.

102 *GB*, V, pp. 326, 8.

103 *GB*, V, p. 271.

104 *GB*, V, p. 287.

105 See Leskov, 'The Left-handed Artificer', in *The Enchanted Pilgrim* (London, 1946), pp. 251–82.

106 *SW*, 3, p. 161.

107 *SW*, 3, p. 150.

108 *SW*, 3, p. 144.

109 *SW*, 3, p. 149.

110 *SW*, 3, p. 149.

111 *SW*, 3, p. 162.

112 *SW*, 3, p. 162.

113 *SW*, 3, p. 146.

114 *SW*, 3, p. 150.

115 *GB*, V, p. 307.

116 See Adorno's letter to Benjamin from 6 September 1936 in *GS*, VII:2, p. 864.

117 *GB*, V, p. 305.

118 *GB*, V, p. 320.

119 *GB*, V, p. 320.

120 *GB*, V, p. 303.

121 *GB*, V, p. 367.

122 *GB*, V, p. 373.

123 *GB*, V, p. 302.

124 *GS*, 3, p. 488.

125 *GB*, V, p. 366.

126 *GB*, V, p. 402.

127 *GS*, 3, p. 503.

128 *GB*, V, p. 426.

129 Walter Benjamin, *Das Adressbuch des Exils: 1933–1940* (Lepizig, 2006), pp. 94–5.

130 *GB*, V, p. 443.

131 *GB*, V, p. 457.

132 *GB*, V, pp. 457–8.

133 *GB*, V, pp. 458–9.

134 *GB*, V, pp. 466–7.

135 *SW*, 3, p. 262.

136 *SW*, 3, p. 267.

137 *SW*, 3, p. 266.

138 *GB*, V, pp. 480, 503. To Margarete Steffin he claimed to have 'discovered' Jochmann, a claim that would upset Werner Kraft, who thought he had got onto Jochmann first and that Benjamin had acted deceitfully in claiming him as his own, when he had borrowed Jochmann's books from him. Kraft broke off all relations (*GB*, V, pp. 504–5). Benjamin insisted in March 1940, when the controversy flared up again, that Kraft had known of Jochmann before him, but he knew of him independently of Kraft (*GB*, VI, pp. 421, 426–89).

139 *GB*, V, p. 480.

140 *SW*, 4, p. 361.

141 *GB*, V, p. 490.

142 *GB*, V, pp. 500–1.

143 *GB*, V, p. 516.

144 *GB*, V, p. 527.

145 *GB*, V, p. 530.

146 *GB*, V, p. 535.

147 *GB*, V, p. 543.

148 *GB*, V, pp. 531, 544, 550.

149 *GB*, V, p. 544.

150 *GB*, V, pp. 549–50.

151 *GB*, V, p. 572.

152 *GB*, V, p. 590.

153 *GB*, V, p. 620.

154 *GB*, V, p. 606.

155 *GB*, V, pp. 621–2/*GB*, VI, p. 30.

156 *GB*, V, p. 639.

157 *GB*, V, p. 638.

158 *SW*, 4, p. 124.

159 *GB*, VI, p. 10.

160 *AP*, p. 271.

7 Writer's Block, 1938–40

1 *GB*, VI, p. 38.

2 *GB*, VI, p. 54.

3 *GB*, VI, p. 43.

4 *GB*, VI, p. 62.

5 For the development of the radio project, see T. W. Adorno, *Current of Music. Elements of a Radio Theory*, ed. Robert Hullot-Kentor (Frankfurt, 2006); T. W. Adorno, *In Search of Wagner* (London, 2005).

6 Cited in *GB*, VI, p. 34.

7 *GB*, VI, p. 80.

8 *GB*, VI, p. 72

9 *GB*, VI, p. 65.

10 Geret Luhr, ed., *'was noch begraben lag': Zu Walter Benjamins Exil. Brife und Dokumente* (Berlin, 2000), p. 232.

11 Luhr, *'was noch begraben lag'*, pp. 43–4.

12 *GB*, VI, p. 74.

13 *SW*, 4, p. 126.

14 *SW*, 4, p. 130.

15 *SW*, 4, p. 130.

16 *GB*, VI, pp. 89–90.

17 *GB*, VI, pp. 934.

18 *GB*, VI, p. 152.

19 *GB*, VI, pp. 129–30.

段落引用

20 *GB*, VI, p. 133.

21 *GB*, VI, p. 132.

22 *GB*, VI, pp. 138–9.

23 *GB*, VI, p. 138.

24 'Conversations with Brecht', in Walter Benjamin, *Reflections* (New York, 1978), p. 213.

25 *GB*, VI, p. 168.

26 *GB*, VI, pp. 142–3.

27 *GB*, VI, p. 168.

28 *GB*, VI, p. 167.

29 *GB*, VI, p. 174.

30 Adorno's letter is in *sw*, 4, pp. 99–105. Benjamin's response follows, pp. 105–12.

31 *sw*, 4, p. 109.

32 *sw*, 4, p. 106.

33 *sw*, 4, p. 107.

34 *sw*, 4, p. 107.

35 *GB*, VI, pp. 197–209.

36 *GB*, VI, pp. 60–61.

37 *GB*, VI, p. 70.

38 *sw*, 4, p. 145.

39 *sw*, 4, p. 147.

40 *sw*, 4, p. 145.

41 *GB*, VI, p. 198.

42 *AP*, p. 476.

43 *AP*, p. 473.

44 *AP*, p. 474.

45 *GB*, VI, pp. 226–7.

46 *sw*, 4, p. 223.

47 Frank Jellinek's translation of Brecht's poem, rendered as 'Cover Your Tracks', is in John Willett and Ralph Manheim, eds, *Bertolt Brecht; Poems 1913–1956* (London, 1979), p. 131.

48 *sw*, 2:2, p. 701.

49 *sw*, 4, p. 233.

50 *GB*, VI, p. 215.

51 *GB*, VI, p. 232.

52 *GB*, VI, p. 232.

53 *AP*, p. 14.

54 *AP*, p. 15.

55 *GB*, VI, p. 235.

56 *AP*, p. 14.

57 *GB*, VI, p. 236.

58 *GB*, VI, p. 249.

59 *GB*, VI, p. 244.

60 *GB*, VI, p. 247.

61 *GB*, VI, p. 253.

62 *GB*, VI, pp. 258–9.

63 *GB*, VI, p. 263.

64 *GB*, VI, p. 281.

65 *GB*, VI, p. 303.

66 *GB*, VI, p. 282.

67 *GB*, VI, p. 294.

68 *GB*, VI, p. 294–5.

69 *GB*, VI, p. 303–4.

70 *GB*, VI, p. 304.

71 *GB*, VI, p. 304–5.

72 *GB*, VI, p. 306.

73 Luhr, *'was noch begraben lag'*, pp. 52–3.

74 *SW*, 4, p. 357.

75 *GB*, VI, p. 318.

76 *GB*, VI, p. 319.

77 *GB*, VI, p. 327.

78 *GB*, VI, p. 323.

79 *GB*, VI, pp. 330–31.

80 *GB*, VI, p. 334.

81 *GB*, VI, p. 335.

82 *GB*, VI, p. 347.

83 *GB*, VI, p. 370.

84 *GB*, VI, p. 373.

85 *GB*, VI, p. 376.

86 *GB*, VI, p. 379.

87 *GS*, III, p. 588.

88 *GB*, VI, p. 379.

89 Horkheimer, 'The Jews and Europe', in *Critical Theory and Society: A Reader*, ed. Stephen Bronner and Douglas Kellner (London, 1989), pp. 77–94.

90 *GB*, VI, pp. 400–1.

91 *GB*, VI, p. 413.

92 *GB*, VI, p. 420.

93 *GB*, VI, pp. 418–20.

94 *GS*, III, p. 593.

95 *GS*, III, p. 591, 595.

96 *GS*, III, p. 591.

97 *GS*, III, p. 594.

98 *GB*, VI, pp. 431.

99 *GB*, VI, pp. 435–6.

100 *SW*, 4, p. 390.

101 *SW*, 4, p. 402.

102 *SW*, 4, p. 403.

103 *SW*, 4, p. 394.

104 *SW*, 4, p. 471.

105 *SW*, 4, p. 415.

106 *SW*, 4, p. 416.

107 *GB*, VI, p. 470.

108 *GB*, VI, p. 473.

109 *GB*, VI, pp. 477–8.

110 *GS*, V:2, p. 1197.

111 Lisa Fittko, who led the party, provided a full account of the crossing. See *AP*, pp. 946–54. See also the recollections of another member of the party, Carina Birman, *The Narrow Foothold* (London, 2006).

112 *GB*, VI, p. 483.

8 Afterwords

1 *SW*, 3, p. 385.

2 Documents found by Ingrid Scheurmann dispute Henny Gurland's claim that she paid for the grave. See *Neue Dokumente zum Tode Walter Benjamins* (Bonn, 1992), p. 15.

3 *Neue Dokumente zum Tode Walter Benjamins*, p. 40.

4 See Detlev Schöttker, ed., *Schrift, Bilder, Denken: Walter Benjamin und die Künste* (Frankfurt, 2004). See also reviews of the exhibition under this name held in Berlin's Haus am Waldsee in 2004–5.

5 One of the latest rambles in this genre is Michael Taussig, *Walter Benjamin's Grave* (Chicago, 2006).

6 *GS*, I:3, p. 1421 (excerpted).

7 *GS*, I:3, p. 1224.

8 Wizisla, *Benjamin und Brecht*, p.275.

9 See Reinhard Markner, 'Walter Benjamin nach der Moderne. Etwas zur Frage seiner Aktualität angesichts der Rezeption seit 1983', *Schattenlinien*, 8–9 (1994), pp. 37–47.

10 Jürgen Habermas, 'Bewußtmachende oder rettende Kritk – die Aktualität Walter Benjamins', in *Zur Aktualität Walter Benjamin*, ed. Siegfried Unseld (Frankfurt, 1972), pp. 174–223. (Translated into English as 'Consciousness-Raising or Redemptive Criticism: The Contemporaneity of Walter Benjamin', *New German Critique*, 17, Special Walter Benjamin Issue (Spring, 1979), pp. 30–59.)

11 See, for example, Bernd Witte,'Benjamin and Lukács. Historical Notes on the Relationship Between Their Political and Aesthetic Theories', *New German Critique*, 5 (1975), pp. 3–26.

12 Hans Magnus Enzensberger, 'Baukasten zu einer Theorie der Medien', *Kursbuch*, 20 (1970), pp. 159–86.

13 For bibliographic details, see Burkhardt Lindner, ed., *Benjamin Handbuch: Leben – Werk – Wirkung* (Stuttgart, 2006), p. 28.

14 Sebastian Kleinschmidt, ed., *Walter Benjamin: Allegorien kultureller Erfahrung. Ausgewählte Schriften 1920–1940* (Leipzig, 1984).

15 Gershom Scholem, *The Story of a Friendship* (New York, 1981).

16 Gershom Scholem, *On Jews and Judaism in Crisis* (New York, 1976), p. 187.

17 See the 720 pages of Lindner, *Benjamin Handbuch: Leben – Werk – Wirkung*, for a

recent vast effort to orient the entire field of Benjamin research by recommending thematically organized bibliographies and overviews of his life, work and influence. See also 'Benjamin's Finale; Excavating and Re-membering', in Esther Leslie, *Walter Benjamin: Overpowering Conformism* (London, 2000).

18 *GS*, III, p. 592.
19 *GS*, III, p. 592.
20 *SW*, 3, p. 102.
21 Benjamin, *Moscow Diary*, p. 53.
22 *SW*, 4, p. 396.

Select Bibliography

Benjamin's Writings in German

Gesammelte Schriften, 7 vols, with the assistance of T. W. Adorno and Gershom Scholem, ed. Rolf Tiedemann and Hermann Schweppenhäuser (Frankfurt am Main: Suhrkamp, 1972–89)

Correspondence

Gesammelte Briefe, 6 vols, ed. Christoph Gödde and Henri Lonitz (Frankfurt am Main: Suhrkamp, 1995–2000)

Facsimiles and Archival Materials in German

Walter Benjamin. 1892–1940, exh. cat. of the Theodor W. Adorno Archive, Frankfurt am Main, in association with the German Literature Archive, Marbach am Neckar; ed.Rolf Tiedemann, Christoph Gödde and Henri Lonitz (*Marbacher Magazin* 55), 3rd revd and expanded edn (Marbach am Neckar, 1991)

Benjaminiana: Eine biographische Recherche, ed. Hans Puttnies and Gary Smith (Giessen: Anabas Verlag, 1991)

Neue Dokumente zum Tode Walter Benjamins, Ingrid Scheurmann (Bonn: AsKI 1992)

'was noch begraben lag': Zu Walter Benjamins Exil. Briefe und Dokumente, ed. Geret Luhr (Berlin: Bostelmann & Siebenhaar, 2000)

Walter Benjamins Archive, ed. Ursula Marx, Gudrun Schwarz, Michael Schwarz and Erdmut Wizisla of the Walter Benjamin Archive at the Academy of Arts Berlin (Frankfurt am Main: Suhrkamp, 2006)

Das Adressbuch des Exils 1933-1940 (Leipzig: Koehler & Amelang, 2006)

Writings in English

Collections
Reflections, Introduction by Peter Demetz (New York: Harcourt Brace Jovanovich, 1978)
One-Way Street and Other Writings, Introduction by Susan Sontag (London: New Left Books, 1979)
Illuminations, Introduction by Hannah Arendt (London: Fontana 1992)
Selected Writings, I: *1913–1926*, ed. Marcus Bullock and Michael W. Jennings (Cambridge, MA: Bellknap Press of Harvard UP, 1996)
Selected Writings, II:1 and 2:2: *1927–1934*, ed. Michael W. Jennings (Cambridge, MA: Belknap Press of Harvard UP, 1999)
Selected Writings, III: *1935–1938*, ed. Howard Eiland and Michael W. Jennings (Cambridge, MA: Belknap Press of Harvard UP, 2002)
Selected Writings, IV: *1938–1940*, ed. Howard Eiland and Michael W. Jennings (Cambridge, MA: Belknap Press of Harvard UP, 2002)

Themed Collections and Single Volumes in English
The Origin of German Tragic Drama, Introduction by George Steiner (London: New Left Books, 1977)
Understanding Brecht, Introduction by Stanley Mitchell (London: New Left Books, 1983)
Charles Baudelaire: A Lyric Poet in the Era of High Capitalism (London: New Left Books, 1983)
Moscow Diary, with an Afterword by Gary Smith [originally an edition of the journal *October*] (Cambridge, MA: Harvard UP, 1986)
The Arcades Project, ed. Rolf Tiedemann (Cambridge, MA: Harvard UP, 1999)
On Hashish (Cambridge, MA: Harvard UP, 2006)
Berlin Childhood around 1900, with an introduction by Peter Szondi (Cambridge, MA: Harvard UP, 2006)
The Writer of Modern Life: Essays on Charles Baudelaire (Cambridge, MA: Harvard UP, 2006)

Correspondence in English

The Correspondence of Walter Benjamin and Gershom Scholem, 1932–1940, ed. Gershom Scholem (New York: Schocken, 1989)
The Correspondence of Walter Benjamin, 1910–1940, ed. Gershom Scholem and T.W. Adorno (University of Chicago: Chicago, 1994)
Walter Benjamin and T.W. Adorno, *The Complete Correspondence, 1928–1940*, ed. Henri Lonitz (Cambridge, MA: Harvard UP, 2001)

Selected Writings on Benjamin in English

Andrew Benjamin and Peter Osborne, eds, *Walter Benjamin's Philosophy; Destruction and Experience* (Manchester, 2000)
—, and Beatrice Hanssen, eds, *Walter Benjamin and Romanticism* (London, 2002)

Norbert Bolz and Willem Van Reijen, *Walter Benjamin* (Atlantic Highlands, NJ, 1996)

Momme Brodersen, *Walter Benjamin: A Biography* (London, 1996)

Susan Buck-Morss, *The Origin of Negative Dialectics; Theodor W. Adorno, Walter Benjamin and the Frankfurt Institute* (Brighton, 1977)

—, *The Dialectics of Seeing: Walter Benjamin and the Arcades Project* (Cambridge, MA, 1989)

—, 'Aesthetics and Anaesthetics: Walter Benjamin's Artwork Essay Reconsidered', *October*, 62 (Fall 1992), pp. 3–41

Howard Caygill, *Walter Benjamin: The Colour of Experience* (London, 1998)

—, Alex Coles and Andrzej Klimowski, *Walter Benjamin for Beginners* (London, 1998)

Margaret Cohen, *Profane Illumination; Walter Benjamin and the Paris of Surrealist Revolution* (Berkeley, CA, 1993)

Terry Eagleton, *Walter Benjamin or Towards a Revolutionary Criticism* (London, 1981)

David S. Ferris, *The Cambridge Companion to Walter Benjamin* (Cambridge, 2004)

Gerhard Fischer, ed., *With the Sharpened Axe of Reason: Approaches to Walter Benjamin* (Oxford, 1996)

David Frisby, *Fragments of Modernity* (Cambridge, 1985)

Helga Geyer-Ryan, Paul Koopman and Klaas Yntema, eds, *Benjamin Studies/Studien* I: *Perception and Experience in Modernity* (Amsterdam, 2002)

Graeme Gilloch, *Myth and Metropolis: Walter Benjamin and the City* (Cambridge, 1996)

—, *Walter Benjamin: Critical Constellations* (Cambridge, 2001)

Jürgen Habermas, 'Walter Benjamin: Consciousness-Raising or Rescuing Critique (1972)', in J. Habermas, *Philosophical-Political Profiles* (Cambridge, MA, 1983), pp. 129–64

Beatrice Hanssen, *Walter Benjamin's Other History: Of Stones, Animals, Human Beings, and Angels* (Berkeley, CA, 1998)

—, *Walter Benjamin and the Arcades Project* (London, 2006)

Carol Jacobs, *In the Language of Walter Benjamin* (Baltimore & London, 1999)

Martin Jay, *The Dialectical Imagination: A History of the Frankfurt School and the Institute of Social Research, 1923–1950* (Boston & Toronto, 1973)

Michael Jennings, *Dialectical Images; Walter Benjamin's Theory of Literary Criticism* (Ithaca, NY, 1987)

Lutz Koepenick, *Walter Benjamin and the Aesthetics of Power* (Lincoln, NE, 1999)

Margarete Kohlenbach, *Walter Benjamin* (Basingstoke, 2002)

Siegfried Kracauer, 'On the Writings of Walter Benjamin' (15 July 1928), in *The Mass Ornament: Weimar Essays* (Cambridge, MA, 1995)

Richard J. Lane, *Reading Walter Benjamin: Writing Through the Catastrophe* (Manchester, 2005)

Ulrich Lehmann, *Tigersprung: Fashion in Modernity* (Cambridge, MA, 2000)

Esther Leslie, 'Souvenirs and Forgetting; Walter Benjamin's Memory-work', in *Material Memories; Design and Evocation*, ed. Marius Kwint, Jeremy Aynsley and Christopher Breward (Oxford, 1999), pp. 107–22

—, *Walter Benjamin: Overpowering Conformism* (London, 2000)

—, 'The World as Image and Thing', *Twentieth Century Literature and Photograph*, edited by David Cunningham, Andrew Fisher and Sas Mays (Newcastle, 2005)

Michael Löwy, *Fire Alarm: Reading Walter Benjamin's 'On the Concept of History'* (London, 2006)

Eugene Lunn, *Marxism and Modernism; A Historical Study of Lukács, Brecht, Benjamin and Adorno* (Berkeley, CA, 1982)

Laura Marcus and Lynda Nead, eds, *The Actuality of Walter Benjamin* (London, 1998)

John McCole, *Walter Benjamin and the Antinomies of Tradition* (Ithaca, NY, 1993)

Jeffrey Mehlman: *Walter Benjamin for Children; An Essay on his Radio Years* (Chicago, 1993)

Pierre Missac, *Walter Benjamin's Passages* (Cambridge, MA, 1995)

New German Critique, no. 48 (Fall 1989), Walter Benjamin Issue; includes Beth Sharon Ash, 'Walter Benjamin: Ethnic Fears, Oedipal Anxieties, Political Consequences', pp. 2–42; Ackbar Abbas, 'On Fascination: Walter Benjamin's Images', pp. 43–62; Rey Chow, 'Walter Benjamin's Love Affair with Death', pp. 63–86; Margaret Cohen, 'Walter Benjamin's Phantasmagoria', pp. 87–108; Christiane von Buelow, 'Troping Toward Truth: Recontextualizing the Metaphors of Science and History in Benjamin's Kafka Fragment', pp. 109–34

Peter Osborne, ed., *Walter Benjamin: Critical Evaluations in Cultural Theory* (London, 2004)

Dag Petersson and Erik Steinskog, eds, *Actualities of Aura: Twelve Studies of Walter Benjamin* (Svanesund, 2005)

Julian Roberts, *Walter Benjamin* (London, 1982)

Christopher Rollason, 'The Passageways of Paris: Walter Benjamin's *Arcades Project* and Contemporary Cultural Debate in the West', in *Modern Criticism*, ed. Christopher Rollason and Rajeshwar Mittapalli (New Delhi, 2002), pp. 262–96

Gershom Scholem, *Walter Benjamin – The Story of a Friendship*. (New York, 2003)

Gary Smith, ed., *Benjamin: Philosophy, History, Aesthetics* (Chicago, 1989)

Gary Smith [editor], *On Walter Benjamin* (Cambridge, MA, 1991)

Michael Taussig, *Walter Benjamin's Grave* (Chicago, 2006)

Sigrid Weigel, *Body and Image-Space: Re-reading Walter Benjamin* (London, 1996)

Rolf Wiggershaus, *The Frankfurt School: Its History, Theories, and Political Significance* (Cambridge, MA, 1994)

Bernd Witte, *Walter Benjamin: An Intellectual Biography* (Detroit, 1991)

Irving Wohlfarth, 'Et Cetera? The Historian as Chiffonnier', *New German Critique 39* (Fall 1986), pp. 147–86

Irving Wohlfarth, '"Männer aus der Fremde": Walter Benjamin and the "German-Jewish Parnassus"', *New German Critique 70* (Winter 1997), pp. 3–85

Richard Wolin, *Walter Benjamin; An Aesthetics of Redemption* (New York, 1982) [reissued with a new introduction in 1994]

Web Resource

The Walter Benjamin Research Syndicate
http://www.wbenjamin.org/walterbenjamin.html

Photo Acknowledgements

The author and publishers wish to express their thanks to the following sources of illustrative material and/or permission to reproduce it.

Photos by the author: pp. 224, 227; copy of book from author's collection: p. 61 (Weimar: Landes-Industrie-Comptoir, 1801); collection of the author: p. 96; postcards from the collection of the author: pp. 16, 21, 22, 24, 41, 94, 95, 129, 151, 215; photo Stefan Brecht: p. 189; photos © Hamburger Stiftung zur Förderung von Wissenschaft und Kultur: pp. 97, 102, 110, 120, 122; photo Regine Koerner: p. 219; photo Sasha Stone, 1927, by kind permission of Serge Stone: p. 73; photos Studio Joël-Heinzelmann: pp. 7, 99; photos courtesy Walter Benjamin Archiv, Akademie der Künste, Berlin: pp. 7, 12, 15, 17, 19, 50, 73, 97 (Sign. Dr 516), 99, 102 (Sign. Dr 526), 110 (Sign. Ms 361), 120, 122 (Sign. 221), 140, 189.